Lessons in
People
Management

Tom Mochal and Jeff Mochal

Lessons in People Management

Copyright ©2005 by Tom Mochal and Jeff Mochal

Reviewers: Tracee Leeka, Lindsay Mochal

Library of Congress Cataloging-in-Publication Data

Mochal, Tom, 1957–

Lessons in people management / Tom Mochal and Jeff Mochal.

p. cm.

ISBN 1-4196-0854-1

1. Management.   I. Mochal, Tom 1957 - , Mochal, Jeff, 1974 –

All rights reserved. No part of this work may be reproduced or transmitted in any form or by any means, electronic or mechanical, including photocopying, recording, or by any information storage or retrieval system, without the prior written permission of the copyright owner and the publisher.

Printed and bound in the United States of America

Trademarked names may appear in this book. Rather than use a trademark symbol with every occurrence of a trademarked name, we use the names only in an editorial fashion and to the benefit of the trademark owner, with no intention of infringement of the trademark.

For information on translations, please contact TenStep, Inc. directly at 4390 Laurian Drive, Kennesaw, GA 30144. Phone 770.591.9860, fax 770.591.9860, email admin@TenStep.com

The information in this book is distributed on an "as is" basis, without warranty. Although every precaution has been taken in the preparation of this work, the author(s) shall have any liability to any person or entity with respect to any loss or damage caused or alleged to be caused directly or indirectly by the information contained in this work.

This book is dedicated to my wife, Pam, and our children, Lindsay, Sean, and Ashley. Pam provides constant support and keeps me from getting too carried away with my work. Our children are growing too fast, but make us proud every day.

—Tom Mochal

This book is dedicated to Erika Mochal - my wife, my love, my life. Thanks for your constant support and encouragement.

—Jeff Mochal

Contents by Story

1	Identifying the Cause of Team Conflicts with the Barracuda	1
2	Keep an Open Mind About Teleworking	4
3	Linda Learns Techniques to Resolve Conflicts	9
4	Mark Needs to Learn to Listen	12
5	Stan – A Good Guy but Weak Performer	17
6	Jerry is in an Ethical Dilemma	22
7	Look All Around You for Performance Feedback	26
8	Reflecting on Professional Development on Super Bowl Sunday	31
9	Dawn Needs to Firm Up Her Group's Flextime Options	36
10	The Office Romance Turns Sour	40
11	Sexual Harassment is a Burning Issue - Extinguish it Quickly	44
12	"Frustration Culture"	49
13	Team Members May Look Like Adults but Act Like Babies	54
14	Everyone is Replaceable – If You Prepare	58
15	There is No "I" (Isolation) in "T-E-A-M"	63
16	Leaders are Born *and* Grown	67
17	Stop the Guessing Game on Performance Expectations	72
18	Work Twenty-Four Hours a Day, or Delegate	76
19	Value Diversity – It Makes Business Sense	80
20	"Lead!"	84
21	Mort is Getting Involved in Politics, but He is Not Running for Office . . .	89
22	Doing the Expected is not the Way to be Promoted	94
23	You Can Let an Employee Go – And Feel Okay About It	98
24	Morale Problems are Everyone's Problems	102
25	High-Performance Teams are a Hole-in-One	106
26	Manager – Heal Thyself	112
27	"Coach" Arnie Needs Some Coaching	115
28	Contractors are People Too?	118
29	Take Time Out for Time Management Skills	122

Contents by Story

30	Can't We All Just Get Along?.................................	126
31	In Praise of Technical Nerds.................................	130
32	Jorge is Losing Recognition to the Non-Participants.................	135
33	Fear and Loathing in the Purchasing Department....................	139
34	There's a "Good Old Girl" on the "Good Old Boy" Team.............	144
35	Delayed Feedback Causes Delayed Problems......................	148
36	Meet Bob, the "Can't Do" Manager............................	153
37	Jack the New Guy is Shaking Things Up.........................	157
38	What's Wrong Here? The Organization Failed, but Every Staff Member was Successful..	161
39	There's Nothing to Fear – Except Your Job!......................	166
40	Rose the Clerk Made a Mistake – Fire Her!......................	171
41	Marcia Needs to Get Formal with Fred..........................	174
42	Everything's Personal with Marvin..............................	178
43	Tricks or Treats for Isaac's Project Team........................	182
44	The First Snow Won't Cover Up Joe's Mistake.....................	186
45	Use Multi-Tasking to Make Everything Take Longer................	190
46	Phyllis Fills in Nicely in the Mentor Role.......................	194
47	Warren Actually Wants to Work on the Most Important Projects First....	200
48	Chris Risks Much with His Ideas for Compensation Changes..........	205
49	"Give it Up" to a Self-Managed Team...........................	208
50	Morale Problems Don't Take Holidays...........................	212

Contents by Lesson

1	Resolve a Conflict by First Understanding the Cause	2
2	Use Facts to Assess the Viability and Effectiveness of Teleworking	5
3	Understand the Cause of a Conflict First, Then Look for Conflict Resolution Techniques	10
4	Utilize Active Listening as the Key to Effective Communication	13
5	Give Fact-Based Feedback Routinely, Not Just During Formal Reviews . . .	18
6	Maintain Your Personal Ethics	23
7	Use 360-Degree Reviews to Get a Thorough Understanding of Employee Performance	27
8	Encourage Your Staff to Take Responsibility for Their Personal and Professional Development	32
9	Ensure Flextime is Good for the Business as Well as the Individual	37
10	Act Quickly When Personal Problems Turn Into Performance Problems . . .	41
11	Deal with Sexual Harassment Issues Sensitively but Swiftly	45
12	Push Your Organization to Practice What it Preaches	50
13	Deal with Babies on the Team in a Professional Manner	55
14	Have a Transition Plan Today to Handle Turnover Tomorrow	59
15	Don't Allow Team Members to Isolate Themselves	64
16	Identify, Mentor and Grow New Leaders	68
17	Set and Manage Expectations at Both a Group and Personal Level	73
18	Expand Your Ability to Get Things Done Through Responsible Delegation	76
19	Hire a Diverse Workforce Without Compromising on the Best Candidates	81
20	Lead Your Staff – Don't Just Manage Them	85
21	Learn to Influence Others Without Moving to the "Dark Side" of Office Politics	90
22	Encourage Staff to Take on New Challenges to Get Ahead	94
23	Be Open and Fair with Poor Performers – Including Parting Ways if Necessary	99
24	Don't Ignore Morale Problems – Turn Them Around	103
25	Strive to Create High-Performance Teams	107
26	Understand that Your Attitude Rubs Off On the Entire Team – For Good or Bad	113

Contents by Lesson

27	Coach Your Staff so That They Can Mature and Grow	115
28	Manage Contractors Effectively, But Differently Than Your Employee Staff	119
29	Increase Your Effectiveness with Strong Time Management Skills	123
30	Proactively Resolve the Personality Problems of a Dysfunctional Team	127
31	Understand Your Technical Staff and Manage Them Accordingly	131
32	Take Credit for Your Successes	136
33	Use a Multi-Faceted Approach to Implement Culture Change	140
34	Be Sensitive to Differences When Managing a Diverse Staff	145
35	Provide Clear Performance Feedback on a Timely Basis	149
36	Encourage and Embrace Process Improvement Suggestions	154
37	Make Sure People Know You and Your Expectations When You are New to an Organization	158
38	Unleash the Power of an Aligned Organization	162
39	Make Sure Your Organization Can Survive a Staff Reduction	167
40	Look at Processes, Not People, to Solve Quality Problems	171
41	Escalate a Performance Problem with a Formal Plan	174
42	Recognize the Difference Between Logical and Emotional Feedback	179
43	Proactively Manage to the Strengths and Risks of a Virtual Distributed Team .	183
44	Be Honest and Upfront When Dealing with a Mistake	187
45	Minimize the Inherent Weaknesses of Multi-Tasking	191
46	Teach Your Staff How to Resolve Problems	195
47	Use Portfolio Management Techniques to Ensure People are Allocated to the Right Work	201
48	Be Very Savvy When Implementing At-Risk Compensation Plans	205
49	Use Self-Managed Teams	208
50	Respond Carefully to Significant Morale Problems	212

Story #	Timeline	Title	Lesson(s)	Character
1	January 5	Identifying the Cause of Team Conflicts with the Barracuda	Resolve a Conflict by First Understanding the Cause	Linda Martin
2	January 8	Keep an Open Mind About Teleworking	Use Facts to Assess the Viability and Effectiveness of Teleworking	Noah Henson
3	January	Linda Learns Techniques to Resolve Conflicts	Understand the Cause of a Conflict First, Then Look for Conflict Resolution Techniques	Linda Martin
4	January	Mark Needs to Learn to Listen	Utilize Active Listening as the Key to Effective Communication	Mark Thornburg
5	January	Stan - A Good Guy but Weak Performer	Give Fact-based Performance Feedback Routinely, Not Just During Formal Reviews	Olivia Riordan
6	January	Jerry is in an Ethical Dilemma	Maintain Your Personal Ethics	Jerry Ackerman
7	Last Friday in January	Look All Around You for Performance Feedback	Use 360-Degree Reviews to Get a Thorough Understanding of Employee Performance	Erin Christianson
8	First Weekend in February	Reflecting on Professional Development on Super Bowl Sunday	Encourage Your Staff to Take Responsibility for Their Personal and Professional Development	George Benes
9	First Monday in February	Dawn Needs to Firm Up Her Group's Flextime Options	Ensure Flextime is Good for the Business as Well as the Individual	Dawn Jackson

Story #	Timeline	Title	Lesson(s)	Character
10	Second Week in February	The Office Romance Turns Sour	Act Quickly When Personal Problems Turn Into Performance Problems	Bill Rodriguez
11	Third Week in February	Sexual Harassment is a Burning Issue - Extinguish it Quickly	Deal with Sexual Harassment Issues Sensitively but Swiftly	Ellen Davies
12	February 23	"Frustration Culture"	Push Your Organization to Practice What it Preaches	Mary Kendrick
13	February 26	Team Members May Look Like Adults but Act Like Babies	Deal With Babies on the Team in a Professional Manner	Gentry Braman
14	March 3	Everyone is Replaceable – if You Prepare	Have a Transition Plan Today to Handle Turnover Tomorrow	Betty Kennedy
15	Second Week in March	There is no "I"(Isolation) in "T-E-A-M"	Don't Allow Team Members to Isolate Themselves.	Jerry Ackerman
16	Third Week in March	Leaders are Born and Grown	Identify, Mentor and Grow New Leaders	Dave Huntley
17	Third Week in March	Stop the Guessing Game on Performance Expectations	Set and Manage Expectations at Both a Group and Personal Level	Janie Tudor
18	Late March	Work Twenty Four Hours a Day, or Delegate	Expand Your Ability to Get Things Done Through Responsible Delegation	Steve Buckner
19	Late March	Value Diversity – It Makes Business Sense	Hire a Diverse Workforce Without Compromising on the Best Candidates	Marvin Hendricks
20	Early April	"Lead!"	Lead Your Staff. – Don't Just Manage Them	Al Singleton

Story #	Timeline	Title	Lesson(s)	Character
21	Second Week in April	Mort is Getting Involved in Politics, But He is Not Running for Office	Learn to Influence Others Without Moving to the "Dark Side" of Office Politics	Mort Blackwell
22	Second Week in April	Doing the Expected is Not the Way to be Promoted	Encourage Staff to Take on New Challenges to Get Ahead	Perry Williams
23	Second Week in April	You Can Let an Employee Go – And Feel Okay About It	Be Open and Fair with Poor Performers – Including Parting Ways if Necessary	Penny Williams
24	Second Week in April	Morale Problems are Everyone's Problems	Don't Ignore Morale Problems – Turn Them Around	Annette Venezuela
25	Third Week in April	High-Performance Teams are a Hole-in-One	Strive to Create High-Performance Teams	Jimmy Purdue
26	Last Week in April	Manager – Heal Thyself	Understand That Your Attitude Rubs Off On the Entire Team – For Good or Bad	Bert Zucker
27	First Thursday in May	"Coach" Arnie Needs Some Coaching	Coach Your Staff So That They Can Mature and Grow	Arnie Appleby
28	Second Week in May	Contractors Are People Too?	Manage Contractors Effectively, But Differently, Than Your Employee Staff	Laura Adamson
29	May 12	Take Time Out for Time Management Skills	Increase Your Effectiveness With Strong Time Management Skills	Judy Masterson
30	Third Week in May	Can't We All Just Get Along?	Proactively Resolve the Personality Problems of a Dysfunctional Team	Doug McDonald

Story #	Timeline	Title	Lesson(s)	Character
31	June 2	In Praise of the Technical Nerds	Understand Your Technical Staff and Manage Them Accordingly	Meg Roberson
32	Third Week in June	Jorge is Losing Recognition to the Non-Participants	Take Credit for Your Successes	Jorge Herndon
33	End of June	Fear and Loathing in the Purchasing Department	Use a Multi-Faceted Approach to Implement Culture Change	Abbey Smith
34	July 3	There's a "Good Old Girl" on the "Good Old Boy" Team	Be Sensitive to Differences When Managing a Diverse Staff	Wes Foggerty
35	End of July	Delayed Feedback Causes Delayed Problems	Provide Clear Performance Feedback on a Timely Basis	Marcia White
36	End of July	Meet Bob, the "Can't Do" Manager	Encourage and Embrace Process Improvement Suggestions	Bob Drudge
37	Beginning of August	Jack the New Guy is Shaking Things Up	Make Sure People Know You and Your Expectations When You are New to an Organization	Jack Brewer
38	Middle of August	What's Wrong Here? The Organization Failed, But Every Staff Member was Successful	Unleash the Power of an Aligned Organization	Owen Martin
39	End of August	There's Nothing to Fear – Except Your Job!	Make Sure Your Organization Can Survive a Staff Reduction	Sam Edmonds
40	September	Rose the Clerk Made a Mistake – Fire Her!	Look at Processes, Not People, to Solve Quality Problems	Murphy Martinson

Story #	Timeline	Title	Lesson(s)	Character
41	October 1	Marcia Needs to Get Formal With Fred	Escalate a Performance Problem with a Formal Plan	Marcia White
42	Second Week in October	Everything's Personal With Marvin	Recognize the Difference Between Logical and Emotional Feedback	Tonya Zucker
43	October 31	Tricks or Treats for Isaac's Project Team	Proactively Manage to the Strengths and Risks of a Virtual Distributed Team	Isaac Danielson
44	First Week in November	The First Snow Won't Cover-up Joe's Mistake	Be Honest and Upfront When Dealing with a Mistake	Joe Abernathy
45	November, week of	Use Multi-Tasking to Make Everything Take Longer	Minimize the Inherent Weaknesses of Multi-Tasking	Jay Bondermann
46	End of November	Phyllis Fills in Nicely in the Mentor Role	Teach Your Staff How to Resolve Problems	LaTasha Adams, Phyllis Drummond
47	First Week in December	Warren Actually Wants to Work on the Most Important Projects First	Use Portfolio Management Techniques to Ensure People are Allocated to the Right Work	Warren Yount
48	Second Week in December	Chris Risks Much with His Ideas for Compensation Changes	Be Very Savvy When Implementing At-Risk Compensation Plans	Chris Carpenter
49	December, last day of the year	"Give it Up" to a Self-Managed Team	Use Self-Managed Teams to Empower Staff (But Don't Leave Them Totally Alone)	Jed Holley
50	December, last day of the year	Morale Problems Don't Take Holidays	Respond Carefully to Significant Morale Problems	Gerry Tyson

About the Authors

Tom Mochal has over 25 years of people management and project management experience and is currently president of TenStep, Inc., a project management and methodology consulting and training company. Tom has published hundreds of columns, and has presented and trained on project management and lifecycle topics around the world. He has developed a complete project management methodology called TenStep (http://www.tenstep.com), a methodology for implementing and supporting project management within companies called PMOStep (http://www.pmostep.com), a methodology to help companies implement portfolio management (http://www.portfoliostep.com), and a project lifecycle methodology call LifecycleStep (www.lifecyclestep.com). Tom's prior experience included positions at Eastman Kodak, Cap Gemini E&Y, The Coca-Cola Company, and Geac Computers.

Jeff Mochal has more than eight years experience in the public relations and marketing industries, creating and managing high-profile and highly-successful projects. He is an experienced communications and marketing strategist and currently works as Public Relations Manager for Hardee's Food Systems, Inc. in St. Louis, Mo. His prior experience came in Los Angeles, where he worked at Brener Zwikel and Associates, a sports marketing and PR agency, on accounts such as Showtime Boxing, American Motorcycle Association and PONY Shoes.

Jeff and Tom also collaborated on an earlier book called Lessons in Project Management, Apress 2003. For hard copies or electronic copies, contact TenStep, Inc. at 770.591.9860 or admin@TenStep.com.

About the Reviewers

Jeff and I want to thank the following people who helped shape the final product by pointing out all of our mistakes.

Lindsay Mochal coordinated the logistics for putting the entire book together and getting it published. Lindsay graduated from the University of Georgia with a degree in International Business (summa cum laude).

Jeff and I also want to thank **Erika Mochal**, **Tracee Leeka** and **Sean Mochal** for their final reviews. They helped catch many of the small things the rest of us somehow missed.

Introduction

Like many of you, I have had a number of managers in my career, including team leaders, project managers, supervisors, directors, Chief Financial Officers and many more. My managers have included men and women and, in my opinion, they have come with all sorts of strengths and "opportunities for improvements" (just can't get myself to say the word "weaknesses"). I tended to get along with all my managers and, as far as I know, they all tended to get along with me. In that respect I have been lucky, or perhaps it is just my nature. I always worked as hard as I could for all of my managers and I think that was appreciated.

As I moved into the management ranks, I constantly tried to improve my people management skills, and I likewise started mentally critiquing the managers I reported to. I tried to emulate the behaviors and skills that I admired in others, while vowing to do better in areas where I thought my managers came up short.

Here is one example: I once saw my manager meeting with a staff member, Janie, when another staff member came up with a problem that needed to be resolved quickly. Most managers would just turn their head and their attention to the crisis and assume that Janie would understand. This manager did something else. He looked at Janie and explained that this new situation was time critical and needed his attention. He further explained that this circumstance did not diminish the fact that his meeting with Janie was important. He asked Janie to wait for a few minutes and told her that he would extend the meeting time to make up for the disruption.

Needless to say, the manager helped resolve the crisis in a few minutes, yet still made Janie feel she was very important. In fact, the way the manager handled the disruption probably made Janie feel even more important than if the problem had not come up at all. The event also left an impression on a certain young manager – me. To this day, I also try to maintain focus with people I am talking or meeting with and I do not easily allow distractions to get in the way. When an interruption must be addressed, I similarly apologize in advance and assure the person I am meeting with that I value them and their time.

Another example was a manager that was very results-oriented and pushed his subordinates to be creative and solve their own problems. Sounds good right? Not when this philosophy was taken to an extreme. When a younger employee had a problem, he was told to figure it out. Likewise, when a salesman had difficulty making a sale to a tough client, he would say something like this—"We hired you to be a salesman. We are paying you to be a salesman. Your job is to sell. So figure out how to do it." Imagine that you were on the other end of that kind of advice. I think it would be natural for you to feel unsupported and your morale would probably be pretty low. In fact, the entire staff tended to feel that way.

I learned from this experience as well. I learned this was not the best way to manage staff, and I have always tried to be supportive when problems arise. Do I do the work for my staff when they are in trouble? No, of course not. Do I offer advice and coaching to help the person resolve the problem? Absolutely yes!

Looking back over the past years, I am sorry to say that I have probably learned more things to avoid from my prior managers than I did techniques to imitate. As you read this book, you should think about your management style and techniques as well. You should ask yourself whether your staff will look back on you as being one of their best managers. Will you be seen

Introduction

as one of the worst? Or are you one of the vast army of managers that leave no real lasting impression on your staff or the company?

Please don't get me wrong. I am not saying you need to be everyone's friend. In fact, if you are the best manager in the world, you will still find that some people still don't like you. But does most of your staff respect you as a good manager and leader?

I was not the perfect manager in every situation. I tried to be, but I couldn't be Superman all the time with every person. The question I would ask you is whether the "not enamored" people are in the majority on your staff. I have had many managers where that was the case.

Jeff and I have written this book to give you a sense for what is required to move from the vast, faceless ranks of management zombies into the "best manager" category. In my opinion, there are two components required to be a "best manager." The first is simply to treat people with respect. This means treating people like they are important and not simply a subordinate. This includes listening to your staff and focusing on them when you are in a discussion. It means recognizing their professional needs and looking for ways to help them grow. It means not surprising them with bad performance feedback at review time when you never mentioned anything about it before. It means all this and much, much more.

The second component of being a "best manager" is to understand and practice good people management techniques. I was perhaps lucky that I worked for companies that actually invested in management training. I have also read management books, listened to tapes while riding in a car, and taken self-taught classes. Management techniques include things like gathering 360 degree review feedback, understanding how to manage virtual teams and teleworkers, recognizing whether a person is responding emotionally or logically, knowing how to implement culture change, etc.

You need the complete package to be totally successful. If you know the techniques but don't care about people, you will not be a successful people manager (in fact, you might still go far, but you will not be on anyone's "best manager" list). Likewise if you respect people but don't know the right management techniques, you will struggle responding to the needs of your staff. However, if you have a respect for the people that work for you, and you have a good knowledge of how to apply situational people management practices and techniques, I think you will have a winning combination.

They say that the essence of a person is made up of that which is directly experienced, plus that which is read. I think there is some truth to that statement and this book was written based on that philosophy. This book is a sort of first-hand diary that chronicles one year in my life as a management coach. You can learn by "experiencing" situations at my company where managers faced the same types of events that you are facing. If you experienced some of these situations before, you can compare how you responded against the advice I gave to a manager in a similar situation. If you encounter tough people-management situations in the future, you will now have two sources to pull from – your own prior work experience as well as the situational lessons in this book.

After you read this book, keep it handy so that you can refer to it often. We have not covered every situation you will ever encounter, but we have covered a lot of ground. This book goes so

Introduction

much further than the typical "working with difficult people" advice. In fact, my belief is that in many cases it is not the person that is difficult – it is the situation itself. I have found that if you treat people with respect and if you can pull the right management techniques from your toolbox, you can typically resolve most any people management situation successfully.

Jeff and I hope you enjoy this book, learn the lessons and apply them on your job.

… Welcome to Dickens, Illinois. The people that live here think it's the best place in the world….

Story 1:

Identifying the Cause of Team Conflicts with the Barracuda

Early January in the state of Illinois, I have discovered, is a time for cautious optimism. The turning of the New Year opens windows of new possibilities in the hearts and minds of people, and there is always a sense of urgency and excitement in the air to get started. At the same time, Mother Nature turns the temperature dial down, and snow, freezing rain and bitter cold days and nights are still the norm. The result is tempered excitement.

That is how I found myself the morning of January 5. It was a Monday morning, and the first day back to work after the long New Year's holiday break. It was also the beginning of a new role for me at Mega Manufacturing. I had been working at Mega for 15 years, and had spent the last three years working as a project management coach for the company. Working in that role allowed me the opportunity to teach people how to be more effective project managers.

This year, my superiors at Mega asked me to switch away from project management, and focus my coaching on people management. It was another exciting opportunity for me to work with managers at the company, and also allowed me to spread my wings a bit and take on a new challenge. The new opportunity excited me, but I was also cautious. Projects, after all, are inanimate. People are not. I knew my new role would require me to analyze people, rather than projects, and I was curious and apprehensive at the same time as to how managers would respond to me.

I didn't have a lot of time to be nervous, though, as my first meeting was at 8:30 with Linda Martin in the Sales Department. She arrived at my office door a few minutes early, so we agreed to walk to the break room for a cup of coffee before getting down to business.

"How was your New Year?" I asked as we walked down the hall.

"It was very busy," Linda replied. "We had family in town, so Jack and I spent a lot of time cooking, cleaning, entertaining, planning and all that." Jack and Linda lived in an upscale part of town and had been married for eight years. Linda was the Department Manager in the Sales Office, and she was a real barracuda. In doing my research on her and her department, I discovered she has ranked in the top 5 percent of the company for sales in nine of her 10 years with the company. Her only "down" year was her second, when she took a month-long leave of absence for her wedding and honeymoon. Even with that time off, she still managed to rank in the top 10 percent by the end of the year.

"Sounds like you didn't get much rest," I said as we filled our coffee mugs.

"At this point, I am used to it," she said with a sarcastic smile. "We had a crazy end to the year, so it was kind of hard to relax over the break. I am actually glad I was able to keep busy!"

As we got back to my office I shut the door and took a seat behind my desk, moving aside some files to concentrate on our meeting.

1

Story 1: Identifying the Cause of Team Conflicts with the Barracuda

"So why don't you tell me about the conflicts that surfaced before the holidays. Sounds like the time off has not resolved things."

"That's an understatement," she began. "You know, when I took a leadership position within the Sales Department last year, I really thought I would be able to handle the demands of being a salesperson, as well as the demands of being a manager. I thought people would be more responsive to my direction. Instead, I find myself constantly in conflict with people on my team, and at the same time trying to resolve conflicts among others in the group. My salespeople are resistant to my ideas, and they don't seem to listen or follow when I give orders."

I could see the problem already. "You know, Linda, Mega Manufacturing is not a branch of the military," I said with a smile. She laughed and seemed to relax a bit. "Resolving conflicts does not always mean barking out orders and expecting people to blindly follow. Good managers have to first establish a context for conflicts before they attempt to resolve them. Do you have a clear idea of the nature of the conflicts?"

"Not at all," she said, opening her notepad.

"Then I think we should start here first. I will schedule an appointment for us next week to discuss conflict resolution techniques. But let's deal with first things first."

Lesson #1 – Resolve a Conflict by First Understanding the Cause

If you are a manager, you can't help but be in conflict situations at times. Some managers are more successful in resolving conflicts than others. They do this naturally by calling on their facilitation skills, having empathy for the other person's opinion and displaying a desire to determine how both parties can end up in a win-win situation.

Other managers are not very good at conflict resolution. In fact, their attempt at resolving conflict usually makes the situation worse than before. Some managers draw conflict like a magnet. They have an opinion on everything and insist their way is the best way – perhaps the only way. Sometimes an entire organization is generally poor at conflict management and the organization ends up under performing as a result.

Conflicts can occur between any two (or more) people. Even a mild-mannered person can come into conflict with another person. In fact, you may not even recognize when these events happen because the mild-mannered person may decide to give in to avoid the conflict. (Avoiding the situation is one way to resolve a conflict. It is not necessarily a good approach at all times, but it is one of several possible responses).

As a manager, you will see conflicts amongst your staff members as well as between yourself and others. Technically, whenever two people have a difference of opinion, a potential conflict exists.

Story 1: Identifying the Cause of Team Conflicts with the Barracuda

That last sentence above is key to understanding conflict resolution. On the surface, we typically think of conflict as bad. However, conflict by itself is neither good nor bad. Conflict just means there are differences between two or more people. In many instances, the differences are a good sign that people are engaged. If there are not challenges or differences of opinion, there is no reason to believe the best and most effective actions are always being taken.

There are definitely some conflicts in Linda's department. The Sales organization has plenty of opinionated, strong-willed employees. They are outgoing by nature and they are generally very competitive. It's not surprising that their conflicts can become more exaggerated than other organizations. In many respects it takes a cool head to manage a group of people like this. However, Linda is discovering she is not always up to the job.

My coaching to Linda focused on two areas. First, she needs to make sure she understands the nature of the conflict. Second, she needs to understand that there are a number of techniques to resolve conflicts (more on this aspect in Chapter 3).

The first part of resolving a conflict is simply to recognize what the conflict is and what is at stake. This involves framing the conflict situation in the following terms:

- **Context.** In many instances, managers strive to help resolve a conflict without really understanding the context. You need to know the background and situation that lead up to the conflict before you can resolve it successfully. If you are a party to the conflict, you will need to fully understand the other person's assumptions.

- **What is at stake?** This requires understanding the stakes at two levels. First are the obvious consequences of resolving a conflict one way versus another way. Second is to try to determine what the personal consequences might be in terms of lost prestige, hard feelings, etc. If the obvious consequences are not a big deal, you may want to take the personal consequences into account when resolving a conflict.

- **Roles.** Sometimes people are involved in a conflict situation where they really don't have a major stake in the outcome, while some people have much more on the line. For instance, you sometimes find a technical expert in conflict with a non-technical person over a technical matter. When you review the situation, you realize the non-technical person really doesn't have the background required to overrule the technical expert. The non-technical person can surely challenge the technical recommendations, but he or she can be overruled if he or she does not have the obvious technical qualifications.

As a manager, you will deal with conflict from two unique perspectives. The first is where people who work for you are in conflict, and it is up to you to resolve the situation. The second is when you are one of the parties in conflict. In both cases, knowing a good, logical process will help you resolve the conflict successfully.

Story 2:

Keep an Open Mind about Teleworking

By Thursday of my first week as People Management Coach, I felt like I had established a good relationship with several of the managers in different divisions at Mega. Just as it was when I started as a Project Management Coach, once people realized I was there to help, and not to judge or evaluate, they began to open up more and became more comfortable asking for assistance.

Of course, having worked for such a long period of time at Mega, I had already established strong relationships with much of the management staff. There were some new people who I did not know as well, but by far the majority of managers at Mega had been with the company for several years and worked their way up the ladder. One such person was Noah Henson.

Noah had worked in the IT Department for 15 years, and was now managing a group of 10 people. He had a reputation for being a bit of a curmudgeon, and was often slow to adapt to the changing world, but was working on being more open-minded. Last year, when I was still a Project Management Coach, Noah and I discussed some strategies to improve morale and productivity. His team was suffering from long hours working on complicated projects, and was starting to fall behind on deadlines and miss milestone dates. His client was upset at the missed deadlines, and Noah was searching for a way to get his project back on track.

I had not spoken to him since our initial meeting, but had heard he gained permission to implement a pilot program in his group to allow for teleworking. Initially, two of the 10 people on his team were allowed to telework. One worked two days a week from home, while the other worked four days at home. I was curious to hear from Noah how this program was working. He arrived at my office at 2 p.m.

"How are you, Noah?" I asked as he shook my hand.

"I'm OK Tom. How are you?"

"I'm doing great, thanks. I must admit I am real curious to hear how things are going on your project and with your team. I don't remember the two of us talking about teleworking during our initial meeting, but I heard you were testing a pilot program."

"That's right. When you and I met, you discussed the importance of face-to-face communication, and suggested that better, more personal communication between my team and me could result in improved expectations and morale."

"I recall that conversation. So how did you end up with this new program?"

"Well, when I met one-on-one with my staff, I realized that many of them were struggling with the workload, and didn't think they could meet project deadlines. When I drilled deeper, though, I found out that Peter, for example, spent several hours a day answering phone calls from the client and dealing with other internal distractions. Beth, another person on my team, had a personal issue with a sick mother and would often have to leave for several hours during

Story 2: Keep an Open Mind about Teleworking

the day. On top of that, her cubicle is directly across from the help desk area, and the constant chatter was causing her to have trouble concentrating on her work."

"Wow," I said. "It sounds like opening the communication door resulted in a lot of feedback!"

"Correct. So I decided, having talked to everyone on the team, to give teleworking a try. Peter and Beth are the first people participating in the test, and the feedback from them both has been tremendous. Now I have two more people on the team inquiring about it."

"That sounds great," I replied.

"I am not so sure," Noah said with a sigh. "That's why I came to see you today. I know Peter and Beth enjoy teleworking, but I am not confident they are being as productive at home as they would be here."

"Really? What do you base that on?"

"Well, neither of them is here when we have impromptu team meetings, for example."

"I see. Let me ask you this: What is the current status of your team's project?"

"We're back on schedule. Maybe even a little ahead of schedule actually."

I gave Noah a few minutes to actually hear and think about his last comment before proceeding.

Lesson #2 – Use Facts to Assess the Viability and Effectiveness of Teleworking

Many organizations have integrated teleworking (also called telecommuting) into their work environment, usually with success. There are a number of tangible and intangible benefits associated with a telework policy. First, teleworking is perceived as a quality of life benefit. People are generally happier if they have an option to work at home one or more days per week. It allows them to avoid daily commuting, keeps office distractions to a minimum and allows people to focus on their work for a larger block of time. It also allows people to be more productive. Additionally, teleworking can be used as an incentive to increase retention among current staff, and lead to easier recruiting of new staff.

There are also practical benefits to this work option. In offices with many teleworkers, internal common areas can be established to decrease the overall office space needed. Common areas, rather than dedicated office space, can be used by teleworkers on the days they are in the office. Likewise, more teleworkers results in fewer parking spaces and fewer lights used, etc. If your office is small, like a sales branch, you may not need a traditional office at all. Perhaps you can get by with leasing a small office space instead.

There are also some real and perceived barriers to teleworking. For instance, there may be incremental hardware and software costs to get connected. If you offer an option to work from home, you need to support remote access to your internal network. You might also need to provide hardware and software to ensure your organization can support teleworkers at their homes. With the advances in telecommunication capabilities, however, and with the low cost of hardware, these concerns typically can be overcome.

Story 2: Keep an Open Mind about Teleworking

Of greater concern with teleworking is the cultural aspect. There is a general perception that less personal interaction on the part of teleworkers will lead to problems associated with teamwork and advancement. Teamwork, after all, comes from actually interacting with your fellow teammates. You can be assigned to a team, but if you are working off-site you have a harder time bonding with others. If you are teleworking one day per week, this is usually not a problem. If you are working at home two or more days per week, it can become a problem – especially if multiple people are teleworking.

Working together as a team implies that people struggle together, share the same experiences, care for each other as people and complement each other's strengths. Working in teams is more productive when compared to the same number of people working independently. It is harder to gel as a team if many people are not physically present.

Advancement is also a concern for teleworkers. It is common for people who telework to feel they are getting passed over for advancement opportunities they might otherwise have had if they were physically in the office. Sometimes the old saying "out of sight, out of mind" holds true. If you are not around and do not have as much personal interaction, it is easy to be overlooked when new opportunities arise. This is not a concern when the entire team is teleworking, but if some people are and some aren't, the people who are working at home may inadvertently get left out of some advancement opportunities.

After stating some of the benefits and perils of teleworking, the question all managers need to ask is whether teleworking is right for their group. That is the question Noah is considering. He has tried to be a progressive manager and perform a teleworking test to see if the program could work in his group. However, right now Noah is dealing with one of the biggest barriers to teleworking – his own management mindset and biases. Like many managers, Noah is more comfortable with his people being in the office. His bias is that if he can see people, they are more productive than if he can't see them. Actually it goes a little further than that. His bias is that if they are in the office they are more productive than if they are at home. Of course, there are days when Noah never sees his people at all. They could just as well be working at home, but just knowing they are in the office makes him more comfortable.

Of course, let's not kid ourselves here. Many people cannot, in fact, work as well at home as they can in an office. These people cannot work without the structure and discipline of the office. When they are at home, they find themselves wandering from work activities to house cleaning to yard work to shopping and back to work again. Many people will readily admit they have a hard time working at home for just that reason. Having small children at home is problematic as well. Yes, it saves money by not having to pay for childcare, but small children can also make it very difficult to focus on the work at hand.

Story 2: Keep an Open Mind about Teleworking

The challenge for Noah is to make a fact-based decision on whether the program is working. Right now, his bias for having people in the office is taking over, but he has no firm facts one way or another. With a little planning, Noah could have saved himself from this dilemma, but it is not too late to put some structure in place to help him make a good decision. He can go through the following process:

1. First, determine whether a person has the kind of job that can be done at home, given the right logistics and management structures are in place. Many jobs can be done more than adequately while teleworking and some cannot be done as well. In fact, some can actually be done better at home. Salespeople tend to work effectively out of their homes since they spend much of the day on the phone or traveling anyway. People managers have a harder time working at home because they miss the personal interaction of working with their team. On the other hand, many people managers like to work at home one day a week to get away from the office interruptions.

2. Next the manager should determine how they would manage the teleworker. This is difficult when you initially start, but gets easier once you have good, consistent processes in place. The manager and employee need to agree on:

    - The number of teleworking days.
    - The specific teleworking days to ensure adequate coverage in the office.
    - The process for assigning work.
    - The best way for the teleworker to communicate with the manager, as well as with the rest of the team.
    - The way the manager will validate the effectiveness of the teleworking program is.

3. Lastly, the manager needs to track the teleworking program and provide feedback to the teleworker and the rest of the team. Generally speaking, the same criteria should be used to evaluate the teleworker as is used to evaluate people in the office. Hopefully you have to make very few compromises. Each situation is different, but the following considerations will be common:

    - If someone needs the employee, are they accessible at home just as they would be in the office? In fact, if someone calls the employee, they may not realize the person is teleworking that day instead of sitting at their desk. If emergencies arise, the teleworker may be expected to be in the office.
    - When work is assigned, the manager and employee should agree on a due date. This date should be met, whether or not the person is teleworking for all or part of that time.

If Noah follows these few steps, he should be able to determine how effective the teleworking program is. He should start to track whether the teleworkers are available as needed and whether they are continuing to get their work done on time. If they can meet these criteria, he

Story 2: Keep an Open Mind about Teleworking

should feel comfortable that the people are just as effective as when they are in the office. If they cannot hit their committed target dates and if they are not accessible when needed, he will have some facts to make a different decision.

If a person can be just as productive at home (if not more productive), plus have more control over their work environment, it should make business sense to continue or even expand the program.

Story 3:

Linda Learns Techniques to Resolve Conflicts

I was looking forward to my second meeting of the year with Linda Martin. Based on our first conversation, I had decided to do a little more research on my own, and with Linda's permission I met separately with several of her team members in the Sales office. As anticipated, I found them all to be frustrated with Linda as a manager. They all respected her as a salesperson, and most of them actually admired her for her accomplishments, but none of them felt great about her management style.

The good news was the situation had not yet deteriorated past the point of no return. Team members were willing to work with Linda to make the situation better, and were anxious to see changes. Sometimes things get so bad people simply are not willing to work together anymore. But that was clearly not the case here. In fact, most people wanted to have a better relationship with Linda, in the hope that she would share her experience and skills to help them be better salespeople.

Linda arrived at my office wearing a black business suit and white button-down shirt. She always dressed professionally, even though Mega had switched to business casual several years ago. In her line of work, though, meetings could come up quickly, and she always wanted to look professional. I noticed several of her team members had also started wearing suits and ties, so clearly her philosophy in that regard had caught on.

When we sat down to talk, Linda asked me what kind of feedback I had received from her teammates. I could tell she was generally interested in the feedback, and was not looking to know who her enemies were.

"Actually, Linda, I heard a lot of great things from your team members," I began. She smiled in a way that clearly made me think she was not expecting that statement. "Several people spoke well of you, and everyone was hopeful that internal conflicts could get resolved amicably. In fact, when I questioned them about several of the conflicts you are dealing with, most were willing to back down from some issues, and focus their energy on others."

"That's interesting," she replied. "Do you have examples?

"Indeed. You mentioned to me that casual Fridays were a big issue on your team. In fact, you listed it third on the list of conflicts your team was having."

"That's right. I am not a fan of dressing casual while at work, but several people have voiced heated opinions saying it is not right for them to have to dress up when others at Mega are wearing jeans. I just don't think that is a valid…"

"Let me stop you for a minute Linda," I interjected. "Would it surprise you to learn that everyone I spoke to on your team said they would drop this as an issue if they could have their thoughts considered on other issues?"

"Yes! That does surprise me," she responded.

Story 3: Linda Learns Techniques to Resolve Conflicts

"I think you have a better understanding about the nature of your conflicts. Now we need to discuss techniques to resolve them so you all can move forward."

Lesson #3 – Understand the Cause of a Conflict First, Then Look for Conflict Resolution Techniques

After you understand the nature of a conflict (see Lesson 1), you will have an opportunity to choose the best technique to resolve the situation. There are a number of active and passive techniques that can be used to resolve conflicts. These first three options are used most often and are the main reasons why most conflict situations don't escalate into anything major.

- **Avoid**. In this technique, one party thinks his or her point of view is not worth pursuing. This could be because the other person's case is stronger, or because the conflict is not worth the time. In other words, the consequences are not severe enough to fight over. Another reason is that one party does not feel comfortable pressing his or her case in a conflict situation. As a result, the person tends to avoid all conflict. This is usually not a good situation, since many times good points of view are lost.

- **Defer.** Many conflicts are not worth fighting over because one party realizes the consequences are minor or marginal. In fact, some people tend to give in on what they perceive to be inconsequential matters, so they can fight harder on matters more important to them. In this approach, a person will defer on a number of small issues and then look for a sense of reciprocation when he or she feels strongly in another area of conflict.

- **Compromise**. In this approach, one or both parties agrees there is some merit in the other point of view and both change their stance to come closer to the thinking of the other. In many cases, this allows the best ideas from both sides to be combined into a final solution that is even better. This is a great approach and is the reason why conflicts should not necessarily be discouraged. In many cases, initial conflicts will result in better solutions if a compromise is reached.

If these three techniques don't resolve the conflict, there are two more that can be used, depending on the situation.

- **Use organizational power.** If you are a manager and need to resolve a conflict among your staff, you may have to listen to both sides and then make a decision as best you can. There is nothing wrong with this. It is part of being a manager and a leader. If you are part of the conflict, you might also need to resolve the situation using organizational power. As a manager, you may just need to make a final decision based on your experience and responsibilities. This does not have to be a "my way or the highway" approach. You can still make a decision, explain it to all parties, recognize the difference of opinion and hopefully help everyone feel good about the resolution.

Story 3: Linda Learns Techniques to Resolve Conflicts

- **Facilitation.** The last technique, facilitation, is used when none of the other approaches work and both sides feel strongly about their positions (depending on how formal the facilitation is this technique can also be called arbitration). For whatever reason, compromise doesn't work and neither party wants to defer or avoid the conflict. Also, neither party has organizational power, or if they do, they prefer not to utilize it.

  Facilitation is a process that relies on an outside party (a facilitator) to help. The facilitator starts with a process similar to the one described above, making sure the context of the conflict is understood similarly by both parties, the assumptions are similar, the consequences are agreed to, etc. Then each side can make their case independently and formally. The facilitator does not resolve the conflict, but works as a neutral party to try to get the two sides together. Ultimately, the objective of facilitation is to try to resolve the conflict to the satisfaction of both sides. If that still cannot be done, the parties may have to live with the consequences of the unresolved conflict. If the conflicting parties agree, they can also ask the facilitator to resolve the conflict one way or the other. This is an arbitration role.

  This technique is probably not appropriate for most conflicts that arise in a company. You can imagine that if two employees are having a conflict, the manager is typically not going to call in an outside facilitator. If the employees cannot work out the conflict, the manager will usually step in and resolve it. This would not be through the use of an arbitrator, then, but through the use of organizational power, as described in the prior technique.

I am going to offer some follow-up coaching sessions with Linda to help her deal better with conflict situations. I will even see if Linda will allow her entire team to attend the sessions. I think managers must know how to resolve conflicts effectively, but it is a good skill for her group to understand as well. In this case, Linda was using her organizational power on many small decisions where the consequences were marginal. In many of these instances, she should give her opinion, but then defer to the people closer to the action. Deferring or compromising on many of these decisions will put her in a better position when she really needs to use organizational power. She should also coach her people to avoid, defer and compromise in areas that are not as important to them. People can then use more formal techniques to resolve conflicts that are, in fact, meaningful.

Story 4:

Mark Needs to Learn to Listen

One truth about the town of Dickens is that people love their sports. High school football and basketball are both very popular in the town, as is professional football. Chicago was only a few hours from Dickens, and I didn't know anyone in the town who wasn't a lifelong, die-hard Bears fan. My wife Pam and I had been to only one game this season, but it turned out to be one of the best games of the year as the Bears knocked off the Minnesota Vikings in overtime.

That win all but locked up the Midwest Division for the Bears, and the following week they were playing in a first-round playoff game at home. The excitement in the town was palpable. Some town leaders even organized a pep rally downtown, near the Mega Manufacturing campus, but it snowed heavily and few people attended. One of the few who did, however, was Mark Thornburg. Mark was born and raised in Chicago, and I would bet my life he had never left the state of Illinois. I remember watching a Bears game in December a few years back, and seeing Mark on TV. He was one of the crazy guys in the end zone wearing no shirt in the below-zero temperature.

When I met with him on Wednesday, he was wearing a Denim shirt with a terrible Bears tie. Mark stood about 6-foot-5 with broad shoulders and a chiseled face. He was an avid hunter and fisherman, and loved the great outdoors. He and his wife bought a log cabin house about 20 minutes outside of Dickens in a wooded cul-de-sac by a lake.

As I entered into his office, Mark was on the telephone but waved for me to come in. We had scheduled a 30-minute meeting starting at 2:30 and I was a few minutes early. Normally I prefer to wait outside until a person has finished his or her conversation, but Mark's insistent hand gestures made me believe he was about to hang up. Not wishing to eavesdrop on his conversation, I admired some of the Bears paraphernalia in Mark's office. After a few minutes, he finally hung up and I took a seat across from his large desk.

"So Mark, who do you like this weekend?" I asked sarcastically.

"Very funny Tom. I tell you what, man, this is going to be our year. We finally have a quarterback who can lead us to the Super Bowl, and the defense is playing great right now. We are clicking on all cylinders!"

"Oh we are, are we?" I said wryly, drawing the conversation back to work.

"Well, the Bears are doing great, but you are right in that my team is not doing as well. I just don't know what the problem is. Lately, people have seemed tired and unmotivated. Our client has us on a very aggressive work schedule, and I know people are frustrated by it, but the bottom line is we have to get the work done. What have you been hearing?"

Mark had asked me to speak to his team members last week, and the purpose of today's meeting was to go over their feedback.

Story 4: Mark Needs to Learn to Listen

"For the most part, Mark, you are correct. There is some frustration about the demanding schedule. But I have observed something even more interesting I think."

Just then Mark's phone rang. Without hesitation he picked it up. I got up to excuse myself, but Mark again held up his hand and motioned for me to stay. The tone of his conversation hinted that he was talking to a friend about getting tickets to the Bears game. He finally hung up after about three minutes.

"So anyway, Tom, as I was saying, I know morale is down because of the hectic schedule, but we all just have to get over it and get the job done."

"Well, before your call came in, I was about to go into some more detail about other comments I received during my individual meetings with the men and women on your team. You might be surprised to learn the team has a few problems with your managerial style, and what they perceive as an aloofness and lack of caring about their feelings."

"I really can't believe that," Mark said, looking disappointed. "I've always told those guys that I have an open-door policy. They can come to me any time and get their feelings out in the open without fear."

We talked some more. I went back to the rest of the team feedback, stating the team did not think Mark took their suggestions seriously. Mark noted that most of the suggestions were unworkable and would have required him to make schedule changes he felt were inappropriate. I noted that a number of team members felt he made commitments to them that he did not keep. Mark started to get agitated and stated he always follows up on his commitments, but that perhaps some people are confused as to what is being agreed to.

Mark's phone rang again, and again, without hesitation, he answered it. "Patrick!" he shouted into the phone. "Are you ready for the big game or what? I am so fired up, man, I can't tell you."

With that I motioned to Mark I was leaving. I wrote down a note and handed it to him. It stated simply – "Let's reschedule when you can dedicate time to receive this team feedback."

Lesson #4 – Utilize Active Listening as the Key to Effective Communication

One of the skills of a good manager is to be a good communicator. In many organizations, the measure of this skill has to do with:

- Expressing yourself plainly and clearly.
- Communicating effectively with your clients, customers and vendors.
- Communicating well with your managers and subordinates.

Many organizations also include written communication skills as a management competency requirement. Sometimes this skill is rolled into the general communication category and sometimes it is a separate skill area.

One part of communication that is often missed is the listening side. It has been said that the best communicators are actually the best listeners - not the best speakers. Remember that

Story 4: Mark Needs to Learn to Listen

communication is a two-way process of expressing and receiving information between a speaker and a receiver. The speaking part is only half of the communication model. You must, in turn, listen carefully to the other person to make sure you understand what he or she is trying to say as well.

In a sense, speaking is the easier of the two sides of the conversation. When you talk, you know what you are trying to say. However, when you listen, you must understand what the other person is saying. This requires you to use your understanding of the background, context and assumptions behind the communication. For many people, this is the harder part of the communication model.

"Active listening" is the term used to describe this proactive listening process. You need to really focus on what is being said to know how to respond and to make sure you are identifying and capturing requirements accurately. There are a number of techniques associated with active listening.

- **Look at the speaker.** This is important to help make the speaker feel at ease. Make eye contact when you talk, and let the other person make eye contact with you when he or she talks.

- **Invest the time.** One aspect of being a good listener is that you prepare yourself to spend dedicated time with someone else. If you have a meeting scheduled for 30 minutes, be prepared to dedicate the 30 minutes. If someone comes into your office with a problem, move your work aside to dedicate time to him or her. Don't take phone calls as Mark did. It is hard, perhaps impossible, to focus on the conversation when you are doing other things as well. Even if you can keep focus, this behavior tells the other person that you don't think they are important enough to give your complete attention.

- **Show an interest.** One of the worst things a manager can do is act like he or she really would rather be somewhere else. This happens when a manager looks at his or her watch, glances at other work on the desk, etc. This leads other people to shut down and wonder why they are wasting their time. Instead, be engaged verbally and non-verbally. Non-verbal techniques that show an interest include things like leaning toward the other person, nodding when appropriate to signal you understand, smiling appropriately to make the other person feel at ease and maintaining a good, positive, upbeat attitude.

- **Clear your biases.** When we hear information, we filter it and make sense of it based on our own background and experiences. For instance, if we say that we are having car trouble, we don't expect to have to describe what a car is to the other person. We assume that the person's background and experiences allow them to understand the definition of a car.

  On the other hand, sometimes this background and context can become a bias. This happens when we have our own point of view and we start to selectively hear the parts of the discussion that will support our view. When this happens, for good or bad, you are not listening effectively.

Story 4: Mark Needs to Learn to Listen

- **Draw the speaker out.** In many cases, the other person may not have the best communication skills and the person also may be uncomfortable talking to you as a manager. Using the above techniques can help you make the other person more comfortable. Good follow-up questions will help you better understand what he or she is trying to say.

There are good verbal and nonverbal techniques to help you become a good active listener. These include::

Non-verbal:

- **Listen!** First, make a conscious attempt to spend as much time listening as possible. Resist the urge to give your opinion or to spend a lot of time talking. Active listeners allow the other person to talk.

- **Let the other person speak (within reason).** It is important not to cut him or her off. Let the other person express his or her entire opinion or statement. If he or she is in the middle of a line of thought and gets interrupted, it can be very annoying and may cause him or her to lose the line of reasoning.

- **Observe the non-verbal expressions.** It is said that the majority of information expressed in a discussion is communicated non-verbally. That is why it is easier to express yourself in person than it is through a phone conversation. So look for the non-verbal clues as well. If the person you are talking to is leaning back with their arms crossed, for instance, it may be a sign they are resisting your ideas or disagreeing with you. If a person is getting red-eyed, it is probably a sign that they are upset.

- **Avoid using distracting non-verbal expressions.** Just as you should observe the non-verbal behavior of others, you should be cognizant of your own non-verbal behaviors. Bad non-verbal expressions on your part can jeopardize the discussion as well. This includes things like:

    - Rolling your eyeballs to signal disagreement or disbelief.
    - Checking your watch often to show you wish you were somewhere else.
    - Yawning to show you are bored or tired.
    - Playing with objects like a pencil to show you are preoccupied or bored.
    - Tapping your fingers to show impatience or boredom.
    - Crossing your own arms to show resistance to what the other person is saying.
    - Placing your feet on the desk. This can be a sign of disrespect to the other person or saying that you don't care about being professional.

Verbal:

- **Encouraging statements** to show your interest and to keep the other person talking about an important area. For example, just saying "Hmmm, I see" shows the other person you are engaged in the discussion.

Story 4: Mark Needs to Learn to Listen

- **Restating and summarization.** Restating means you repeat what you have heard to validate you understand. Summarizing means you take a lot of information and restate the major points to validate you heard correctly.
- **Reflecting.** This is similar to restating, except you bring the other person's feeling into the mix. This includes statements like "I see you are passionate about this idea. Let me make sure I have the information right," or "You seem to feel..," or "My perception is you don't think this is a good idea."

My discussion with Mark showed he could use some coaching on active listening. The first thing that struck me, of course, was that Mark did not have the courtesy of dedicating his time to me. We had a prearranged meeting; however, he felt free to take other calls during our meeting. I was trying to coach him on the need to focus on the person he is talking to, and this little demonstration will help drive home that point. This is the type of behavior from Mark that results in the perception from his team members that he doesn't really care about what they are saying. So my personal observation lends credence to this team feedback.

As I expected, Mark called me soon after I left and apologized for the interruptions. He offered to meet with me later that day and I agreed on the condition that he would dedicate the meeting time to the discussion at hand. He began to understand the perception it gives when he allows interruptions at a meeting. Of course, there are exceptions. For instance, if Mark's manager or his sponsor calls, Mark may need to pick up the phone. However, he should keep these interruptions to an absolute minimum, note the importance of the interruption and apologize for the interruption in advance.

Another problem Mark was having with his listening skills was not removing his biases as to the causes for the team morale decline. Mark believed the morale problem was simply a matter of a heavy work schedule. My feedback to Mark was the schedule was part of the problem, but his behavior was also part of the problem. Based on my conversation with Mark, I could see he was trying to reinforce the feedback about the work schedule, since that fits his prior bias. He was tending not to acknowledge the team feedback having to do with his own behavior.

In addition, Mark needed to understand the outcome of his team meetings, including any commitments he was making. He should make it a point to recap the outstanding action items coming out of his meetings, and he or the other person should document any commitments made in an e-mail just to be sure the commitments are understood. If that happens and the commitments are not met, then Mark has another problem. However, right now, it appeared Mark was making commitments or agreeing to actions from the other person without fully realizing what was being said.

Mark is not a lost cause. People can learn to be good listeners even if it is not in their basic nature. Active listening is a critical management skill. Your staff will put up with a lot, including tight schedules and long hours, if they feel you are concerned about them as people and listen to their concerns, suggestions and needs with an open mind.

Story 5:

Stan – A Good Guy but Weak Performer

With the Bears beating up on the Philadelphia Eagles during Sunday's NFL playoff game, I knew what the Monday morning conversation would be around the water cooler. As I walked into the break room for my morning coffee, there were already a few interns talking with some of the managers in the Marketing department, dissecting the key plays of the game and offering insights and analysis into next week's match-up.

"Who won the big game, boys?" I said jokingly. "Was it the Baltimore Colts again?"

The two Marketing managers smiled, although the three interns looked confused (as if I needed another reminder of how old I was). While pouring my coffee, I was pleasantly surprised to bump into Jerry Ackerman – an old friend of mine who I had the pleasure of working with a lot in my days as a Project Management Coach. Jerry was widely recognized as one of the better project managers at Mega, and I took a degree of pride knowing I had helped with his development.

Jerry and I talked for about 10 minutes, and he told me about a new project he was working on. The project was only a few months old, but I could tell by his demeanor there was some sort of problem. He looked over his shoulder more than once while we spoke briefly about the situation, and I began to get the sense something important was going on.

"Tell you what, Jerry, why don't you make an appointment and come and see me tomorrow in my office where we can talk in private?" He agreed with a nervous smile, and we shook hands as he walked out of the break room.

I was thinking about him back at my desk when a knock on my door broke my trance. It was Olivia Riordan, the IT Manager in the application support group, and she was a few minutes late for our 9 a.m. meeting.

"Am I disrupting you?" she said shyly. "You look like you are in deep thought about something."

"I'm terribly sorry, Olivia. No, you are not interrupting. Please, come in and have a seat."

She closed the door behind her and took a seat on the sofa in my office. Most people prefer to sit in the chairs in front of my desk, but I had known Olivia for about four years and she was a very laid-back woman. Not wanting to appear rude, I got out from behind my desk and pulled a chair closer to the sofa.

"So what's happening down in IT these days?" I offered to get the discussion going.

"Things are really going well for me and for the department, with only one problem. His name is Stan Hooper." Olivia sank back into the couch and let out a sigh. I didn't know much about Stan, other than he had been at Mega for just over a year. I was surprised to hear Olivia's problem was employee-related, as I considered her to be a strong manager. She was recently

Story 5: Stan – A Good Guy but Weak Performer

promoted to a supervisory position in the IT Department, and was managing a team of eight specialists.

"Why don't you give me more detail, Olivia? What exactly is the trouble with Stan?"

"He's just not cutting the mustard," she began. "He's a real nice guy, and he gets along great with everyone, but he is constantly behind on his work and missing deadlines. Not only that, but he is not a good communicator, and he is terribly disorganized."

I could tell from her tone that Olivia was serious about the problem, and she was clearly thinking about termination as an option. Olivia emphasized the importance of multi-tasking in her group, and spoke anecdotally about Stan's inability to focus in this type of environment. As she spoke, a question popped into my head. I waited for her to conclude her thoughts and asked.

"Stan isn't new to the company. How did he do in his last performance review?"

"That's the problem, Tom. His last manager gave him a satisfactory review, and did not mention anything about his inability to meet expectations. When I asked his old manager about this, he implied that the problems existed during his first review, but he didn't have the heart to say anything because 'Stan tries real hard and is a good guy.' Those were his exact words!"

"It sounds like Stan's old boss did him a major disservice by not pointing out these deficiencies during his review. It might not be fair that this was passed along to you, but don't do Stan another disservice, Olivia. You are a great manager and you need to bring these issues up to Stan right now. Don't wait for his next review."

The remainder of our time focused on the proper way to proceed.

Lesson #5 – Give Fact-Based Performance Feedback Routinely, Not Just During Formal Reviews

The world is made up of people with various skills and talents. Often, people's talents drive them to work in certain areas where they excel. In other cases, their individual talents and the jobs they perform are not aligned. Many people have the general skills and the drive required to overcome a lack of alignment.

If everyone excelled in the job they were asked to fulfill there would be much less need for the Human Resource staff. However, it doesn't always work like that. Some people are not able to meet expectations and managers must not feel guilty about working with them to try to turn things around. Such may be the case with Stan. It appears he is not able to meet the expectations of Olivia, his manager. That is not a good thing. It appears Stan's performance has been lacking for a while, perhaps ever since he came into the group. Unfortunately, Stan's old manager did not provide honest performance feedback and he did a disservice to Stan by failing to bring this to his attention.

Olivia, however, is better about providing honest performance feedback and is not afraid to bring this issue to Stan's attention. In fact, Olivia needs to address this performance issue since

Story 5: Stan – A Good Guy but Weak Performer

it keeps her group from providing maximum business value. Olivia also knows this feedback should be given now and should not wait for the next formal performance review.

Olivia's question really is how best to proceed. Her inclination would be to place Stan on a performance plan, but I warned her that was not the place to start. Although the performance problem may have been around for a while, it is probable Stan will be hearing about it for the first time. So there is some preliminary work that needs to be done to properly set the stage for this discussion.

As a management coach, I don't want to get into the position of assuming Olivia's view of Stan's performance is correct. It could be that Stan's performance is fine and perhaps it is Olivia who is not judging the performance correctly. In this particular case, Olivia seems to have validated the poor performance with a prior manager, but again, I have not talked to that second manager, so at this point I am taking Olivia's word.

Fortunately, I can help Olivia address this problem without making judgments one way or the other on Stan. I asked her to consider the following approach,

1. The first step is to start collecting facts. Olivia has told me of some general situations where Stan missed his deadlines, but she has not provided any factual information in terms of specific due dates missed or specific expectations not met. So, this is the place to start. Olivia needs to have a set of facts and examples available when she talks to Stan. These examples cannot be six months old - they need to be relatively recent. Olivia also does not need 10 examples, but she should have at least a couple.

2. Once the factual examples are ready, the second step is to have a preliminary performance discussion. There are three targeted objectives to this meeting:

   - To make Stan aware of the perceived performance problem;
   - To get Stan's feedback and response;
   - To determine a short-term action plan; This is critical and will be the key to trying to turn Stan's performance around.

Olivia may have some ideas for how to proceed, but she cannot firm things up until she hears Stan's side of the story. In many cases, the manager jumps to the conclusion that there is a performance problem, pure and simple. However, there are a number of different reasons why Stan's performance may not be up to expectations. Once Olivia understands the causes, she will be able to create the right action plan. For example:

- Stan may not be clear on the work that is being assigned or he may not be clear on the expectations and due dates. Sometimes when team members miss a deadline, they may tell you they did not realize the work was due at that time.

  If there is confusion on what the expectations are, the action plan would include changes for how Olivia assigns work. This could include having Stan confirm back to Olivia in writing the expectations for deliverables and dates. In the weekly status meeting, Olivia could also discuss assignments and status as a team, and ask each person to state his or her current assignments and due dates to the rest of the team for validation.

Story 5: Stan – A Good Guy but Weak Performer

- Sometimes it is not a matter of "will," but a matter of "skill." Stan may feel he does not have the right skills and experience for his assignments. For instance, one of Stan's assignments was to complete an analysis for a new set of reports. However, Stan may be delivering late because he does not have the right technical skills for his position. He may not understand how to perform the analysis. He would not be the first person that was sent into a position at Mega Manufacturing without the proper skill set.

  If Stan falls into this category, Olivia will need to decide whether she thinks he could do the work better with the proper training. Training could mean a class, computer-based training or even pairing Stan up with someone more experienced. If Olivia and Stan feel that training could help, the training steps should be a part of the short-term action plan.

  If Stan feels he does not have the right skills and Olivia feels he can't be easily trained, they will need to look for other alternatives. One alternative might include replacing Stan with someone with a better skill set for this job and looking for a new role for Stan.

- Stan may be confused as to who should be providing work to him and he may be taking on additional work that is being requested from others. If this is part of the problem, the short-term plan will include an emphasis on how work is assigned and the expectations Olivia has for the assigned work. Perhaps emphasizing the point and providing more structure for Stan will help him focus on his assigned work.

- It may turn out that, in fact, Stan has other critical support work that does take precedence over the work that Olivia has assigned. In this case, perhaps the problem is a lack of proactive communication from Stan back to Olivia regarding his changing priorities. The action plan in this case would include stressing the need for proactive communication. If Olivia knows that Stan is getting pulled off her work to address a production problem, she can reset her expectations or perhaps even assign someone else to the performance problem and allow Stan to continue on his assigned work.

- There may be some other business or personal factors that could explain Stan's performance. For instance, Stan may be taking care of a very sick child or spouse. He may be selling his home and purchasing a new one. He may be having trouble sleeping at night. Olivia should not bring up these potential personal problems on her own, but Stan may volunteer a personal problem contributing to his lack of focus. If personal problems are affecting work performance, the effect should be temporary. In many cases, just having the performance discussion is enough for most people to re-focus and turn the situation around.

Story 5: Stan – A Good Guy but Weak Performer

This initial performance discussion between Stan and Olivia will help determine the next steps. Stan's performance problems may have a root cause that Olivia and Stan can resolve together. Remember that his previous manager did not make Stan aware of this problem before. Perhaps just bringing the performance perception to Stan's attention will help to resolve the situation. Until this initial discussion occurs, it is not possible to know exactly where the problem lies and what solutions might be appropriate.

The first performance meeting between Stan and Olivia should not end before there is a short-term plan for addressing the situation. The short-term plan may require work from both Stan and Olivia. The plan should also include a time to get back together again, perhaps in about 30 days. It is important to get back together to determine whether there has been any improvement in performance. If there has been, then perhaps the situation just needs to be monitored from that point.

If the performance is still not up to expectations, then the second meeting should again explore causes and see if there are more short-term actions that make sense. If there are, Stan and Olivia can implement them as well. However, if Olivia does not think Stan can meet the expectations for the position, she should get Human Resources involved and look at the alternatives available at that time.

Story 6:

Jerry is in an Ethical Dilemma

Jerry Ackerman arrived at my office door right on time for our 10 a.m. meeting. He had recently cut his shaggy hair and now wore it cropped very close to his head. The new haircut made him look somewhat younger, although he didn't need much help as he was only 32. Jerry and I had worked together on several projects last year, and it was amazing to see the amount of growth he achieved.

Still, when I spoke to him briefly in the coffee room yesterday, I knew something bad was going on. Jerry was a worrier when I first met him, but over time I noticed he was mellowing a bit, most likely due to his increased confidence in himself and his project management ability. I shook his hand as he walked toward my desk to take a seat, and I knew right away he was nervous. His palms were sweaty, and there was some sweat beads brewing on his brow.

"Jerry, you've got me a bit worried," I said as I took my seat behind my desk. "What exactly is going on?"

"Well Tom," he replied, "I think I might have gotten myself into a bit of hot water. Something is going on in my project team, and I should have said something right away, but I didn't, and now I feel like the more time has passed, the more difficult the situation has become. I really just don't even know what I can do, and I…"

"Slow down Jerry! You are talking in riddles here. Take a deep breath and start from the beginning."

Jerry inhaled deeply and let the breath out slowly through his nose as he reclined back in his chair. He began talking about a new cross-functional team he had been asked to participate in. The Vice President of Marketing was leading the team, and there were several people from brand management and marketing also on it, as well as Jerry and a few other people from various departments whose opinions were generally valued within the company.

The team's purpose was to interview advertising agencies and make a recommendation on which agency to hire. The task was of tremendous importance to the company as a significant amount of money had been set aside for a major new branding campaign to kick off next year. The budget for the agency was in the $18-$20 million range, and, last I heard, the field had been narrowed to three companies.

"So what exactly is the problem?" I asked.

"I am afraid I have not been completely honest with the group about a relationship I have with a person on one of the agency team's pitching the business. You see, an old college friend of mine, Darren, works for an ad agency and he is participating in the pitch for his company."

Jerry's eyes glanced toward me, and it was clear he was ashamed. My head was immediately filled with questions, but I knew this was going to be a very sensitive conversation and I wanted to choose my words carefully.

Story 6: Jerry is in an Ethical Dilemma

"How strong is your relationship with Darren?"

"I would not say we are great friends, but I went to college with him, and we have stayed in touch, on again off again, through the years."

"Have you given Darren access to any information or any feedback that would give him and his company an unfair advantage over the others?"

"No, we haven't spoken outside of the meetings. But, it seems clear to me that his agency asked him to play a large role in the presentation because of his relationship with me."

"Why do you say that?"

"He disclosed during the first round of interviews that he works full-time on another account, and that his day-to-day involvement with our business would be minimal. He would be involved with the brand strategy and creative direction, but the day-to-day communication would be handled with another woman."

"I see. And do you feel like your opinion has been swayed by the relationship?"

"I don't know. I did not have to say much in the first round of meetings. Several people thought highly of Darren's presentation and wanted his company to come back again for the second round. I did not disagree. Still, though, there is not much consensus on which of the remaining three agencies is the best, and I find myself wondering if my opinion is biased."

"The problem is, Jerry, it does not matter whether your opinion is biased or not. Even if you were as objective as you could be, an impression of impropriety will always exist. What if one of the losing agencies finds out about this relationship and decides to seek legal options claiming they were unfairly hurt because of your relationship?"

"I know, Tom. That's exactly why I needed to see you today. I wish I could go back in time and excuse myself from this process at the very beginning. But I cannot undo what has been done. The question is what do I do moving forward?"

"Ethically, you know the situation isn't right. That's a good start. Now we just need to determine how to move forward."

Lesson #6 – Maintain Your Personal Ethics

Trying to define ethics can be difficult because there are two components. The first is more legal and the second is more personal. The legal side refers to acting in a way that is within the law. More specifically for companies, it means you are acting within company policies. On the surface this seems reasonable enough. However, laws and company policies do not address every activity and every situation that a manager comes upon in the course of a career. In many cases, the policies themselves contain shades of gray; that is, the policies are really guidelines to guide your actions in certain situations.

Story 6: Jerry is in an Ethical Dilemma

One example of normal company policy has to do with not taking bribes, especially in areas where you have decision-making authority. If you take a monetary bribe from a vendor on matters you are deciding, you are obviously on the wrong side of the ethics question. This type of behavior is against your company policy and probably illegal as well.

However, does this policy apply to a vendor that pays for you to attend an industry convention in an attractive location? Perhaps it is not so clear. In fact, there may be business reasons why it would be good for you to be at the conference and you may not have the budget to get there on your own. Is this still a bribe? Let's scale this back a little to include expensive dinners that the vendor pays for. It's not quite so cut and dry. How about a lunch that the vendor pays for? This may be even murkier.

That is why there are two aspects of ethical behavior. The first has to do with the laws of society and the policies of your company. The second side is more personal and helps fill in the gaps when there are not laws or policies that govern the situation. Someone once said that ethics has to do with making sure you act appropriately even when no one is looking. This gets to the core of personal ethics. When you are in a situation that appears to have a conflict of ethics, many times no one will know how you act or the potential repercussions. However, the question is whether you act as if others know, or will find out, about the situation. You have a better chance of acting ethically if you behave as if someone will always find out about the decisions you make.

Let's look back at the prior examples. Should you allow a vendor to pay for you to attend a conference? Think about it in terms of what people would think if they knew. If the conference deals with a subject absolutely within your job description, perhaps it is okay. In fact, perhaps you will be able to make more informed decisions if you have the perspective of the additional information available at the conference. In that case, you should feel prepared to justify your decision if challenged by a co-worker or a manager.

On the other hand, if you attend a conference with a dubious business connection, you might be in trouble from an ethics standpoint. Likewise, if you attend a relevant conference, but end up spending more time on your personal entertainment that you do on conference business, you would also have a hard time from an ethics standpoint. The question is not whether you will get away with it or not. The question is whether you are behaving as if other people will find out. If you are relying on the logic that no one will know, then chances are you are not acting in the highest ethical standards.

Now let's look at Jerry's situation. Jerry is a friend of mine, and I know he is a stand-up guy. He is a good husband and goes to church regularly. However, he had a large hand in his current ethical quandary.

If he would have disclosed up-front that he and Darren were friends, the various stakeholders at Mega and the other vendors could have reacted to this information accordingly. There is no rule against vendors and company employees being friends. It happens all the time. If there was a big concern, Mega could have asked for Darren to be replaced by someone else at the ad agency. Jerry and Darren could still be friends and the vendor evaluation would proceed.

The assignment of Darren as a vendor representative was probably a smart move by the vendor.

Story 6: Jerry is in an Ethical Dilemma

The problem has risen because of non-disclosure. The risk is that the relationship will become known at a later time and the immediate question will be asked as to why the situation was not disclosed. Jerry is also in a quandary now regarding his impartiality. If his team recommends Darren's company as the primary vendor, there will be a big concern that the (undisclosed) personal relationship helped drive the decision. Jerry could avoid that situation by making sure Darren's company did not win the business, but then he is not being fair to Darren's company. There will be millions of dollars, and jobs, riding on this decision. It is not fair to Darren's company for Jerry to purposely guide the decision away from them for the sake of being "impartial."

So, we are left with an ethical dilemma and it is not sitting too well with Jerry. The fact that he feels bad about the situation shows he knows it is not totally right. He is not acting in a way that he would feel comfortable with if the relationship was discovered. Therefore he is on the wrong side of an ethical decision. Since he did not disclose this situation immediately, it is possible that Jerry could be disciplined and removed from the evaluation. Depending on how serious the situation is perceived, this could affect Jerry's performance review and his future opportunities in the company. It could result in his termination. At this point, these are only possibilities. However, if the situation comes out much later from someone else, those potential outcomes are much more certain.

At this point Jerry needs to determine what are his personal ethical standards? Should he act as if someone was looking and make the situation clear now? This would probably be the ethical approach. He might face some consequences and he would have to deal with that. Being on the wrong side of an ethics question usually brings some consequences. It is also possible that his manager might see this as a learning opportunity for Jerry and give him the benefit of the doubt. However, if the situation comes out later or through someone else's disclosure, Jerry's situation will surely be much worse.

After our discussion I knew what Jerry's answer would be – disclosure. I don't think he would have asked to talk to me if he had not already been leaning toward that conclusion.

Story 7:

Look All Around You for Performance Feedback

The last Friday of January was a special day at Mega, as all employees were allowed to wear Chicago Bears attire at work, in support of the town's favorite NFL football team. The Bears had advanced to the Super Bowl and would be playing in the championship game on Sunday. It was neat to walk around the office and see everyone dressed in Bears attire. Even Kenneth Holliday, the chief financial officer and one of the straightest arrows I'd ever met, got in the spirit with a throwback Gale Sayers jersey.

Of course, in a company as large as Mega, I had a feeling I would bump into more than one "odd man out," and the first one I saw was Marvin Hardy. He was wearing blue jeans and a bright orange and blue sweatshirt, with a matching orange and blue hat. Marvin was born in Florida and was a die-hard Miami Dolphins fan – the Bears opponent on Sunday. He was getting some grief for wearing the "enemy's" colors, but most people were good-natured about it.

The second person I saw in Dolphins colors caught me by surprise. It was Erin Christianson, who was born in Maine and went to college at Northwestern. I bumped into her in the third floor large conference room, where pizza and soda were being served as a special lunch.

"I didn't know you were a Dolphins' fan Erin. Where did that come from?"

"My dad, actually," she said as she started in on her sausage pizza. "He played football at Syracuse University with Larry Csonka."

"Wow! I didn't know your dad played football. What position?"

"He wasn't very good, actually. He was a back-up linebacker mostly, although he did start a couple games his senior year when another guy got hurt."

"That's very interesting. A neat story," I said as I sipped on my cup of Diet Coke. "So how are things down in product engineering?"

Erin was one of six project managers in the product-engineering department, working for Rebecca Holden, who I did not know very well. Erin had been at Mega for two years, and she shared with me a concern she was having about her upcoming performance review.

"Rebecca is a very nice woman, but she is also very busy, and she doesn't stay in touch with us on any sort of consistent basis, unless there is a problem. On one hand, it is nice not having a boss looking over my shoulder constantly, but on the other hand, I feel like I get penalized at review time because she doesn't know what projects I have been working on, and she doesn't have much feedback for me."

Story 7: Look All Around You for Performance Feedback

"That seems strange," I said, putting down my pizza slice. "Do you and Rebecca not communicate during the week? Does she not hold team meetings or one-on-one meetings?"

"She tries to, but, again, it is not consistent. I think I am doing good work on my projects, and I don't normally need a lot of instruction. Since I don't often need help, she devotes her time to the other managers who need more supervision."

"That sounds like it should be a positive thing for you."

"It should be, but Rebecca is still my supervisor, and she is responsible for things like salary increases and professional advancement."

"I see. And you think that because Rebecca does not spend as much time with you, it will negatively affect your ability to get ahead?"

"Exactly. Rebecca sees that I can meet deadlines and complete projects within budget, but I don't think she sees my communication skills, my organizational skills, and the other things I do as a project manager."

"Tell you what. Why don't you talk to Rebecca and see if she would be willing to use a 360-degree feedback approach to your upcoming review? This way you can solicit feedback from people who have worked and interacted more closely with you over the last year."

Lesson #7 – Use 360-Degree Reviews to Get a Thorough Understanding of Employee Performance

Performance reviews can be a stressful time for staff. There is a lot at stake. The amount of a pay raise may be based on the review feedback. Bonus payments may be involved, and promotions may be affected. It's no wonder that performance reviews are viewed with a combination of anticipation, desire and dread.

Performance reviews are no picnic for most managers either. It takes a great deal of thought and care to give honest and thorough performance feedback to an employee - even if it is positive. If a manager has to deal with negative performance, his or her anxiety level can be off the scale. Because giving good feedback is difficult, many, if not most, performance reviews are shallow at best.

Of course, it is worth mentioning that the yearly performance review is not the only time a manager should provide feedback. This dialog should happen on an ongoing basis. When employees do something good, they should get positive recognition and reinforcement. Similar constructive feedback should closely follow employee actions that do not meet expectations.

One of the major criticisms of the annual review process is that some managers do not have a good appreciation for the accomplishments their staffs achieve during the year. I say "some" managers because this is different from manager to manager. There are some managers at Mega who are more hands-on in terms of the work that goes on in the group. They are part of status meetings, they are engaged with the client and they meet frequently with the people in their

Story 7: Look All Around You for Performance Feedback

groups. Other managers, like Rebecca, are more hands-off and only get involved with their staff when there are problems. That doesn't mean Rebecca is a bad manager.

Last year, Rebecca's feedback stated that since she did not have to get too involved in Erin's projects, she assumed that Erin was managing her projects well. Since project managers are expected to manage their projects well, Erin's performance "met expectations." This is an example of a "shallow review" that I mentioned earlier. The feedback may be valid on the surface, but there is nothing behind it in terms of meaningful feedback that an employee can use to reinforce or change his or her behavior. In many cases, managers who do not have firsthand observations also end up providing feedback that the employee does not think is valid or relevant. These are the kinds of characteristics that cause a lot of anxiety with the review process.

One way to be as fair as possible with employees is to be sure that performance feedback is not based exclusively on the manager's perception. The manager should seek feedback from other people that the employee works with on a daily basis. This is called a 360-degree review process.

A 360-degree review process formally seeks input from multiple sources. Typically this includes feedback from the rest of the team (peers) and business clients (customers). If the employee is also a manager (functional manager or project manager), feedback is also sought from his or her direct reports.

The 360-degree feedback process is a way to help the manager get a more balanced view of the employee's performance. The real beneficiary of this process, though, is the employee being reviewed. The review process should not be a time when the employee sits back passively to be praised or beaten up. The employee should see the review process as an opportunity to get an outside perception of strengths and areas where they can improve. Ultimately, the employee should take a personal interest in the review process to ensure they can grow professionally and provide more and more value to the company.

Like many companies, Mega Manufacturing has a yearly process for gathering and documenting formal performance feedback for the prior year. Mega still ties annual salary increases, bonuses and other benefits to the results of the performance reviews, so they are important milestones for all employees in the company.

The process of gathering formal feedback from multiple sources seems reasonable enough. Why aren't managers at Mega using this process already? First, it takes extra work and the manager must be willing to invest the extra time to seek and gather the feedback. Second, since this is not the way reviews are typically performed, it requires a change in work habits.

When you change how people do their jobs, a culture change initiative is implied, and Mega has not invested the time and effort to fight this particular culture change battle. Implementing the 360-degree review process will require setting up some processes, putting together forms, educating managers and employees, getting people comfortable completing the feedback surveys, etc. Of course, you have to reinforce the message and prepare to battle the managers and employees who don't want to follow the process for whatever reason. So it is not something that can be implemented overnight.

Story 7: Look All Around You for Performance Feedback

One good thing about Erin's situation is that she and Rebecca can gather this performance feedback without having to worry about implementing a major culture change initiative. Erin and Rebecca can use this process to gather better input for Erin's review, since Rebecca does not have good firsthand feedback. The process goes something like this:

- Rebecca or Erin sends out simple, standard surveys to major business clients, other project managers (peers) and project team members (upward). Each of these audiences may have a customized survey form, or you may have a generic form that can be used by all participants. The survey should have 10 questions at a maximum, plus areas to write free-form comments. I should be able to help them by getting some sample performance feedback forms from the Human Resources group.

- Typically, the surveys and associated comments are returned to Rebecca, since she is the one who will provide the feedback. Completing the surveys is encouraged, but not mandatory. You can also leave a place for the person completing the feedback to place their name, although this is usually optional as well.

- Rebecca consolidates all feedback and free form comments. It is important that the actual review forms not be given directly to Erin since this may stifle the honest feedback you desire.

- Rebecca uses the 360-degree review feedback, as well as her observations, as input into the performance review. Rebecca also has some additional input based on the past years accomplishments.

- During the actual review, Rebecca provides her overall review feedback based on all of the diverse feedback received. She should also provide a spreadsheet to Erin with the detailed feedback results. Rebecca should throw out any comments that would help Erin identify the reviewer, unless that feedback is vital to the review.

Of course, all personal feedback is based on perceptions. That is true when the manager provides the only feedback, but it is also true with a 360-degree review process. The difference is that the feedback is more real and more valid when it is captured from different perspectives and from different people. If the manager's feedback is reinforced by clients, direct reports and/or peers, it is much harder to ignore.

The 360-degree review process should help ease Erin's concerns about not getting valid performance feedback from Rebecca. This process will not guarantee Erin a high rating, but it should give Rebecca a better sense for how Erin is perceived by the people she works with on an ongoing basis.

Story 7: Look All Around You for Performance Feedback

Ultimately, giving performance feedback is still the job of the manager. That responsibility is not delegated to the people providing input. However, getting performance feedback from these various sources gives the manager more information, which he or she can use to provide more valuable performance feedback to the employee. This information, combined with other more objective, performance-based results, should allow a manager to provide meaningful feedback to the employee.

Story 8:

Reflecting on Professional Development on Super Bowl Sunday

Super Bowl Sunday arrived the first weekend in February and found the Chicago Bears taking on the Miami Dolphins in a clash of the two best teams in football. To celebrate the day, my wife Pam and I invited several friends and colleagues over to watch the game on our big screen TV. It was a snowy day in Dickens with temperatures in the teens. Still, the opportunity to watch the big game on the big screen was too good to pass up for most, so we had a big crowd.

George Benes and his wife Maria were the first couple to arrive. George was wearing a Bears jersey that looked a little small on him, with old jeans and an old pair of Nike running shoes. George worked in the Sales Department and had been with Mega for about 14 years. He was in his early 40s and did not own many new things. I had heard several of his clients and colleagues calling him "dinosaur" because of his unwillingness to change with the times.

I offered to take the Benes' coats and put them in our guest room. On my way down the hall, I noticed George was following me and looked like he wanted to talk about something.

"Something on your mind, George?" I offered as we walked down the hall. He smiled and pointed into the bedroom, looking over his shoulder to make sure his wife had moved into the living room.

"Actually, Tom, I was wondering if we could talk shop briefly before the others arrive," George began, closing the door behind him.

"I prefer to discuss business at the office, George, but I can make an exception if the matter is urgent."

"I would really appreciate it," he replied. "The matter truly is important. I think I might be on a path to termination at Mega."

"Really? Why do you think that?"

George began to talk about a new Customer Relationship Management (CRM) package that Mega had purchased and installed, and his inability to use it correctly. He mentioned that the entire staff went through two full days of training on the software, but he didn't feel that things were explained well enough and he needed more personal instruction on how to use the new tool.

In the course of our conversation, George also mentioned that he had not had much experience with computers in general, and had no idea how to access the Internet or how to send an e-mail.

"I prefer to do business the old-fashioned way I guess," he said. "I like to meet face-to-face with people and leverage my contacts to meet new people and set up sales meetings. Nowadays, though, meetings are scheduled via e-mail, and most of my colleagues are using PDAs to track

Story 8: Reflecting on Professional Development on Super Bowl Sunday

schedules and appointments. They are also researching companies on the Internet and getting easy access to a wealth of information that I simply do not know how to access."

"You know George, the Internet is not really a new fad any more, nor are computers and e-mail. Haven't you been the least bit curious about how to use these tools to help do your job better?"

"That's the thing, Tom. I feel like I do my job perfectly well. I am not the top sales person in our office, but I am not the worst either. I haven't seen the need to do things differently. Besides, if the company wants me to do things differently, then it should pay for adequate training to make sure I am able to meet its new expectations."

"I thought you said you received training on the new CRM package?"

"I did, but it wasn't good enough, obviously."

"I think I am getting the picture. Although I sympathize with your current situation, George, I think you need to reexamine how you got to this point. The truth is, you are more responsible than Mega for your professional growth."

Lesson #8 – Encourage Your Staff to Take Responsibility for Their Personal and Professional Development

I have heard other employees complain that Mega Manufacturing does not provide them with enough training. They basically stay in the same job year after year, and keep their noses clean. Sometimes people like the job they are in, but they sometimes feel like they are stuck and not able to learn new things. However, they keep doing what they have always been doing and think that someday their manager will tap them on the shoulder and tell them it is time to go to a training class. Then one day they do get tapped on the shoulder. However, the tapping leads to a meeting with their manager and a layoff notice.

On the surface, employees might think training is the responsibility of the company. After all, many types of training have a cost and it is typically expected that the company pays if the subject is work-related. For instance, if a company asks an employee to work in an area that requires new skills, it would not be uncommon for the company to provide training (or to pay for the training). This happens all the time on projects. One of the responsibilities of project managers and other people managers is to evaluate the skills of their people and ensure the team has the right skills to do their jobs in a way that provides the maximum value to the company.

However, think about that last line a little more and notice where the emphasis is. One of the responsibilities of a manager is to make sure the members of his or her team have the right skills to get their jobs done. In many cases this means having people with the right skills to provide primary and backup coverage for all areas of responsibility. In many cases it requires people to be multi-functional and have talents that will allow them to fill many roles.

However, the key point is that a manager must look out for the business and make sure the people on the team have the right skills to meet the business needs. A manager also has

Story 8: Reflecting on Professional Development on Super Bowl Sunday

responsibilities for helping people grow so they are of more value to the company in the future. Again, the emphasis is on growing people to meet current and future company needs.

A manager has much less responsibility for the development of employees for simply altruistic reasons. That is, managers are not responsible for helping people grow professionally and personally, unless there is a tie to a business need. That is why there are so many people who have outdated skill sets. It's not because their managers are not doing their duty. If an employee is doing his or her job fine, the manager does not have an obligation to invest in training.

However, the manager does have an obligation to make sure all of his or her employees understand that they are responsible for their own development. If an employee is in a position where his or her development is also aligned with the needs of the company, the employee may find the company investing in the development as well. However, regardless of these alignments, each employee must understand that they must take responsibility for their own personal development and growth.

Let's look at the situation with George and his boss, Pat Henderson. Pat is concerned because George is not utilizing the new CRM tool sufficiently. Customer Relationship Management tools attempt to automate and formalize much of the sales cycle. In theory, this should benefit George since it will automate much of the sales information he keeps manually today. The CRM package will also make more information available to George than he has today.

From Mega's standpoint, having detailed sales information in the system will allow sales managers to track sales throughout the organization and make better decisions on the state of future sales, as well as what's working well and what isn't. However, the employees and the company can't gain this value if the sales information is not entered into the system.

So, why is George struggling? Pat expects George to adhere to and follow the same standards and CRM requirements as the rest of the sales staff. However, it looks like George is a lot farther behind in his training needs. George has not taken personal responsibility for keeping up his skill set. Part of his struggle is simply because he is not used to the user interface of the new system. He is not comfortable with the forward and backward navigation buttons on a web browser. He is not used to pull-down boxes, hyperlinks and all the other paradigms that most salespeople take for granted.

Likewise, the CRM tool puts a lot of power in the hands of the salespeople and their PDAs. George was provided a company PDA two years ago, but has never used it. This tool, once seen as an extravagance, is now a required part of the job. George is again out in the cold. So, who is responsible? Is it Mega's responsibility to teach George the fundamentals of navigating on the Internet or using a PDA?

I'm actually concerned for George. His sales numbers are not spectacular. He has been steady, but not a sales whiz like he was in the past. In fact, part of the reason for George's flat sales may

Story 8: Reflecting on Professional Development on Super Bowl Sunday

well be because of his aversion to developing personally and taking advantage of new tools and techniques. It would not surprise me if Pat's discussion with George is the first step of what might turn out to be a process that ultimately leads to termination. After all, the company is not going to invest $20 million in a CRM package and then not use it because sales people are not entering the information they should.

The answer to all of this, of course, is that you don't want to be in this position and your staff doesn't want to be in this position either. Although your job as a manager is not to take responsibility for everyone's personal and professional growth, you should make opportunities and resources available. There are many learning events other than training classes that can help, including:

- **Magazines**. Every field and industry has specialty magazines. For George, this would include magazines that are sales specific. Many of these magazines are free or available for a nominal cost. Employees can read about companies in their industry, best practices, success stories, new ideas, etc.

- **Books**. Books go into much greater lengths to describe new thinking and ideas. A book might go into great detail about how to better manage sales cycles, for instance, but they will not have the stories on what is going on today. Many companies have libraries with professional and technical books. Of course, the public library should be considered a resource as well.

- **Seminars and webinars**. Vendors and user's groups are always sponsoring seminars, and many of them have been transformed into webinars. Again, many of these events are free. It just takes some time to attend, but they typically only last for anywhere from an hour to a day.

- **Mentoring**. Mentoring involves pairing up with others who have skills in areas that you do not. Sales organizations love success stories. Encourage your team to find people that have been particularly successful, meet with them and ask them to explain what they are doing. Most people love talking about what they do and are glad to comply.

- **Self-teach classes and Computer Based Training (CBTs).** Most companies have computer based training or videos available for employees to utilize. Mega Manufacturing has a number of technical and business libraries with all kinds of interesting things to learn. Again, typically these just take time to pursue, since the company has already purchased them. Employees should take advantage of them to learn about new things or new skills that will help them in their job.

- **Other**. There are other opportunities for personal development. People just need to use their imaginations. These include joining professional associations, internet training, attending night classes, listening to speakers at your local college, distance learning, etc.

Of course, you should not forget formal training classes. Sometimes they are the best option if the skills learned can be applied directly to the job today. Encourage employees to seek out training opportunities and bring them to your attention. Companies usually have some money available for training. They just want to spend it where it will do the most good. If your

Story 8: Reflecting on Professional Development on Super Bowl Sunday

employees could use training in an area that will help the company, and if they can apply the training on their jobs, they should go ahead and propose it to you.

George came to see me and was hoping that I would see how unreasonable his manager was. However, the best I can offer is my sympathy and my advice to him that he needs to get proactive very soon or it may be too late for him at Mega.

Story 9:

Dawn Needs to Firm Up Her Group's Flextime Options

Most people at Mega had a hard time concentrating the Monday after the Super Bowl. There was an eerie quietness in the lobby when I walked in, and as I walked to my desk the silence in the hallways was quite deafening. Having watched the game myself, I knew the malaise was a direct result of the Bears heart-breaking defeat to the Dolphins on a last-second field goal. The Bears scored the go-ahead touchdown with only a minute left, but a great kickoff return lead to good field position for the Dolphins, and they completed two passes before making a 53-yard field goal to end the game.

Logging into my e-mail, I noticed that my 9 a.m. meeting with Evan Gillespie had been cancelled. At 9:35, I began to wonder if Dawn Jackson was going to show up for our 9:30 meeting. As I dug through my drawer for a company directory to give Dawn a call, she showed up.

"Sorry I am late, Tom. We had a few people show up late this morning for work, and another woman called in sick, so we've been scrambling to cover for everyone."

"I guess last night's loss has really got people in a funk," I said with a smile.

"Well, I wish I could say this sort of behavior from our group was atypical. Unfortunately, it is not. In fact, that is why I scheduled this meeting."

Dawn was fairly new to Mega, but I had heard from several people that she was a competent manager who was fair and flexible. She worked in Accounts Receivable and was responsible for a team of eight women and three men. She brushed back her brown hair as she started explaining the specifics of her situation.

"When I first started at Mega, I spoke to the team about expectations and what we needed to work on as a department. One of the big concerns from the group was the ability to balance professional and personal commitments. I know everyone has a private life. In fact, everyone but three people in the department is married. In addition, half of the people in the department have more than two kids."

"That's interesting," I said. "It sounds like scheduling is a big concern for your people."

"Exactly," she responded, straightening up as if she wanted to jump right into that topic. "To accommodate their needs, I decided to implement flextime for our department. This allows Peter and Julie to come in early and leave early, for example, while Sara and Jennifer come in an hour late and stay an hour late."

"Sounds good so far. So what is the problem?"

"Honestly, I am just having a hard time managing it. Sometimes we don't have the right people in the office to deal with customer calls, and there have been many times when employees do not stick to the flexed schedules we arranged."

"What do you mean?"

"Well, I don't wish to name names, but suffice it to say that the employees seem to think as long as they work eight hours each day they can come and go as they please. As a result,

Story 9: Dawn Needs to Firm Up Her Group's Flextime Options

the employees who have been allowed to work from 7 a.m. – 4 p.m. with an hour lunch will sometimes work those hours, but they'll also sometimes work 8-5 or 9-5 without taking lunch."

"I see. Well, that is definitely a problem Dawn. I think you and your employees are confusing flextime with free time. The flexible part of flextime is allowing your employees to work off normal office hours. However, once they have established the hours they are going to work, they need to adhere to those hours."

Lesson #9 – Ensure Flextime is Good for the Business as Well as the Individual

Flextime is a work concept that is becoming increasingly more popular. It is not necessarily new, however. Some companies have been doing it for years. If you let a person come in early and leave early for a doctor's appointment or a child's game, you are employing a basic form of flextime.

Generally speaking, flextime refers to the ability of people to work the number of weekly hours the company expects, but gives them flexibility on when the hours are worked. Usually people are given flexibility within some general boundaries. For instance, your company may set general hours of work to be 6 a.m. until 7 p.m. During this 13-hour period, everyone is expected to be on-the-job for nine hours, which includes eight hours of work and one hour of lunch. Flextime would occur within this general 13-hour window.

There are many variations, but the following examples illustrate the point.

- An employee works better in the morning and prefers to work from 7 a.m. until 4 p.m. each day.

- You live in a city with bad commuting traffic. A number of people work from 6 a.m. until 3 p.m. and a number of other people work 10 a.m. until 7 p.m. to get in before or after the morning and afternoon rush hours.

- You have a mother that needs to carpool a group of children to school once per week. She normally comes in at 8:30 a.m. every day, except on Thursday. On Thursday, she comes in an hour late since it is her turn to carpool and she works an hour later that day.

- Your company allows people to work four 10-hour days (actually they are in the office eleven hours, including lunch) and take a three-day weekend.

All of these are examples of flextime. Your company or your organization is giving people more control over their lives and their schedules by allowing a level of flexibility regarding when people are physically in the office. Note that this is not the same as teleworking, since the people who utilize flextime are actually in the office.

Flextime is based on letting employees have some level of control over their schedules. Many people work non-standard scheduled but are not working flextime. For instance, you may have a customer service organization that needs to be available from 8 a.m. through 9 p.m. The

Story 9: Dawn Needs to Firm Up Her Group's Flextime Options

company will need to set the work hours to make sure there is coverage in the morning and at night. This is not an example of flextime since the company sets the hours, not the employee.

Flextime provides intangible benefits to a company. People are generally happier when they have more control over their lives, which leads to better morale, and should translate into better employee retention. Likewise, happy employees are generally more productive employees. If the company is getting the regular number of hours it expects, the situation can be a win-win for everyone.

Why then is Dawn uncomfortable about the way flextime is working in her group? Because she is not proactively managing the flextime program and she is not controlling it to make sure the business needs are being met. Remember the prior comment that flextime can be a win-win for both the company and the employee? In fact, it has to be that way. If either the company or the individual is in a perceived "lose" situation, the program will not be successful.

The following questions must be taken into account in a flextime program:

- Can the job be performed using flextime, or are there limits on the flextime parameters? This is the first question to ask. Some jobs can be done at any time. For instance, if you are an IT programmer, you may be able to sit at your desk and bang out code at almost any given time of the day. However, if you are in a job like customer service, you will probably need to be working at the time when customers are likely to call. In Dawn's case, they provide basic customer support from 7 a.m. until 5 p.m. Since they have 10 hours to cover, she does have the ability to work with people on flexible hours. If some people prefer to work 7 a.m. until 3 p.m. (with no lunch), while others prefer to work 8 a.m. until 5 p.m., she can definitely attempt to accommodate them.

- Are the business needs covered? The question here is whether you can accommodate flextime requests from all employees and still meet your business commitments and expectations. Sometimes you can and sometimes you can't. This is the first area that Dawn needs to address. She has allowed flextime in her group, but it sounds like she is not meeting her business expectations. If she had an equal number of people working early and working late, she would have been fine. However, it sounds like too many people are arbitrarily working later, which is resulting in not having adequate coverage in the morning.

- Are flextime hours stable or ad-hoc? Flextime should not imply that employee's hours are ad-hoc and that people come in on any given day whenever they want. Flextime just allows an employee to reset his or her schedule. Once an employee asks for and receives approval for flexible hours, those hours must be adhered to. In other words, the flexible hours now become the schedule the employee is expected to meet. For example, if you have an employee that receives permission to work 7 a.m. until 4 p.m., the employee must be in by 7 a.m. each day. He or she cannot come in late and leave late on a regular basis. The employee needs to meet his or her commitment to the flexed schedule to keep the entire department running smoothly.

Story 9: Dawn Needs to Firm Up Her Group's Flextime Options

Dawn also has a problem in this area. It sounds like she is not sure when some of her people will be working on any given day because she has not held them accountable. This is unacceptable.

- Are people meeting their commitments and expectations? Flextime does not work for everyone. Some people work better with more structure and discipline. These are the people that say they want to come in early to beat traffic, and then they consistently come in late because they have a hard time getting up in the morning. Some people say they want to leave late but then they start failing to meet their commitments because they have a hard time focusing late in the day. In these examples flextime may be contributing (or be the cause of) a performance problem.

Dawn has got a mess on her hands now, but she can take steps to remedy the situation. Using the four questions from the previous page, Dawn should quickly put together a plan like the following:

1. Make sure all jobs in her department are eligible for flextime. It may turn out that they are, but she may discover that some jobs require people to work a "standard" business day. She should document her findings to make sure they are fact-based and can withstand a challenge from the affected people.

2. Determine the coverage she needs from a business perspective. Right now her group is not supporting the business needs adequately because they are not adhering to their flex schedule. For her group, this will probably mean more people will need to be available in the morning. If she explains the coverage problem first and then asks the group for help, she may well find that some people will be fine with moving to the earlier start time. If she cannot find the coverage she needs, she can look for people to cover the earlier start time in shifts. If this still causes problems, she may be able to require some people to work early based on some standard criteria like seniority. Flextime needs to be a win for the employees and a win for the company. If the business needs cannot be met, flextime cannot be allowed either.

3. Assuming she can get her business needs covered, the next step is to formalize and document everyone's work hours. It may be fine for an employee to work 10 a.m. until 7 p.m. However, the employee needs to be accountable and responsible to work those hours. They cannot come in early and leave early or come in late and leave late. Once the flextime schedule is set, Dawn is counting on each employee to be in when they are supposed to be. Dawn needs to stress this point with her staff. If an employee cannot be responsible for working the hours he or she committed to, there is a potential performance problem.

4. Lastly, Dawn needs to be sure that all employees are meeting their performance expectations. For example, each employee must provide superior customer support regardless of whether a person is working flextime or not. If people are not meeting expectations, they should be dealt with through a performance management process.

Dawn should go back to her team and regroup on the flextime. She will then be in a much more comfortable position managing it and controlling it.

Story 10:

The Office Romance Turns Sour

My first "big" challenge as a People Management Coach came the second week of February. The first month of the year brought several challenges, but none of them were as personal as what Bill Rodriguez was faced with.

Bill was a project manager in charge of a six-person project team in the IT Department. Bill and I went way back, and I considered him a friend as well as a colleague. Bill started in the IT Department and was under my supervision for almost a year before being switched to another team. His wife and my wife often volunteered together at a local food bank.

During the years I have known him, Bill has always showed a cool head and an ability to work well under pressure. His hair was a bit more gray and thinner than when we first met, but his positive attitude and good sense of humor were still the same. When we met for lunch, I knew the problem must have been sensitive enough that he didn't want to talk about it at work.

We sat in a booth at a local sandwich shop and got down to business.

"I tell you what Tom, I've got a real sensitive problem on my hands."

"Is there a problem with the client Bill?"

"I wish it was that simple," he said with a half-smirk on his face. "No, I am afraid this problem is internal. It has to do with Sam and Martha."

"Ah," I said, anticipating, I thought, the problem. "I had heard those two were dating. Last I heard it was getting pretty serious. Is their romance causing problems?"

"No, they were great when they were 'in love,'" he said, making quote marks with his fingers. "But you have not been following this soap opera closely enough. You see Sam and Martha broke up about two weeks ago. Ever since, our work area has been quieter than a funeral held in a library. The tension is so thick you can cut it up and serve it on toast."

Bill always had a way with words, and his description of the situation left little question in my mind about how bad things had gotten.

"Have you spoken to either of them about this?"

"And say what? 'I need you guys to start dating again?' 'Do it for the good of the team?' I am not their love counselor, I am their boss. How do I go about talking to them about their personal lives?"

"Wait a second now. You don't need to dig into their personal lives, but you cannot ignore the fact that they are causing a professional problem on the job. You are correct – you are their boss, and you are also several other people's boss. If your team members are not acting in a professional manner, or if they are not working as they should, you need to address it right

Story 10: The Office Romance Turns Sour

away. Send a message now that you expect them to meet the expectations of the job. Maybe you can nip this in the bud. If not, you'll have to bring in HR and escalate this issue."

Lesson #10 – Act Quickly When Personal Problems Turn Into Performance Problems

Most companies have some kind of policy about whether couples can work together (the term "couples" is used to indicate married couples, common-law couples, same-sex partners, etc.). Many companies will not hire the spouse of an employee that already works at a company. Of course, that policy does not help when two people meet at work and later become romantically involved. Many companies also have policies against employee dating, especially if one employee is in a supervisory role over the other. These policies are common because they protect companies from the situation that Martha and Sam find themselves in now.

It is not uncommon for there to be friction between people that work together. It happens all the time. Sometimes one employee's personality rubs someone else the wrong way. Sometimes the stress of long hours will cause even friendly people to bicker. Some behavioral consultants will even tell you there should always be a little personal conflict since it shows people have some emotional attachment to what they are doing.

So even in normal circumstances, personal conflicts arise. Part of the responsibility of a good manager is to recognize when this conflict exists and try to eliminate it, or at least minimize it to an acceptable level. Bill's situation is different because of the very personal nature of the situation. This is not just a situation where one employee rubs another one the wrong way. This conflict has some emotion behind it. Co-workers who are romantically involved can be on the top of the world and brighten everyone's day. However, if the relationship goes sour it can adversely impact the entire team as well.

Bill's question to me was whether he should get involved in this personal situation. He knows this is a problem area but he is not sure how much flexibility he has in dealing with it. He is also wondering if he should have stepped in to begin with when the two team members started dating.

Let's start at the beginning. Should Bill have done anything when the two team members started to date? The question here is whether Mega Manufacturing has any Human Resources policies in this area. In this case, the company does not have any formal policies. We have all kinds of policies and guidelines to deal with couples, but we have no official policies about dating. So, the answer to the first question is "no." There is nothing official Bill could have done when Martha and Sam started dating.

Some project managers may have felt comfortable talking to both of them about the potential hazards of mixing their personal and business lives, but no one takes that discussion seriously when a romance is starting. Bill is not the best communicator in the company either, so that discussion would have been hard on him. Likewise, Bill could have talked to Martha and Sam about the company's policies on couples working together, but that would have been way too

Story 10: The Office Romance Turns Sour

premature. Martha and Sam are not going to want to talk about rules for couples when they are first dating and Bill would not have been able to handle the discussion anyway.

The second question Bill posed is one where he does have some responsibility. Bill is rightly concerned about getting involved in Martha and Sam's personal lives. If Martha and Sam's relationship had remained personal, in fact, the situation would be no one's business. Unfortunately, Martha and Sam have made their problems the company's problems as well. Their personal situation has spilled over into their work environment. The situation is impacting the morale of the project team and the success of the project. At this point, Bill definitely needs to step in. Bill is the project manager and he is also the functional manager on his team. The project team is feeling the stress of Martha and Sam's personal relationship and this is clearly unacceptable.

The key to managing this situation for Bill is to deal with the problem as a performance problem, not as a personal problem. Team members who cause morale problems and do not meet deadlines need to be dealt with on that basis. Bill does not have to get into the personal nature of the conflict at all. Bill needs to deal with this as he would any other performance-related issue. This involves a clear process.

1. **Verify the facts.** First, Bill needs to be certain of the nature of the problems. He has received feedback from multiple team members that the personal friction between Sam and Martha is starting to spill over and become noticed by the rest of the team. He is certain of this situation, even if it is just the perception of some team members. Second, Bill has been warned of a morale problem by these same team members, so he again has some perception-based information that the personal friction is causing morale to drop – not just Martha and Sam's, but others in the team as well.

    Third, Bill knows the project deadlines are starting to slip. He doesn't have all of the facts here yet, but he should determine the cause as quickly as possible. After investigation, he may discover the problems with the deadline are totally unrelated to the personal issues. However, there is a good likelihood that the deadline problem is being caused by Martha and Sam, or the missed deadlines may be the direct result of morale problems that they are starting to cause.

2. **Provide Performance Feedback.** Once he has a better set of facts, Bill needs to sit down with both Martha and Sam individually and provide performance feedback. Managers should provide performance feedback on an ongoing basis to their direct reports, not just once a year during the formal performance review. The tone of the performance discussion does not have to be negative or threatening. Bill just needs to make both people aware that their behavior is causing problems on the project. Bill then needs to document the discussion and the date and time it was held. He should save this document in case the performance problems are not addressed.

3. **Discuss Next Steps.** Bill should get a specific commitment from Martha and Sam to improve the situation today. This is not a problem that needs a week to fix. Bill's

Story 10: The Office Romance Turns Sour

expectation needs to be that both of their behaviors will change as soon as the meeting is over and Bill needs to make sure that Martha and Sam understand that as well.

In the short-term, the question is whether this performance-based feedback will do the trick. In many cases this initial discussion is all that is needed, especially with people that are typically solid performers like Martha and Sam. In this scenario the conflict situation goes away; team morale improves; the project ends successfully; and Bill throws away the notes he made after the performance feedback meeting. Bill is a management hero!

Of course, you can never be sure with people, and you cannot always predict how they will respond in any given situation. If the problems continue, then Bill again needs to deal with them as he would any performance problem. He should utilize any and all options available to him in that regard. He will need to determine if this is still a common problem between the two of them or if only one person needs to be dealt with. This will again be based on the facts at the time. In this scenario, Bill will need to take a different course.

1. Bill will need to have a second, more serious performance discussion centering on the problems and the fact that Martha and Sam were not able to meet the commitments they made at the first meeting. The second performance meeting should definitely be documented.

2. Bill will need to notify his manager, as well as Human Resources and let them know of the situation. He will likely get more feedback on next steps and options. This is probably going to include:

   - Close, continued monitoring of the situation.

   - Escalating performance feedback to Bill's manager and Human Resources. A meeting with either of these parties should convince Martha and Sam of the seriousness of the situation.

   - Potentially reassigning one or both of them. This may be considered if there are other positions available and if they have had a solid performance track record in the past.

   - Placing one or both of them on probation. This will give them formal warning to keep this problem out of the work environment.

In a smaller company, this type of behavior might get one or both of them fired immediately, but a large company like Mega Manufacturing cannot be so arbitrary. However, a process can be initiated that would end in termination if the situation is not resolved.

The bottom line is that Mega does not have formal policies addressing co-workers getting romantically involved. However, the company does have policies affecting employee performance. If the personal situation spills over into a performance issue, it will be dealt with from that perspective.

Story 11:

Sexual Harassment is a Burning Issue – Extinguish it Quickly

"Difficult Challenges" was turning out to be the theme for me in February. A week after helping Bill Rodriguez deal with two of his employees who were dating and subsequently broke up, I was now faced with something even more difficult – sexual harassment.

Ellen Davies was a first level supervisor in one of our local manufacturing plants. She had recently been promoted after working five years on the assembly line. Ellen was an easy-going woman with a great work ethic and a winning personality. She tended to get noticed first for her long blonde hair, but her bright smile and warm personality were what stuck with you.

When she showed up at my office for our afternoon appointment, I was quite surprised by her nervous handshake. She looked over her shoulder before walking into my office, and asked if it would be OK to close the door. I normally do so anyway, but the fact that she asked, coupled with her unusual demeanor, led me to believe something was not right.

Actually, my first clue that this meeting was going to be sensitive came from the e-mail I had received from Ellen two days prior to scheduling our meeting. She asked if I could meet with her "just to talk" and said she would rather not say what the topic was until we met. This usually means the topic of conversation will be HR-related.

"Please have a seat Ellen," I said as she stood wringing her hands. "Can I get you some water or coffee?"

"That's OK Tom," she replied, looking over the two chairs in front of my desk for what seemed like an unusual amount of time before finally picking one to sit in. "I really appreciate your willingness to talk with me. Before we begin, though, I need you to promise me that what we discuss will be confidential and just between us."

"That is a difficult request, Ellen. First, you should know that I am not a lawyer or a priest, and therefore I am not given legal protections to ensure absolute confidentiality. Second, I have ethical responsibilities to the company that must be honored. If, for example, you were to tell me you had stolen money from the company, I could not ethically keep that a secret."

"I understand Tom," she said, now squirming in her seat and clearly re-thinking if she should proceed with the conversation.

"Look, something is obviously troubling you very much. I am here to help as much as I can. Why don't you take a deep breath and then let me know what is going on?"

She took the deep breath like I had suggested, and then followed it with another one.

"I am being sexually harassed at work," she said quietly, looking away from me. I noticed a tear running down her right cheek which she wiped away stoically. I gave her a moment to gather herself before continuing. Sexual harassment is a very sensitive and serious subject, and

Story 11: Sexual Harassment is a Burning Issue – Extinguish it Quickly

I knew my first course of business was to find out from her exactly what she perceived to be happening.

"Tell me exactly what is going on so I can fully understand the situation."

Ellen began talking about how she had always been "one of the guys" over at the plant. Since her promotion, however, several of "the guys" have started treating her differently. Ellen's promotion requires her to dress in a more businesslike, professional manner, and several of the guys she once worked with were making comments to her daily about her appearance. These comments had progressed to the point where sexual overtones were now present. She also reported being the butt of several "dumb-blonde" jokes since her promotion.

At first, Ellen thought the guys were just giving her grief because of her promotion, and just joking around with her. All comments were made with a smile and a laugh, but lately she said she felt several comments had crossed the line, and what was once playful humor is now constant harassment.

The conduct of the men on the assembly line was bad enough, but as she continued talking, she disclosed that her new management peers – all men – were also making comments. Her peers would mention her name with snide comments during the weekly meetings. The department manager did not join in, but he didn't help or discourage the comments either.

Ellen ended the conversation with a tone of exasperation and frustration. "I know if I make a formal complaint, the guys will all deny any wrongdoing and claim to be just joking around. They will say I am being too sensitive. I know, too, that if I say anything it will just make matters worse. My girlfriends say I should call a lawyer, but part of me wishes I could go back to working the assembly line. I just don't know what to do."

Lesson #11 - Deal with Sexual Harassment Issues Sensitively but Swiftly

When I heard about Ellen's situation, I was initially quite surprised. I know harassment still goes on in the workplace, but with all the sensitivity training our managers attend, I thought we were beyond that type of problem at Mega. Perhaps I was too naive. On the other hand, it is probably a good sign that this is the first time I have encountered the problem, and a sign that our company culture is moving in the right direction – even if everyone has not yet gotten on board.

Sexual harassment is as old as the workplace itself. However, it has only been in more recent times, perhaps the last half of the 20th century, that the term "sexual harassment" was formally coined. Leading companies started to recognize that harassment was counterproductive to the smooth running of the company and many of them started to focus on eliminating the problem. Companies that weren't enlightened enough to stop the problem on their own soon had a financial incentive to do so, as women started to sue their employers and win large judgments to compensate for humiliation, pain and suffering.

Frankly, Mega Manufacturing was not one of the leading companies in fighting sexual harassment. After all, as a manufacturing company, Mega had a management staff of mostly

Story 11: Sexual Harassment is a Burning Issue – Extinguish it Quickly

men, and many of the men had a "boys will be boys" attitude. However, the executive management staff at Mega was not stupid, and they realized many years ago that this was an area that needed to be worked on from a cultural perspective. This culture change started 20 years ago, which is another reason why it is surprising we still run into problems today.

Harassment occurs in many forms. Men harassing women is still the most common, although every combination is possible. Women can harass men, although the instances are fewer. In addition, men can harass men and women can harass women. In the classic sense, this harassment has purely sexual motivation. However, in many cases, the harassment is not based on sexuality, but on power instead. In Ellen's case, for instance, there could be a feeling on the part of the men that Ellen is not deserving of her promotion, and this is one of their ways of reminding her that she is "just a woman."

There are two general recognized forms of sexual harassment:

- **"Quid pro quo sexual harassment."** These are situations where the harasser requests sexual favors in exchange for providing an employment benefit. This is usually a case of a manager making sexual advances to a subordinate. The manager implies (or blatantly states) that he or she can influence a raise, promotion or other benefit in exchange for a sexual favor. This is sexual harassment plain and simple.

- **Hostile work environment.** In this situation, an employee feels intimidated or even threatened because of a continual stream of sexual jokes, comments, innuendo, cartoons, etc. The result is that an employee cannot perform at his or her peak, and his or her opportunity for advancement and promotion are handicapped. It is rare that the harassment is of a hard-core sexual nature, and, when pressed, the harassers will typically defend themselves by saying they were just joking. In fact, in Ellen's case, the harassers might even prefer that Ellen defend herself by giving them the same treatment back. Of course, if that happens, then the men would probably feel emboldened to take the harassment to a higher level, since Ellen is also playing the game. So, Ellen definitely does not want to go there. If managers are aware of the problem but do not address the situation, the company itself will be found at fault and could be liable for damages.

After listening to Ellen, I have become very concerned about the situation. Of course, I have just heard one side. However, in these types of situations, that is the place to start. My first action is to explain to Ellen that our company's policies on sexual harassment are clear – we don't stand for it. The consequences for this behavior, if proven, are also very clear – immediate termination. This policy even extends to our union workforce.

Story 11: Sexual Harassment is a Burning Issue – Extinguish it Quickly

However, Ellen has also placed me in a difficult situation. She has described a disturbing situation, but she has also attempted to handcuff me from trying to help her. Her request for me to treat the conversation as confidential is her attempt to ensure that I do not do anything without her knowledge. Obviously she is afraid of the situation getting out of control and perhaps getting to a point where people will take retribution against her for reporting it.

So, after discussing the situation with Ellen, I gave her advice on the next steps she should take. She should talk to her manager and make him aware that she believes the group is creating a hostile work environment. Based on the training that all managers receive, her manager should take the initiative immediately to remedy the situation. The manager should also know that retribution is also strictly forbidden in our policies. So, if things don't get cleaned up in a hurry, the situation will need to be escalated.

If a discussion with her manager does not do the trick, Ellen has an option to escalate the problem to the next level of management or go straight to the Human Resources Department. I assured Ellen that if the situation gets to HR, there will be definite attempts at intervention. Of course, the HR Department will verify the facts first, but some actions will be taken.

Now for the other dilemma I have – Ellen's request that I keep the situation confidential. Most of the situations where I provide coaching remain confidential; however, in this case, I do not have that luxury. After all, I am a manager in the company. Therefore, if this harassment continues and Mega ends up in a court case, I might be brought into the matter as well. My manager would then be asking questions about why I did not do something.

My discussion with Ellen ended with an understanding that Mega Manufacturing will not tolerate this type of behavior and neither will I. I did, however, tell Ellen I would let her attempt to deal with this situation first. Therefore, I agreed to do nothing for two weeks. She has two options for addressing the situation.

1. She should talk to her manager about the situation. If the manager addresses the problem, then I will stay out. I will, however, call her every two weeks to monitor the situation. If the harassment is not stopped immediately, Ellen should bring the situation to the attention of the Human Resources Department.

2. If Ellen does not feel comfortable talking with her manager, she can bring this directly to the Human Resources Department. This will give visibility to the situation as well.

If Ellen does not take this situation to her manager or to the Human Resources Department, I will be obligated to raise visibility to the situation – perhaps keeping Ellen's name out of it, but perhaps not. This may seem extreme, but this is an extreme problem that the company will not tolerate. If I knew that an employee was considering committing violence, I would have an obligation to bring it forward immediately. Sexual harassment is also something about which I cannot keep quiet.

Story 11: Sexual Harassment is a Burning Issue – Extinguish it Quickly

**Editor's Note: This chapter does not address all the nuances and complexities of sexual harassment. This chapter is also not meant to be a legal primer on the subject. Suffice it to say that all managers should recognize workplace harassment of all types and address the situation swiftly and decisively. It is not only the right thing to do from a personnel perspective, it is also essential for the financial well-being of the company.

Story 12:

"Frustration Culture"

The flu bug came to Mega Manufacturing during the month of February, sending home several employees in the Marketing Department at first before slowly spreading its way around the company. I had managed to avoid the bug at the beginning of the month, but my luck changed the morning of Feb. 23rd and I had to call in sick. I managed to maintain some of my workload via conference calls during the three days I was out, but many meetings had to be moved and rescheduled.

Being home with the flu is no fun, especially for someone who enjoys work as much as I do. My job as a management coach at Mega had really recharged my batteries and given me a fresh perspective on my job and my company. It felt good to know that Mega valued me as an employee and that the company was genuine in its desire to keep people like me happy and rewarded.

The same was not true for Mary Kendrick, an old friend who worked as a sales rep for a medium-sized IT consulting company in Dickens called Micron Consulting. Mary left Mega Manufacturing about 14 months ago to accept a position at Micron.

I spoke with Mary on the telephone from my home office after lunch.

"Are you sure I am not disturbing you, Tom?" she asked when I called. "Maybe you should get some rest and we can talk next week. This is not urgent."

"Don't be silly," I responded. "Besides, I've been in bed for two days now. It will do me good to get back in the game a little."

Mary was a sweet and caring woman with three kids and a house in the suburbs. Her husband Ralph managed a local grocery store and their kids were all very athletic. Rusty, the oldest, was one of the better basketball players at Dickens High School. The turnover rate at Mega is well below the national average, and I know several executives were sad to see Mary go. At the time, though, I remember her saying that Micron had a fantastic, employee-friendly culture, and she felt like the change could be good for her career.

"So how are things at Micron? Are you running the company yet?"

"Far from it," she responded with a voice of frustration. "In fact, it has been a very rough year for us, and we're all feeling a lot of pressure to bring in new business opportunities."

"Sounds rough. How is management responding to the slow time?"

"Well, that's actually the reason for my call," she began. "You see, one of the big reasons I felt comfortable leaving Mega for the position at Micron last year was because the company went on and on about how much it valued its employees. 'Employees are our number one asset' people kept telling me."

"And now?" I asked, even though I could guess the answer.

49

Story 12: "Frustration Culture"

"Now the employees feel more like a liability instead of an asset. The company is laying people off left and right, and denying people training opportunities to learn new skills."

Mary went on to say that the cutbacks were starting to have a very real effect on employee morale. Many of her colleagues were "grumbling" behind closed doors about whether the company was genuine about its desire to put employees first.

"When I first got here and business was good, things were amazing. I went to two training seminars in the first two months and really learned a lot of new business techniques that I apply daily in my job. When business slowed, however, the company did nothing to protect its 'number one assets.' Instead, they simply began laying people off with two week's pay."

"That's really too bad," I responded, excusing myself while I blew my nose. "It sounds like the employee-centric nature of the company is only as good as its profit-making capability."

Lesson #12 – Push Your Organization to Practice What it Preaches

One of the reasons employees don't like working at their companies is they feel the company is not intellectually honest with them. The company says one thing and does another. It has lofty ideals or principles - on paper. However, there is no follow through to actually implement policies and processes to back up the words.

Many companies also do not commit funding to back up their principles. They may say their employees are number one, but what they really mean is that employees are number one as long as it does not cost the company anything. Likewise, many companies say their customers are king, but in practice they mean customers are king as long as they pay their bills on time and don't ask for anything extra.

This disconnect can happen at any level in a company when the top managers don't practice what they preach. It can occur within a division, department, team or project as well.

The term "culture" refers to "how we do things around here." In a narrow sense, culture refers to the formal and informal policies and procedures that define how you do your job. More broadly, culture includes how you relate to your managers, peers and clients. It refers to how people treat other employees, vendors, customers, contractors, etc.

A culture is not written in a company's newsletters or posted on the wall in short slogans. After you have been with an employer for a while, you start to get a sense for how decisions are made and how people treat each other. That reflects the company culture.

When people say they don't like their "job," usually they are referring to the specific role they have today. They may have had great jobs in the past, but they might not like the work they are performing now.

On the other hand, when people say they don't like their "company," what they are really

Story 12: "Frustration Culture"

saying is they do not like the culture of that company. They don't like what the company stands for, the way people treat each other, the policies, the politics, etc.

The term "frustration culture" describes the way employees feel when a company's actions don't follow its words. Frustration is the most common feeling that people have in those circumstances. Sure they are angry and they may not be motivated, but it all stems from a deep frustration with the intellectual inconsistencies.

Let's look more closely at a couple of hypothetical companies like Mary's. These two examples will illustrate the point.

Company A, a consulting company, has a Mission Statement that says employees are its number one asset. Without its employees, the company would not exist. However, the reality is that employees are Company A's number one asset as long as they are billable. If a consultant comes off an assignment and is without work for a few weeks, he or she was likely to be let go. Company A also touts its ability to train employees in new skills. However, training is funded at each local branch. If the branch is behind its profit targets, training is one of the first areas to be cut.

Company A also highlights the variety of assignments consultants can receive, which allow the consultant to pick up many skills in a shorter period of time. But, in reality, since all assignments are from customers looking for specific skills, it seems you can rarely get new work outside of your current skill set. Most of the employees in Company A start to pick up a negative perception of the company after they have been on board for a few months.

Now let's look at Company B. They are in this same consulting business and have many of the same company goals and principles. However, Company B has a reputation for keeping people "on the bench" a long time when necessary if no work is available. When the bench costs are high, they ask employees to work four-day weeks and take a vacation day on the fifth – a much better alternative to employees than a layoff. Company B also has a real commitment to training, even paying to send people to outside classes and paying for certification. Company B also looks for outsourced project opportunities. If Company B manages an outsourced project for a fixed price, it has the flexibility to bring in consultants that don't have a perfect skill match. This allows consultants to pick up new cutting edge skills, which Company B is then better able to market to client companies. Employees love working for Company B.

Both of these companies make money. Both have been around a long time. However, Company A is an example of a place with a "frustration culture." It says one thing and does another. Its literature talks about its commitment to employees, but that commitment is only an inch deep when company profits are on the line.

In this context, the actions of Company A are not even the problem. The company just needs to get its words aligned with its actions. For instance, instead of saying that employees are number one, it should state that stockholders are most important. Many companies are aligned that way. This provides a better sense for how decisions are made when profits drop. Instead of talking about all of the training opportunities available, the company should provide rich opportunities for self-study and then stress the importance of consultants taking responsibility

Story 12: "Frustration Culture"

for their own skill development. It should also put policies in place for the downtime between assignments. The company should state upfront that everyone is entitled to four weeks of bench time per year (or two weeks, or whatever length is appropriate). That way, if an assignment is coming to an end and the consultant does not have another assignment identified, he or she knows what the expectations are ahead of time.

Mary sounds like she works for a company like Company A. It should not be a surprise that she is frustrated and uneasy. We don't know the motivation for why decisions are being made as they are, however, at this point, Micron's motivation is not as important as the perception.

Mary has some decisions to make. The next time a customer asks her to talk about her company: she is going to be uneasy talking about how it is employee-centric. All the glowing words she spouted off in the past will be difficult to back up now with conviction. She also is going to have to come up with a good story if customers ask about the ongoing layoffs.

It's hard for a person in Mary's position to make changes to the principles, culture and business priorities of an entire company. However, she should at least have a dialog with her Branch Manager about her concerns. It may turn out that the Branch Manager also has similar concerns and may be willing to implement some local changes to help local employees and customers. On the other hand, if the Branch Manager is unwilling or unable to do anything, that will tell Mary something as well. The Branch Manager should at least be able to provide more perspective on the financial situation and why the company is making cuts. This may at least help Mary rationalize the decisions.

Mary will then have the same options everyone has when they don't feel comfortable with their employer. One option is for her to reconcile herself to the inconsistencies and come up with a good rationalization that helps her feel better. For instance, she can always fall back on the belief that some cutbacks and layoffs are preferable to the entire branch losing money and closing down. Many employees make this choice and decide that the positive experiences associated with their company (including the compensation) are more valuable than the frustration of working for a company whose actions don't match its words.

Her other option is to look for an opportunity elsewhere.

Most companies are good to work for. However, the good places to work usually tell employees upfront what is important and, in fact, try to execute according to stated principles, goals and strategies. These companies try their best, and if they falter from time to time, that does not make them bad.

The type of people I typically work with (middle and senior company managers) have more options available to them than Mary in resolving these inconsistencies. Managers set the mission, goals and principles in their organization. These managers need to honestly evaluate their company's actions and words. If the words and slogans don't match the actions, they have more of an ability to lobby for change.

At the same time, managers also need to evaluate their own personal actions and words. Individual managers may have a limited ability to change the entire culture, but each of them

Story 12: "Frustration Culture"

has an ability to change his or her department. They can at least model the right behavior in their own department and then look for ways to move the culture upward and outward.

Story 13:

Team Members May Look Like Adults but Act Like Babies

After spending three days out of the office with the flu, I was anxious to return to work and begin meeting with some of the people I had to reschedule with while I was out. Gentry Braman was my first scheduled meeting of the day, and he showed up a few minutes before 9 a.m.

Gentry was fairly new to Mega and was a first-level manager of a small group of seven financial analysts. He was a tall man, about 6'3", with shaggy sideburns and dark-rimmed glasses. His overall demeanor presented a man of great strength and assuredness, although I found out quickly that looks can sometimes be deceiving.

While taking his seat, Gentry confided in me that he had not received any real training in people management, but that he considered himself a very fair person who was confident in his abilities to lead, while also open to suggestions from his teammates. When he started at Mega, he spent a great deal of time learning from the analysts on his team, relying on them to show him the ropes. He also spent a lot of time learning what each person was responsible for and what the processes and procedures were for completing work assignments.

"I saw a few things right away that I disliked and wanted to change, but I kept quiet in an effort to learn everything fully first before implementing changes," he said.

"Did you see a lot of things that needed drastic change?" I asked.

"Not really. The group dynamics were sound and the people very professional. I did, however, see some internal processes that I thought could be improved and did, after time, begin to implement some changes."

"That seems reasonable," I said. "So what is the problem?"

"Well, there are a couple people on the team who have been very resistant to the changes. They are constantly complaining and whining and undermining my authority. If they had suggestions for other ways to proceed, I would be open to those suggestions and the feedback. But they seem content to just sit back and complain."

"That's not good."

"No, it's not," he replied, leaning forward. "And I'm afraid it has gotten worse, which is why I thought I better see you. The negativity and resistance from these two is beginning to affect the group and cause some negative morale changes. People are overall less content and now others are also showing signs of resistance. I think the two are really beginning to rub off on the others."

"It sounds like the time has come to act," I said. "Let me give you my thoughts and suggested next steps."

Story 13: Team Members May Look Like Adults but Act Like Babies

Lesson #13 – Deal with Babies on the Team in a Professional Manner

Many managers have encountered situations where a team's effectiveness is compromised by the behaviors of one or two people. If you are lucky, the resistance is above board. In fact, in my own experience, it always made me feel good when my management decisions were constructively challenged. By "constructively," I mean that the challenge was made openly, along with the reason for the challenge. Usually, the individual making the challenge had another alternate idea. It shouldn't surprise you to know that sometimes the alternate idea was better than my own.

I didn't mind the up-front challenge for two reasons. First, usually when I make a decision, I ask the team if everyone understands the decision and is okay with it. As a manager, you cannot make statements like that ("are you okay with this?") if you are not prepared to listen openly when people are not okay with it.

Secondly, I always felt it was a good thing when team members were comfortable enough to bring a challenge. Keep in mind that the alternative is that people will still complain about you and your decisions – only it will be in the form of non-constructive complaining behind your back. It is a good thing if your relationship with your staff allows them to feel comfortable enough to challenge you to your face.

Unfortunately, Gentry has two people that appear to want to act the other way. They are in disagreement with some of the things Gentry is doing, but instead of reacting positively and constructively to make things better, they are acting covertly and negatively. Gentry's comments are telling. He says the two employees are complaining and whining and that they are starting to hurt the overall morale of the group. This is not the type of behavior you would expect from professionals such as financial analysts. In fact, it is a behavior more commonly associated with children or even babies. Basically, they don't like what is going on and so they are crying about it.

Of course, at this point we don't know all the facts of this situation. My coaching to Gentry will start out by asking him to validate the behaviors of the people involved so that both of us can be sure of the situation. However, let's assume now that Gentry's observations are substantially correct – we have a couple of professionals on the team that are behaving like babies.

The situation above is an example of baby-like behavior, but there are other signs as well. These behaviors include:

- Complaining about things instead of offering constructive alternatives
- Resisting change and not being open to new ideas on how to improve things
- Making excuses and rationalizing problems instead of taking responsibility
- Wanting the authority to make decisions but then not accepting responsibility when the decisions don't work out
- Grumbling that they don't have time for any more work, but have all the time in the world to complain

Story 13: Team Members May Look Like Adults but Act Like Babies

- Dumping problems on the manager's desk without any suggestions or ownership
- Thinking everyone is screwed up except themselves

It is frustrating to have a vision and plan for your team and then not be able to make it happen because some people are working against you. This is especially difficult when people are acting emotionally and immaturely. However, just as children cannot be allowed to make decisions for the parents, the babies on your team cannot be allowed to undermine your actions. If the situation is not addressed, the babies may become emboldened and grow into full-fledged "brats."

Gentry is an accountant by trade, but his number-crunching skills are not going to help him here. He is going to have to polish his people management skills. There are many types of people, each with different personalities and motivations. Fortunately, there are also many different management techniques for working with all kinds of people.

The place to start is always with the direct approach. Gentry should meet one-on-one with these team members and discuss the situation. This discussion should include the specific observations Gentry has made, as well as his perceptions of the problems being caused. The first meeting doesn't need to be confrontational. Gentry can be persuasive and listen to the response of the staff member. If no easy solution is forthcoming, Gentry will need to be firm about the direction the team is going and he will need to ask the team member to get on board – even if the team member doesn't agree with everything going on.

Gentry has not yet taken this first crucial step. As with many managers, Gentry is not totally comfortable in addressing performance problems. However, it is amazing how many of these situations can be resolved with just one meeting. Remember that Gentry is dealing with professionals that are acting like babies. Sometimes the simple fact that the team member knows the manager is aware of what is going on is enough to get the behavior to stop. Sometimes people turn into babies and don't even know it. Just pointing it out to them might be enough for the behaviors to stop.

Although the initial face-to-face meeting takes care of many problems, it doesn't always work. The manager must then consider this a performance problem. Many managers think that performance problems are only caused when a person is not doing their assigned work. That is not the totality of performance problems. All problems related to what a person is doing and how they do their jobs falls under "performance."

Behaviors such as complaining, stirring up trouble and lowering the morale of the group are definitely areas where your performance management processes come into play. This type of behavior falls under the category of insubordination, or the active defiance of legitimate authority. The problem is that even if the baby seems to be doing his or her job, the poor attitude is rubbing off on others, and when morale declines, the team's efficiency and effectiveness will decline as well.

Story 13: Team Members May Look Like Adults but Act Like Babies

Once you move this to the category of a performance problem, the next steps become more obvious. These actions include:

- Meeting again with the team member(s) to discuss specific behavior observations and consequences. Note that this is now the second time discussing this problem. The conversation should be documented and specific short-term action items should be assigned to address the problems. The staff member must understand that the next step will be a formal performance plan.

- The next escalation point would be to formally get the Human Resources Department involved and put together a performance plan.

- If the employee has not met the conditions of the performance plan, he or she may have to be fired.

Just as with all performance-related problems, it is never certain whether the team member has the will and the desire to change. It is possible that they may quit, which might work out better in the long run. It is possible that the person might ask for a transfer and that request can be evaluated. A transfer might be a good alternative; however, if you are just transferring a problem employee to someone else, you should think twice.

The bottom line is that team members need to understand that childish behavior will not be tolerated. Hopefully, a baby can ultimately mature into a person who better understands how to react to situations when they do not agree.

Story 14:

Everyone is Replaceable – If You Prepare

The third day of March was marked by the last day of snow in Dickens (although we did not know it at the time). The weather was slowly beginning to warm up, and even though the snow was falling in heavy flurries, it was melting as soon as it hit the ground. It made for a slow drive to work, but I was happy knowing I wouldn't need to get out the shovel when I got home.

An accident on the Interstate leading into work slowed traffic even further, and I found myself thinking about my son Tim, who would be turning 10 this year. For the last two years, Tim and I have celebrated Spring by taking a father-son golf trip for a long weekend somewhere. Tim enjoyed a lot of different sports, and loved watching football, but his favorite sport to play was golf, and he was getting quite good at it. My wife Pam and I wanted to encourage him, so we agreed that once a year we would take him somewhere new to play.

At first, it was a family retreat. But after the first year, Pam decided to let the two of us go alone. She wasn't much of a golfer, although frankly, neither was I. As I drove to work, I thought a great deal about where we could go this year. I like taking Tim to nice courses, but he is still young and cannot yet play the professional courses he sees on TV. We'd been to some nice courses in Chicago and Indianapolis already, and as I stared at the falling snow, I couldn't help but think of Florida or Arizona or anywhere south as the perfect destination this year.

"You should definitely hit Orlando," said Betty Kennedy, as she took a seat in my office. I had been recounting the story of my long commute and my desire to go someplace warm with my son.

"You could stay at Disney World and I know there are several nice golf courses within driving distance," she continued.

"Tim has never been to Disney, though. If we were there, he'd probably want to go see Mickey Mouse instead of golfing."

"I am sure he would just love it, though, Tom. We took the kids last year and they had such a great time. They have daily parades at the Magic Kingdom, and you can get your picture taken with Snow White and Goofy. It's really a wonderful trip. I have pictures if you want to see."

"Thanks Betty. Perhaps some other time." I knew Betty was not much into sports, and therefore could not understand why I would schedule a vacation just to golf.

"What brings you to see me today?" I asked, trying to turn the conversation back to business.

"I'm actually in a bit of a pickle, Tom. One of my best employees, Roger Matheson, has put in his two weeks notice and is moving to Denver to be closer to his sick father. Of course, I completely understand his reason for leaving, but as I said he is one of my best employees and I am saddened to see him go."

Betty was a Director of Market Research for Mega and she led a team of 12 people doing

Story 14: Everyone is Replaceable – If You Prepare

market research, customer surveys, and long-term sales forecasting. Over the years, I have bumped into many of her colleagues by the water cooler and heard that she was very good at what she did. Her peers spoke very respectfully of her, and she seemed to be a great people manager.

"I'm sorry to hear about Roger and his dad," I said. "But you have built a very solid team, I am sure you guys can get by until a replacement is hired."

"I do have good people on the team, but the timing is what has me really nervous. You see, we are right in the middle of a big project analyzing some market research data that will eventually be used to set the Marketing strategy for the end of this year and into next year. This is a very important project for the company, and Roger's experience and understanding of the marketplace are crucial, I believe, to the success of the project. Roger had several people helping him, but none of them can do what Roger does."

Lesson #14 - Have a Transition Plan Today to Handle Turnover Tomorrow

I guess if the world was perfect, good employees would never leave your company, and bad employees would never get hired. In that kind of world, you would not have to worry about having to fire bad performers and you would not have to replace good workers. Everything would be in balance until each good employee retired after 30 years of service.

Of course, that is not the environment we are familiar with because unfortunately, in some cases, good employees leave, while bad employees stay. This requires you to deal with both performance problems and unwelcome turnover.

There are a number of general reasons people leave companies, including:

- Poor morale, heavy overtime, a lack of training, etc. These are things managers have some control over.

- Lack of career path opportunities, salary structure or poor benefits. These problems are more company-based and hard for an individual manager to overcome.

- A spouse getting transferred, an employee having to move to take care of a sick parent or employees who leave for a perceived better quality of life in another city or state. In these instances, the decision to leave has nothing to do with the company and is mostly outside your control.

- Internal transfer or promotion. These are usually good events for employees, even though they may affect your team negatively.

- Company layoffs or firings. Although initiated by the company, the loss of employees results in these same transition problems.

There are many strategies for increasing employee retention rate. Ultimately, however, all managers will be faced with turnover in their staff. In fact, you should plan on having some turnover every year – no matter how good of a manger you are. Some companies even prefer to have a certain amount of turnover to have an opportunity to bring in new people and get new

Story 14: Everyone is Replaceable – If You Prepare

ideas. In fact, the long-term effect of a controllable level of turnover is probably a net benefit to the company.

If you have done a good job of resource planning in your group, you should have a good primary and backup person for each of the major areas your group is responsible for. In some cases, you are losing primary skills in certain areas, but you may have a solid backup that can come up-to-speed quickly. The primary and backup resource model will make turnover situations much less disruptive.

However, there are definitely problems in the short-term. To put it simply - turnover is disruptive. It means the remaining team members need to compensate for the person who left. It means you have to take the time to hire a new member of the team and get them through a learning curve before they are productive. So, what should you do when unexpected turnover hits?

First take care of the basics. Congratulate the person leaving on his or her new opportunity (even if it is with another company). Of course, you will want to make all the standard jokes about asking if the new company needs anyone else. You will also duly note that the person leaving will now be blamed for all problems for the next three months. This initial banter is expected and lets the person leaving and the rest of the team know that there is no crisis and that you will all work through it.

Next, get down to business. As soon as possible (the same day would be great), call a meeting of all team members, including the person leaving. This is a meeting with a short-term focus, since you probably have two weeks to work through a transition. During this meeting, work through the following process:

1. **Document the responsibilities**

    - Document all of the responsibilities of the person leaving. If you have a job description that will help, use it as a reference.

    - Determine all of the work he or she is responsible for today. This is just a list. Some people have one or two things they are focused on. Other people may have many of their own responsibilities, plus they may be matrixed into many other projects and teams.

    - Check into any ongoing responsibilities. The person leaving may have things they do every month or on a quarterly basis. For instance, they may provide support for a monthly financial process or perhaps they have responsibilities for gathering quarterly manufacturing metrics.

    - Don't forget to document any backup responsibilities. Depending how your group is organized, the person leaving may have had backup responsibilities in certain areas. These backup roles need to be identified and transitioned to someone else as well. For instance, a person may be providing backup administration help for when your primary administrator is out. This backup responsibility will need to be reassigned as well.

Story 14: Everyone is Replaceable – If You Prepare

Sometimes it is hard for people to articulate everything they do. They are busy every day, but it takes a while to retrace their steps and see exactly what they are responsible for on an ongoing basis. This is one reason you want other team members in the room. Between the person that is actually leaving and the rest of the team, hopefully all of the current and ongoing responsibilities will be identified.

2. **Determine what happens to the responsibilities.** Next look at the list of responsibilities and see what needs to become of them. There are a number of options for the transition.

    - The person leaving may get some work completed before he or she leaves. This work can then come off the list. You need to monitor the work though, to make sure it actually is completed.

    - Some work will need to be reassigned to other team members for the short-term until a replacement candidate is found, or until other long-term arrangements are found.

    - Some work will be reassigned for the long-term. This provides an opportunity for some team members to gain additional responsibilities or to gain experience in new areas where they did not work previously.

    - Some work will be dropped – temporarily or permanently. If there are not suitable people to take on new work and if the work itself is not time critical, it is possible the work will be put on hold until a replacement is found. It is also possible that some work will be dropped and not picked up again.

3. **Create detailed transition plans.** Everyone assigned one or more of the responsibilities needs to work closely with the departing teammate to cross-train and learn as much as possible about what needs to be done. Hopefully, you have at least a two-week notice to make these transitions. However, the bottom line is that when the person's last day arrives, all of his or her work must be completed, stopped or transitioned to another team member.

4. **Monitor the transition.** As the manager, you now need to monitor the situation to make sure that the transition activities are performed before the person leaves. It is often the case that good transition plans are created, but then people get too busy and before you know it your team member has departed and your transition plans are not completed.

As mentioned earlier, although there is usually short-term disruption associated with turnover, there can be long-term opportunity as well. This is where you make lemonade out of your situation. One of the positive aspects about turnover is that it provides opportunities for remaining team members to increase or change responsibilities. For instance, if the person who left was doing IT web development, you may not need to immediately hire another web developer. Maybe this is an opportunity to have another team member assume the web responsibilities.

Story 14: Everyone is Replaceable – If You Prepare

This can cause some short-term pain and decreased productivity, but your team will come out ahead in the long-term. This strategy will also position your team with skilled backups that can be counted on for expertise if other team members leave. Using a current team member to take over for a person leaving may also allow you to backfill for the second person whose responsibilities might be easier to fill. This might also allow you to run the group more efficiently with one less person.

This is the case with Betty as well. There is no question that there will be some disruption as the team loses a current member. There might be a period of a couple months when the team is not performing at its peak. However, there are good and bad ways to transition when people leave that make a difference between the transition being disruptive and disastrous. If Betty gets the team together and focuses on transition in the next two weeks, they can minimize the impact of the disruption. If she does not plan the transition and if she does not monitor the transition, the situation will be much worse.

Turnover is inevitable and sometimes outside of your control. That being said, how you handle the turnover is very much in your control.

Story 15

There is no "I" (Isolation) in "T-E-A-M"

I had not spoken to my good friend Jerry Ackerman since the beginning of the year when he was struggling with a difficult ethical situation revolving around the company's search for a new advertising agency. He and I had communicated via e-mail several times, and I knew his situation had been resolved in an ethical way, but we had not spoken face-to-face since then. He had called me at home when I was out with the flu and we scheduled a time the second week in March to meet for drinks and dinner after work.

We decided to meet at a sports bar not too far from work called O'Patricks. The college basketball season was winding down, and every TV in the bar was tuned to a conference final. We decided to sit at a booth near the Maryland vs. Duke game as we thought it was the one most worth glancing at from time to time.

O'Patricks was a neat Irish pub that had been in Dickens for almost two generations. Old pictures of Patrick O'Patrick, the late father of the current owner, were hung around the bar, along with pictures of Michael O'Patrick, the current owner, and his family. Michael could normally be found behind the bar, but he wasn't working this particular evening, and I did not see his wife waiting tables.

"Do Michael and Melissa have the night off?" I asked our waitress when she came to bring us our drinks.

"They actually took a trip to Ireland with their sons, believe it or not. The kids have never been to their home country, so Mike and Mel decided it was time for them to see their roots."

"Good for them," Jerry said. "Sounds like a neat vacation." Our waitress smiled politely and grabbed her pencil from behind her ear to take our orders. We both ordered the fish and chips before talking about work.

"I am glad everything worked out OK with you and the advertising committee," I said, drinking from my mug of beer.

"I am, too," Jerry replied, "although I was sad to have to leave the team. I suppose it was the right decision, and one that I should have made from the very beginning."

"You did the right thing, Jerry. You could have said nothing at all, but you came clean and did the right thing ethically. Everyone I have spoken to who was on your team said the same thing."

"That's good."

"So now that you are back managing your own projects and teams, how is everything going?"

Jerry spent the next five minutes talking about his latest project, which involved an upgrade of Mega's accounting software. Jerry has updated a lot of software during his time at Mega, so I knew this project would not be too difficult for him. During the course of the conversation,

Story 15: There is no "I" (Isolation) in "T-E-A-M"

though, he mentioned an issue he was having with one of his team members, a guy by the name of Felix Holtkamp.

"It's as though Felix no longer wishes to be part of the team," Jerry said with a sigh. "He still gets his work done, so I know he has not completely abandoned the project mentally, but he no longer interacts with the team and seems to prefer being alone."

"Does the nature of his assignments allow Felix to work independently of others?" I asked.

"Unfortunately, no. You see, I have asked Felix to teach the other team members how to use one of the software integration tools, but he has been resistant and is trying to keep the knowledge to himself. He says that he is the only one that can understand the work."

"That seems odd. What is so challenging about this one integration tool?"

"Nothing, Tom. Felix is just, for whatever reason, resisting me on this one. The people on my team are very competent. I have complete faith that they could learn and understand this if Felix would take a few hours to teach them."

"Sounds like you need to take some action Jerry."

Lesson #15 - Don't Allow Team Members to Isolate Themselves

A project manager once told me that her job would be much easier if she didn't have to deal with people. Some of the biggest challenges on a project are not managing scope or risk, but effectively managing and working with people. I think Jerry is coming to that same conclusion. Of course, many project teams work great. The team members all get along well personally and they all work well together. Unfortunately, that is not always the case.

People problems are sometimes doubly hard for project managers to deal with. First of all, by definition, they have a project to deliver, so people problems can directly impact the budget and schedule. Second, project managers typically focus on the process side of their jobs. That is, they are focused on managing the schedule. When problems come up, they can deal with them through a combination of issues management, scope management, risk management, quality management, etc. On the other hand, companies don't often invest in people management training and coaching for project managers.

Project managers learn how to deal with people from the standpoint of assigning work, keeping up morale and holding people accountable. However, they don't often get training and coaching specifically in people management and dealing with difficult people. This type of training is typically scheduled for the formal management team.

As I talked to Jerry, one of his first thoughts was to recommend that Felix be fired. Although the performance problem may ultimately lead in that direction, it is way too early to consider termination at this point. Not only is it premature in the performance management process, but Jerry admits the project team will suffer if Felix is gone. Part of Jerry's frustration is that he still needs Felix's expertise on the project since Jerry has not been able to get Felix's knowledge spread to others on the team.

Story 15: There is no "I" (Isolation) in "T-E-A-M"

So, where do we start? I think the first place is to look at performance. Since Felix is on a project, the first question is whether his behavior is impacting the project in terms of its deliverables or its deadlines. After discussing this with Jerry, it appears that although there are concerns with some project dates, overall the project seems to be on track.

The next question from a project perspective is whether Felix's behavior may cause problems in the future. If so, then we could consider this a project risk. In fact, at this point, risk is the biggest concern. There are a number of risks, including:

- A risk that Felix's behavior will, in fact, lead to missed deadline dates in the future.

- A risk that Felix's behavior will alienate the rest of the team and that overall cohesion and morale will suffer. This may cause the team's performance to suffer as a result.

- A risk that the lack of knowledge sharing will have a serious impact on the project if Felix leaves.

In addition, there is a potential problem of lost opportunity. This project provides a chance for the organization to spread Felix's technical integration skills. If the skills cannot be transferred to others on this project, the organization may face the same problem on other projects in the future – scarce skills tied up in the head of one person.

Felix's behavior has only worsened in the past few weeks, so Jerry does not think there has been a measurable impact on the project yet. However, he is concerned from the standpoint of risk. Since he has perceived a significant risk, he should address this situation proactively.

The place to start with personnel problems is usually to take the most direct route - a face-to-face discussion. Jerry and Felix should have a frank performance discussion. In this discussion, Jerry can discuss his perceptions of Felix's behavior and why it will (or may) cause problems on the project. Jerry understands the risks to the project and he should communicate these risks to Felix.

One of the benefits of the first meeting is that Jerry can share his concerns and Felix will have a chance to tell his side of the story. You never know how these first discussions will progress. Sometimes they are difficult and don't accomplish what you hope. However, sometimes the person you are talking to will agree with you and tell you the reason for his or her behavior. As a manager, if you know the causes, you might have some ability to help fix them.

Felix may have a problem in his personal life (which he may or may not share). There might be personality problems between Felix and other members of the team. Sometimes people hoard information if they think their job is in jeopardy. Regardless, if you can get some sense as to the cause of a problem, you have a chance of determining a remedy.

In fact, there may be a number of remedies that Jerry and Felix can work on together. This includes trying to build up Felix's communication and people interaction skills, providing continued people-coaching to Felix or changing Felix's job in a way that will allow him to excel. The exact solution will depend on the give and take that comes out of this meeting.

Story 15: There is no "I" (Isolation) in "T-E-A-M"

Jerry and Felix should end the meeting with some concrete commitments for addressing the problem. Jerry needs to feel comfortable that Felix will again start to engage with the rest of the team. Felix doesn't have to win a popularity contest, but he cannot purposely isolate himself either. Jerry must also receive some real commitments for cross-training so that Felix can teach his skills and techniques to other people on the team. If they cannot agree on these points, then the meeting will not have been successful and a further escalation may be necessary. If Felix agrees to a short-term plan of action, but then doesn't follow through, then an escalation may be in order once again.

Keep in mind that Jerry is a project manager. In many organizations, even within Mega Manufacturing, the project managers have limited people management responsibilities, because the team members still report functionally to a true functional manager. This type of organization is called a matrix, and it means that resources are loaned to a project team from functional organizations (like sales, Finance, IT, etc.). The team members report on a "dotted line" to a project manager for the purposes of a project. However, once the project is completed, the team members return to their normal functional groups. In this type of an organization, the project manager would still have the first meeting with the team member. However, the project manager could ask for help from the functional manager to deal with ongoing performance problems.

The first meeting sets the tone for how to deal with the rest of the situation. If Felix responds positively, then perhaps the entire problem will go away. If the situation persists, Jerry will need to deal with this as a performance issue. Being reclusive and hoarding knowledge is counter to what is expected from any employee in the company. Escalating the situation to the level of a performance problem means getting Human Resources involved, documenting the concerns, setting specific targets for behavioral changes, establishing a performance plan, etc.

In this particular case, Jerry can also escalate the performance problem directly to Human Resources. If the situation cannot be resolved, then Felix may ultimately be fired. However, at that point, it will not be Jerry's doing, it will be based on choices that Felix made himself.

Story 16:

Leaders are Born and Grown

I had spent the better part of the weekend working on my tax returns, and was glad to be back at work Monday morning. Owning a home and having a child both come in handy during tax time, but my wife and I both work and we also own several stocks. Figuring out dividends and other investment income and the sheer amount of paperwork involved at tax time is challenging to say the least. When all was said and done, however, we would be getting a nice refund from Uncle Sam, which would once again help fund the golf trip with my son Tim.

Marcus Robertson and his wife were not as lucky. Marcus was 27-years old and had been married for a little over a year. He worked in the Sales Department at Mega and had been with the company for about three years since graduating college from Iowa State University in Ames, Iowa. He and his wife lived in an apartment after getting married, and had just bought their first home together last month. Unfortunately, though, his house wouldn't help him with taxes until next year. With no home and no children, the Robertsons found themselves owing money at tax time.

"It's just not fair," Marcus said. "When we were single, my wife and I each got refunds every year. We never got much, but we certainly never owed. Now that we are married, we owe the government money, and it's a pretty significant amount!"

"Now you know why Dave and I have kids," I said, smiling at Dave Huntley, Marcus' boss, who was standing in the cafeteria line with us.

"I just wish I could deduct my dog Spike," Marcus said, trying to laugh it off although it was clearly bothering him.

As we paid for our food, Marcus excused himself and said he had to eat at his desk because he was expecting an important sales call. Dave and I found a table near a window and sat down to eat our lunches together.

"Marcus is an amazing kid," Dave said as he opened his bag of chips. "He's one of our best sales people and he shows an amazing ability to lead even at such a young age. People really love him and want to help him and follow him."

"That's great, Dave," I said, putting down my tuna sandwich. "Sounds like you've got a guy who will grow into a real leader. Are you doing things now to groom him for growth?"

"I've taken him under my wing in a way, but our department doesn't yet have any formal processes or procedures in place to develop talented people like Marcus. I know Joe over in IT talks a lot about a system that his team has in place, but I am afraid our department doesn't have anything yet."

"Have you thought about trying to implement something? It sounds like you definitely have a need for one."

"Not really, but I think you are right. We do need something more formal in place to develop guys like Marcus. I guess I don't even know where to start. Can you offer any suggestions?"

Story 16: Leaders are Born and Grown

Lesson #16 - Identify, Mentor and Grow New Leaders

Every company needs leaders. Leaders help you get from where you are today to where you want to be in the future. But where do leaders come from? Some people say that leaders are born and not raised. By that they mean that real leaders are also natural leaders and have shown leadership skills from a very early age. They are the informal leaders of your scout troop, the kids who always organize neighborhood baseball games and the captains of your high school sports teams.

But is that really true? Do you have to be a born leader? I don't think so. On the one hand, I do believe that there are many people who are naturals. They exhibit leadership skills at an early age and end up as leaders of organizations and companies. Much of what they accomplish is done on their own. However, they also take advantage of opportunities and mentors when they appear.

On the other hand, I also think most people do not have the right attitude and mindset to be effective leaders. It does not matter how much training and coaching they receive, they are not going to end up on your company's leadership path (in fact, although your company needs leaders, you don't need everyone to be leaders. Too many leaders can cause problems as well).

In the middle of these two groups is another group – potential leaders. These people have leadership skills, but the skills need to be more fully developed. Let's be clear, though – this middle group is not vast. Just as the really good "natural" leaders make up maybe 5% of your organization, this group of "trainable" leaders makes up maybe another 10%.

These people need to be grown and mentored into really top-notch leaders. If they do not receive the right opportunities and the right training, they can easily fall into the vast group of people who never reach their full potential. Not all of these potential leaders will end up making the grade. Maybe only half (5%) will end up moving into upper level leadership positions, where they will join forces with the other 5% of natural leaders.

So how do you grow and develop this pool of leaders? There are some right and wrong ways. Sometimes you take your best technical people and promote them into the management ranks. The thought is that if they can excel technically, they also have the skills required to excel in management. For example, you may promote your best salesperson to be a sales manager, or your best accountant to be the new accounting manager. People like this get promoted into management and leadership positions all the time with little training and preparation. Is it any wonder that many of them fail and are unhappy in their new roles? These moves are not without peril and risk to both the company and the individual.

The better approach is to recognize potential leaders based on their management and leadership skills – not their technical skills. While it is true that many people with strong functional knowledge also end up becoming strong managers and leaders, there is not always a direct connection.

The first step is to identify potential leaders. This is accomplished in a number of ways based on the size of your company and its focus on talent development. In many companies (probably most), the identification of future leaders is left up to the initiative of the current management structure. That is, if you are a current leader in your organization, you will tend

Story 16: Leaders are Born and Grown

to recognize other potential leaders. Then you will normally, consciously or subconsciously, make opportunities for growth available to them. The identification of leaders is a natural tendency of current leaders. That is the easy part. Growing and shaping future leaders takes more time and is where most companies fail.

Although most organizations informally rely on leaders identifying other leaders, the better approach is to have some type of formal process or program in place to look for and develop talented people. In some organizations this program is called a Leadership Track or a Leadership Development Program. This could also be a part of a larger initiative like a Talent Development Program, which seeks to build skills in many key areas, including leadership.

What these programs have in common is that they are formal attempts to seek out talented people and look for ways to grow their skills so that they can reach their full potential. Typically the current leadership tries to identify people within their ranks that look like they can be future leaders in the company. In some cases, it just takes one person to recognize and nominate a potential leader. In other cases, a potential leader is nominated to a committee that meets periodically to evaluate new candidates for leadership development. This same committee also reviews the progress of current leadership candidates to determine if they should still be on the leadership track.

Once a candidate has been identified, your company needs to provide him or her with opportunities for growth. It is important to recognize that this does not mean these talented people get all of the opportunities and all of the training. Everyone in the organization should receive opportunities and training. However, leadership candidates should receive additional opportunities to develop as leaders. The leadership skills training could include:

- **Cross-functional growth.** An example might be a leadership candidate from the Information Technology area that might receive a chance to work in the Finance group. This gives the person a chance to broaden his knowledge of the business and to sharpen his leadership skills by working with new people. This may be an opportunity for cross-functional growth that is not available to many other people in the company.

- **Communication skills.** Solid verbal skills are essential, although basic written skills are required as well. Communication skills include being able to understand and communicate at the level of your audience. For instance, the ability to summarize detailed information for a discussion with upper management, or the ability to take detailed data and communicate direction and trends.

- **Values.** Future leaders should understand the organization's values and be well-grounded in their understanding of what is right and wrong (acceptable behavior and not-acceptable behavior). This is becoming more and more important.

Story 16: Leaders are Born and Grown

- **Creativity.** It is important to be able to think outside the box and see new ways to do old jobs. Not every idea is practical or even good. But future leaders should be encouraged to explore all avenues for providing value. Leaders do not accept that the way things are today is the way things always need to be.

- **Collaboration and influencing skills.** When you lead a functional organization, you may be able to rely on organizational power to get done what you think needs to be done. However, the bigger value comes from being able to work cross-functionally with your peers to get big wins. In these situations you need to collaborate and influence others to accomplish things.

- **Looking for other leaders.** Just as future leaders are identified and groomed, these future leaders also need to understand that the cycle requires them to also look for and groom others to lead further on in the future.

Of course there are other important skills to develop and grow as well. However, the point of leadership development is to identify the skills that the company thinks are important and map those against the skill level of a potential leader. Many of these skills can be learned, but the fact that a candidate is recognized as a future leader means that he has many good foundation skills already.

There are a number of ways that leaders can be developed.

- **Mentoring**. In many companies, future leaders are mentored by current leaders. This is normally the best that can happen since the organization does not have a formal program in place. The value and effectiveness of the mentoring process is based on the time and mentoring skills of the current leader. If the leader is reassigned or leaves the company, the once future leader can again become an unrecognized face in the crowd. If your company has a formal program in place, mentoring can be done on a more formal basis, and new mentors can be assigned if a prior mentor is no longer available.

- **Growth assignments**. In many cases companies give special assignments to people who are recognized as potential leaders. This may include short-term work that exposes the person to new areas and new people, or even full-time rotational assignments that allow a leadership candidate to work in a variety of positions to gain valuable experience in a shorter period of time.

- **Training**. Formal training can go a long way toward building leaders. There are many good classes that provide valuable perspectives and techniques for leading people. This can include formal stand-up training or even e-classes.

- **Books, magazines, newsletters, etc.** There is a wealth of material that you can read on being a better leader and manager. Don't discount these sources of information. Reading books from recognized industry leaders can give you insight that can be applied to your job.

Story 16: Leaders are Born and Grown

In the case of Dave and Marcus, Dave recognizes that Marcus is a future leader at Mega, and he wants to do something formally to get Marcus on the right track. This is a very smart idea. From talking only briefly with Marcus, and from knowing how good he is at what he does, it does not seem unreasonable to think Marcus might explore other opportunities outside of Mega if he feels like he is not being rewarded for his work. To prevent this from happening, Dave should be proactive and not rely on fate or luck to determine future leaders. We spoke a great deal over lunch about programs he can put in place to groom Marcus and other future leaders.

Story 17:

Stop the Guessing Game on Performance Expectations

After lunch I was greeted by 12 e-mails and three voicemails back at my office. As was the case when I first started working as a project management coach, as soon as people found out I was available to help them and that I was not judging them or reporting them to their bosses, they came to me with all sorts of problems. Even some of my superiors were surprised at the amount of time I was spending helping managers with people problems. There was an internal perception that managers did not need people-management help, and that they should concentrate just on their projects, but now they were seeing that managing people was just as important.

As I hit the "send" button responding to the fourth e-mail, I heard a knock on my door. It was Janie Tudor showing up for her 1:30 meeting. She was a few minutes early, but I was at a stopping point and decided to use the extra time to catch up with her. Janie and I started around the same time with Mega Manufacturing and have kept in touch off and on since then. I have always considered her to be a good person and a good manager. She always appeared to be well organized and very knowledgeable.

Janie's husband Herald was a mail carrier who also did some referee work at high school football games. She often had to deal with angry parents at Mega who thought her husband blew a call or caused their kids to lose the "big" game. She always had a lot of patience, as did her husband.

"What's happening Janie? Haven't seen you in awhile." I said as she set her briefcase on the floor next to her chair.

"Nothing new to report. Just the same old - same old really. How are you and Pam and little Tim doing?"

"We are all just fine, thanks for asking. What brings you to see me this afternoon?"

The topic of Janie's conversation – team expectations – caught me by surprise. I always found Janie to be a great communicator, and was surprised to find out her problem revolved around a communication issue.

Janie told me she received feedback from a new member of her team, and much to her surprise, the team member was not sure of the overall purpose of the group. This seemed obvious to Janie, but to the new employee it was vague.

"I can't tell you how shocked I was when he said that," she said. "I was sure that this was an isolated problem and that perhaps there was a miscommunication somewhere."

"Was that in fact the case?"

"Believe it or not, no. In talking with the rest of the group, I found that many people had no idea how what we did impacted the company, or how critical our work is to the company's success. They understood why they were doing their work, but not necessarily why it was important and what they were trying to achieve."

Story 17: Stop the Guessing Game on Performance Expectations

Janie also said that people were not personally clear on what she expected of them. "I always felt the team was not necessarily made up of stellar performers. Now I realize that part of the problem might be that people don't know what is expected of them."

"I think you hit the nail on the head, Janie."

Lesson #17 - Set and Manage Expectations at Both a Group and Personal Level

Janie has run into a problem that is common for a lot of experienced managers – once they feel comfortable with the knowledge level of their job and their organization; they start to make the assumption that everyone else has the same level of knowledge. When they start in a new job, they tend to explain things to people in an organized and detailed manner because it helps them as much as it helps the team member. However, when a manager gets comfortable in his or her job and environment, he or she no longer has the personal need to be so clear and detailed. However, what these managers forget is that even though they no longer need the details, the team members usually still do.

I think Janie is in that position now. She should not be receiving feedback from her staff that they don't know what is expected of them. Janie is a better manager than that. The problem is likely one of complacency. She is not doing a good enough job of making sure others in her group know what is expected of them because she assumes they already know.

My discussion with Janie started at setting expectations for the group and proceeded toward setting expectations on an individual basis.

- **Set goals, objectives and strategy.** To start with, Janie should try to establish goals, objectives and a strategy for her group. The goals talk about what the group is trying to achieve over the next one to three years. They can be somewhat vague. Objectives are very concrete statements that describe what her group is going to specifically accomplish this year. The strategy describes, at a high level, how the group will achieve its goals and objectives. It would be great if Janie could get her team involved in the creation of the goals, objectives and strategy so that everyone understands them and can buy in to them. This process will help establish expectations as to the things that are important for the group to achieve.

- **Communicate the goals, objectives and strategies on an ongoing basis.** The process of setting expectations is not a one-time event. Once set, Janie needs to look for opportunities to make them real. For instance, she might refer to them at each staff meeting. She should also make sure people are aware of how the work they perform aligns toward the objectives and goals. In this way, the purpose of the group and the group's work becomes clearer and more relevant to the team member's daily jobs.

- **Establish clear job expectations.** All team members should understand their job responsibilities. This helps establish expectations for each person. Job descriptions also set expectations about how a person progresses in the organization. A team member

Story 17: Stop the Guessing Game on Performance Expectations

should understand the expectations of their current role and the expectations of other roles in the organization chart. This also allows managers and staff members to have a fact-based discussion on what a person needs to do to reach the next career level in the organization.

- **Define personal objectives.** Janie should sit down with each person on the team and set individual objectives for the year. Many managers at Mega do this, although it is not required in Janie's division. This again helps each person understand what is important for him or her to achieve during the year and helps ensure there are no surprises.

- **Schedule quarterly review meetings**. Janie should set up staff meetings on a quarterly basis to discuss how well the entire group is doing toward their objectives. She should also have quarterly review meetings with each of her direct reports to go over the progress toward his or her personal objectives. This is all a part of setting and managing performance expectations. People get very frustrated when they receive personal objectives at the beginning of the year and then do not get feedback until the year is completed. The problem with that approach is that if people are falling short of expectations, they have no time to recover. If a manager provides feedback on a quarterly basis, there should be no surprises during the formal yearly review process.

- **Set clear expectations for each work assignment.** At a detailed level, Janie needs to make sure that each of her team members knows what is expected of them. Specifically, this means that for each assignment, Janie should identify the people working on the effort, the specific deliverables that are due back and the date when the work is due. She should also provide as much guidance as she can to get them started. Some managers make it a point to then ask the staff members to repeat the assignment back to the manager to ensure that both parties are in synch. As the assignment progresses, Janie can also ask for status updates that will give her a sense for progress. The status reports should also have the deadlines and major deliverables just to make sure that the common expectations are still in place.

These ideas should help Janie better communicate the expectations for the team and for each person. Janie might be surprised by the results. She told me, for instance, that she felt like her team's performance was at a level below top-notch. Perhaps part (or all) of the problem is that her team members don't understand what is expected of them. It would be very easy to miss a deadline, for example, if you didn't know what the deadline was to begin with. Poor or nonexistent communication will also result in deliverables that don't measure up to a manager's unspoken expectations.

Although my discussion with Janie covered a lot of ground, I wanted to try to help her in two ways. First, I want her to make sure that her team members understand the performance expectations of the entire group. This is where group goals, objectives and strategies come in. I also want her to be sure that she is setting expectations appropriately on each assignment she hands out to her team members.

Story 17: Stop the Guessing Game on Performance Expectations

These are all areas within Janie's control. I think her weakness in this area is simply a case of assuming her team members have the same level of knowledge that she does and think the same way she does. That is hardly ever the case. However, with more focus, I have no doubt Janie will be able to help set and manage the expectations of her team members at both a group and personal level.

Story 18:

Work Twenty-Four Hours a Day, or Delegate

Steve Buckner was a new manager in the Finance Billing and Collections group. He had recently been promoted from a position as Senior Financial Analyst, and was admittedly proud. He was smiling from ear to ear when I bumped into him in the hallway in late January after his promotion was announced. It was my understanding that his promotion was very well deserved in that Steve had a reputation as a go-to guy. Whenever people on his team needed help, it seemed like Steve was always willing to go the extra mile.

Last week, however, Steve called me and asked to schedule a meeting to discuss an urgent problem. At the time, he said he was swamped with work and could not make it in that week, but he thought this week would work better. When he arrived at my office, it seemed clear right away that work had not gotten any easier. Steve had bags under his eyes and looked like he had not slept in a few days.

"I don't know what I was thinking," Steve said, running his left hand through his thick brown hair. "Ever since my promotion, it seems like I am working two jobs – my old job as a financial analyst and my new job as group manager. I was here for 12 hours yesterday."

"Are those hours typical?"

"They weren't until I got promoted. Again, though, I feel like I am working two jobs now, and I am really struggling to keep up."

I asked him to describe his day yesterday to me. He said he had to create some financial reports (since he was the one that could do them the fastest), interview a couple candidates for a new position, provide a performance review for a member of his staff, participate in a one-hour status meeting with his manager and update some of the financial procedures for the group. Not only that, he said, but he also had to work on a half-dozen little problems that people brought to his attention during the day.

I began to see the problem.

"Steve, don't you have other people on your team, or are you a team of one?"

"I have several people on my team, Tom. You know that."

"I was joking. The point is, in your new role as group manager, you need to learn to rely on the others in your group more and delegate some of your workload to them."

Steve perked up at the idea of getting help. He took out a pen and paper and asked "Where do I begin?"

Lesson #18 - Expand Your Ability to Get Things Done Through Responsible Delegation

Steve is in a time bind not unlike many other new managers that move up from a "working" position to a management position. In fact, this problem can occur whenever people get

Story 18: Work Twenty-Four Hours a Day, or Delegate

promoted. Being an effective manager requires you to be an effective delegator, and each time you get promoted, you need to be effective at delegating the type of work you used to do in favor of new types of work that are more appropriate at your new level. If you don't do a good job of delegating you will end up in a position like Steve. His promotion has resulted in having to do two jobs – his old one plus his new one.

Delegating work is a specific management skill. It means you assign work to the people that work for you. Delegating specifically refers to assigning work through a manager-subordinate relationship.

The purpose of delegating work is twofold. First, it allows the people under a manager to do the work that they are best qualified for. Second, it frees up the managers to do the types of work that are more appropriate for a person in their position. Let's look at the kind of work that Steve did the prior day to drive home this point.

- **Create some financial reports.** Based on the way Steve described this activity, he should ask a member of his team to create the reports. It appears Steve used to have this job when he was the senior financial analyst. Steve said he was the logical person to do this work since he could do it the fastest. However, this job needs to be turned over to a team member so he or she can become the new "fastest" financial report writer. As a manager, Steve can provide coaching, but he needs to leave the financial report creation to an analyst in his group.

- **Interviewing candidates.** Interviewing is something that a manager should be involved with. The question I need to ask Steve is whether this is a preliminary screening interview or a final interview. As a financial analyst, Steve may have been involved with the screening interview. However, Steve the manager needs to allow his team to do the screening interviews. Steve needs to interview the people that make it through the initial screening process.

- **Provide a performance review for a member of his staff.** This is definitely a management function and one that he cannot delegate to others. In fact, this was a job that Steve probably did not perform before and it is a new process for him. This is another reason for him to be more effective at delegating work so that he can spend more time becoming better at providing performance feedback.

- **Participate in a one-hour status meeting with his manager.** Attending a status meeting with your manager is an activity that cannot be delegated. Everyone needs to communicate with their manager and these status meeting provide that time for personal interaction on a regular basis. Also, there is usually important information distributed at a management status meeting that is not shared with the rest of the staff.

- **Update some of the financial procedures.** Again, this seems to be the kind of detailed work that Steve used to do in his old job. He needs to let go of this type of work and place it in the capable hands of a team member.

Story 18: Work Twenty-Four Hours a Day, or Delegate

- **…a half-dozen little problems.** One of the legitimate responsibilities of managers is to be available to provide coaching and guidance to team members when they encounter problems. However, Steve is taking this too far. Since Steve is so knowledgeable, he feels obligated to actually solve the problem. After all, he can do the work faster than most of the team members. In fact, if we look more closely, we will see that a delegation is taking place here. However, it is going the wrong way. In this example, Steve's subordinates are actually assigning work to him. This is a situation called "reverse delegating" and should be avoided whenever possible.

Steve's team members are bringing problems to Steve's attention. The team members are then delegating the work to Steve (Steve may be volunteering to take on the work, but the result is just the same). This ends up being a disservice to Steve and to his team. Steve ends up getting caught in too many work details while his team members don't get a chance to resolve the problem on their own so that they can deal with similar problems in the future.

Instead, when people come with problems, Steve should provide coaching and guidance. This might include going over the problem with the team member, asking their opinion on how to resolve the situation, providing insight into how Steve would handle the situation, coming up with a plan of attack and then allowing the team member to resolve it. If you ask a person to bring you a proposed solution whenever they bring you a problem, you will find that the person will more easily retain responsibility for getting the problem resolved.

If Steve does not become more comfortable delegating work to his staff, he is going to be in trouble. He is going to make mistakes by doing the detailed work too hastily, plus he is not going to have the time required to perform his new responsibilities. No one will be happy, especially Steve.

Delegation is the art of "letting go." It means that you let go of the more detailed responsibilities that you are so good at and that probably led to your promotion. It means allowing others to do the work you know you can do better and faster – so that they then have an opportunity to do it better and faster.

I mentioned earlier that delegating is a specific management skill. It should be used whenever a manager is promoted to a position of more responsibility. Let's say, for instance, that Steve masters his new job over the next few years and is rewarded with another promotion. He will find he no longer has the time to perform the same kinds of activities he did as a first-level manager. Instead, the responsibilities associated with being a first-level manager need to be effectively delegated to the person at that level. Steve will need to focus on more and more strategic activities and work that has a broader organizational impact.

When you delegate, you will find that you are not so much managing work as you are managing people. The people that report to you take on more responsibilities, under your guidance and with your insight and coaching. An effective manager monitors the people in his group to make sure all the work is being completed. This ensures that the work of the group is being completed successfully, while at the same time allowing him or her to contribute as a manager to the overall strategy and long-term success of the group.

Story 18: Work Twenty-Four Hours a Day, or Delegate

Delegating will allow you to enjoy your job more, be more effective while you are working and reduce your level of stress. Don't be indispensable. Your challenge is to get the group in a position where they don't need you any more. If you can accomplish that, you will be in a position to take on the next challenge (or promotion) that the company sends your way.

Story 19:

Value Diversity – It Makes Business Sense

The only subject more sensitive than sexual harassment to most managers is diversity. After dealing with the first subject earlier in the year, I was now faced with the latter courtesy of Marvin Hendricks, a department manager for quality assurance. Marvin was in his late 40s and had gray, thinning hair. He had worked at Mega for more than 20 years, working his way from a quality assurance technician to department manager.

I met Marvin outside a conference room where he had been called to a meeting with the vice president of his division and several people from human resources. The purpose of the meeting was to formally discuss the issue of diversity at Mega Manufacturing, and the apparent lack of diversity in the QA Department. As we walked back to my office, I found out from Marvin that he had been approached about diversity from HR about six months ago, and since then he had hired six people, none of them a minority. In fact, the new hires brought a total of 35 people to Marvin's group, and only two of them were minorities.

"Ten years ago we didn't have a single woman or minority employee in the whole department," Marvin said. "Today, 40 percent of the group is female, and we have two minorities. We are not ignoring the call to diversity, Tom, but I refuse to hire someone who I don't feel is the best candidate for a position simply because of his or her race or gender."

"You should never hire someone who is unqualified Marvin," I said, taking a seat behind my desk while Marvin shut my office door. "But let me ask you something – are you telling me the last six people you hired were significantly better than other candidates for the position?"

Marvin sat down and thought about the question. He answered that two candidates blew him and everyone else away and were hired without question.

"And the other four?"

He thought for a moment before answering. It turned out he wasn't really sure what, in the end, separated those new hires from the pack.

"You know, Marvin, Mega has been pushing for the hiring of a more diverse workforce for a number of years, for several good reasons. The company has determined that a diverse workforce has several positive business values, and has decided to pursue diversity in all departments."

"You don't need to remind me, Tom. I just got out of a meeting where it was made extremely clear to me."

"Do you disagree with that philosophy?"

"It's not that I disagree. Again, though, I am not willing to hire people who are not as qualified as others simply because of race."

Story 19: Value Diversity – It Makes Business Sense

"But you just said you hired four people recently who did not stand out from the pack during the interview process. Were there no minorities at all in the pack for those four jobs?

"You know what, Tom, I believe there were. I don't consider myself a racist and I am not uncomfortable working with women or minorities. To be honest, I am not sure why we didn't hire for diversity in those instances."

Lesson #19 - Hire a Diverse Workforce Without Compromising on the Best Candidates

The whole issue of diversity is sensitive in many people's eyes. To many people, the focus on diversity is synonymous with the hiring of inferior quality for the sake of meeting quotas. However, the focus on diversity is much more complicated than that.

The place to start is to discuss the case for diversity in terms of business value, since the discussion can go nowhere if there is not business value behind it. No company is going to jump onto the diversity bandwagon if there are not real business benefits. There are really two arguments for the business case for diversity. The first is basic fairness and the second is the long-term business value associated with a diverse workforce.

Let's start with the matter of basic fairness. A company's hiring objective is to always find the best person to fill an opening. This would include looking at internal candidates and external candidates where appropriate. Of course, looking for the "best" candidate can be a highly subjective matter. What does it mean to be the "best" candidate?

Left to their own devices, different managers will have differing opinions about what makes a candidate the "best." In some cases, managers will choose the person with the best set of skills to fill the position. However, in other cases, managers will pick people who are like them. This is a natural tendency and comes from a couple natural, even subconscious biases.

1. A hiring manager tends to rate a person's qualifications using her own background as a measuring stick. After all, if a manager has a certain background and ended up in the position she is in today, doesn't it make sense to look for those same traits in another person? However, typically when the manager makes this type of subconscious decision, she is also making a decision to pick a person that tends to look more like her as well.

2. The other bias slips in under the guise of evaluating how a person will fit in with the rest of the team. This is because in many cases there is not a clear-cut leader in terms of background and skills. If there is not an obvious candidate based on background and skills, the interviewer starts to look for differentiators. One of these differentiators usually has to do with how well a person will get along with the rest of the team. If most of your team fits a certain race and background, there is a natural tendency to think that people with similar traits will get along well, or at least better than people with different traits.

Story 19: Value Diversity – It Makes Business Sense

If teams are left on their own, these two sets of natural biases tend to result in a like group of people hiring a like candidate. That is, they will hire someone with a similar look and background to themselves. In some businesses and some organizations, this results in a bias against workers of the opposite sex. In other businesses, there is not a gender bias, but there is a bias based on culture and race.

Companies, especially large ones, have tried to formalize and standardize the recruiting and hiring process in a way that allows each candidate to be judged based on the same set of criteria. The goal of a standardized process is usually not to hire diverse workers. The goal is to remove as many of the subconscious biases as possible and to ensure that the most qualified candidate is hired. The hiring process usually involves multiple people. The candidates are judged by multiple people using standardized criteria in the hopes of removing as much subjectivity as possible and making the final recommendation as objective as possible.

Many hiring managers take offense at the restrictions the HR Department places on the hiring process. In fact, there is no question that some organizations have developed a burdensome and dysfunctional hiring process. However, many of them are pretty good. They are not designed to be the easiest path to hiring a candidate. They are designed to ensure that every candidate is treated equally and fairly, and that the hiring decision is based on the facts, not the subconscious biases that many of us carry.

So, on the surface, it should not be hard to gain agreement that you want to hire the best candidate and you want to have a fair process for everyone. Hopefully there is not too much argument that this is a good thing.

In addition to the argument about basic fairness, diversity also provides real business value to the company. One of the core assumptions about diversity is that no one would be pushing for it if everyone was the same. However, the fact is that our society as a whole is diverse and all companies exist and sell products in this diverse marketplace. Companies have discovered that diversity translates into being able to exist and prosper in a diverse marketplace. The benefit filters down into at least three specific areas in the company.

- **Exploiting the marketplace.** The basic logic here is that it is hard, if not impossible, to effectively reach a diverse marketplace without a diverse staff. If you are trying to reach Hispanic customers, for instance, it makes sense that you have Hispanic employees helping in product development, sales and marketing. This doesn't mean that every person is Hispanic, but that some are. Likewise for African-Americans, Asian-Americans, etc. Since your market is diverse, you need people with background and understanding in these ethnicities. Together you can effectively attack the diverse marketplace.

- **Making better decisions.** People from the same types of backgrounds can have a tendency to think alike and this can affect the decisions that people make. Managers need a diverse set of opinions to make the best goals, objectives and strategies for the company. Of course, some people are very creative, but it is hard to be creative in areas where you have no background or context. Having a diverse management structure helps drive better company decisions in a diverse world. This should be true even in Marvin's quality assurance group. Marvin thinks he has a good set of quality assurance

Story 19: Value Diversity – It Makes Business Sense

processes in place today, but could they be better? If he had a more diverse group, would these different experiences lead to different ideas about how best to perform the quality assurance function?

- **Hiring better people.** Ultimately there is value in being able to hire the best person, regardless of the person's background. If we looked at Marvin's group 10 years ago, for instance, it would have been hard to say he had the best people available, since he was basically screening out women that represent a sizable percentage of the workforce.

So, what does this mean to Marvin? My coaching to Marvin was also based on these same basic value points. First, I asked him to consider whether the positions in his group were such that white candidates were always the best qualified. His answer, of course, was "no" – there was nothing about the work in his group that would imply that only whites could be successful.

My second question was whether every hiring decision resulted in one candidate being head and shoulders above the rest in terms of background, experience and skills. He replied that it has happened a few times, but normally the decisions are close. Our discussion about diversity normally doesn't take these cases into account. Hiring for diversity does not mean that you hire an inferior candidate over a more qualified one. That does not make business sense, and all of our decisions need to make business sense (exceptions to this basic rule might be necessary if your company is under some sort of legal or court ordered hiring guidelines).

So, according to Marvin, many of the hiring opportunities do not have a definite and obvious "best" choice, and almost every opening has qualified minority candidates. Why is it then that the white candidate gets the nod in almost every hiring decision? Ultimately, it boils down to the internal biases that we looked at earlier. Marvin and his team members are not racist and they are not consciously discriminating. But they have the subconscious built-in bias to hire people like themselves. They make the decisions one at a time, and over a few years the pattern looks obvious. In actuality, if it wasn't for the fact that they always followed the company hiring policy, an outside person might conclude that they were discriminating.

Mega Manufacturing has concluded that there is business value associated with a diverse workforce and Marvin's department is not taking advantage of that value. It is no wonder that Human Resources is starting to push him more. He is losing business value. Still, I pointed out to Marvin that no one has told him to hire non-qualified candidates, or even less qualified candidates. However, Marvin is also being asked to hire for diversity when there is no obvious "best" candidate. Again, he is not taking an inferior candidate, since by his own admission, these are instances where there is not one "best" candidate. However, by hiring for diversity, Marvin can start to get more of the long-term business value associated with the diversity of experiences and points of view. This will make Marvin's quality assurance group better and it will make Mega Manufacturing better.

Story 20:

"Lead!"

In early April I attended a three-day conference on leadership in Chicago at the Hilton Hotel. The purpose of the conference was to discuss new strategies for leading people in the 21st Century and to hear from several well-known celebrities and politicians on how to be an effective leader. The conference was interesting in that many different people offered many different strategies for how to be a good leader. At the end of the day, though, I wondered whether leadership was something that could be taught or whether it was something people were either born with or without. Sort of like a musical gene – you either have it or you don't.

In thinking about Mega Manufacturing, I knew for certain that our CEO, CFO and all our department vice presidents were born leaders. They all had skills and abilities that were an inherent part of their being. They were all very good at setting a direction and getting people to follow it. Over the years, Mega has followed many different strategic courses, but the bar was always set higher and higher by the leaders of our company, and there was always a sense of working hard to be the best among the employees.

But what about those who are not born leaders? I thought a great deal about this during my three-day trip, and had the chance to think about it even further after I got back. My first meeting, it turned out, was with Al Singleton, the project manager on a large project in the IT organization. Al was the master of the project schedule and had all the skills necessary to complete the project on time.

The project, however, was not going as well as it should. Deadlines were being missed and there was a good likelihood that Al would need to re-plan the schedule to show a 30-day project delay.

Al's manager told him the problem was not one of project management skills, but one of leadership. Al's manager felt the team was unmotivated and didn't understand the big picture of how important this project was. They also were complaining about never knowing what was going on and never seeing Al.

"What do you think about your supervisor's comments with regard to your personal team leadership?" I asked.

"That's a tough question. I feel like I can be a leader, although it is not natural to me. I have to try real hard and remember that I am the person in charge. I have tried reading some of the better-known books on leadership, but reading them and putting them into action are two different things."

I smiled at his comment and found myself thinking back to my conference. I knew there were several things I could tell Al – many strategies I could suggest on how to be a better leader – but knowing and doing, as Al mentioned, are two different things.

We continued talking for about 20 minutes, and it seemed obvious to me that Al had mastered all of the project management processes, but he just was not a strong leader.

Story 20: "Lead!"

"I just don't know what to do, Tom. I have people who report to me, so I feel like I am a leader, but my boss doesn't seem to think so, and neither do the people on my team."

"There's one key difference we need to make Al. Having people report to you makes you a manager, not a leader. There is much more to being a leader than just having people who are functionally required to follow you."

Lesson #20 - Lead Your Staff – Don't Just Manage Them

The subject of leadership has been written about at length by thousands of writers over the years. The concept of leadership itself probably goes back to the first humans and in fact is a trait that goes back to the animal kingdom as well. Many animals fight for supremacy and for who will lead and dominate their group.

Of course, the articles, columns and books keep coming (witness this chapter in the book!). The topic of leadership is one that some people struggle with, but it is vital to the success of every organization. Men and women in positions of power should have a pretty good idea of what leadership means. They may not be the best leaders and they may not always be leading in the right direction, but they usually have to understand and exhibit leadership before they can move up to the senior positions in a company or organization.

Not every situation calls for leadership. In fact, it is not really possible to be a leader all of the time. Government leaders are the perfect examples. Most government leaders – senators, congressmen, etc. – could not have gotten to where they are today without being strong leaders. At the same time, however, there are leaders within this group of leaders. There is only one Speaker of the House, for example, and only one person who chairs each of the powerful congressional committees. Therefore, people need to understand their role as leader, including when to lead and when to follow the lead of others.

When we talk about the characteristics of leadership, we usually compare them against the complementary characteristics of a manager. We typically expect our managers to be leaders and, in fact, many managers are good leaders. However, many managers are not good leaders and many leaders are not good managers. The people who can do both are usually the ones who move up in an organization. But these people bring different skills to bear when they are performing in a management role versus when they are showing leadership.

One of the common misperceptions of managers is that since they are "leading" a team of people, they are, in fact, leaders. In many cases, the word "leader" is actually in the job title, for instance "Team Leader" or "Group Leader." However, being a manager of people does not imply you are a leader. Your job title gives an indication of where you fit in the management structure of your organization, but leadership is a characteristic and a skill.

The term "leader" or "leadership" can mean different things to different people. To define the term you really need to identify the characteristics of a leader. These characteristics include:

- **Setting a vision.** If an organization is to be successful over the long term, it must have leaders who can set a vision. The vision always represents a future state that you are trying to achieve. You can never reach your vision because the leaders in the company continue

Story 20: "Lead!"

to raise the bar higher and higher. The company vision from ten years ago might not even keep you in the marketplace now. Vision is important because it sets the direction for the entire organization.

- **Internalizing the vision.** Leaders have the ability to see a vision and understand what it means to them. Remember that people exhibit leadership at all levels of the organization. Your senior management sets the overall vision for the company. Good leaders in the organization work to create an aligned vision for their own divisions, departments, groups and teams.

- **Providing direction.** Perhaps the most important trait of a leader is the ability to actually "lead" a group of people, an organization, a company or a nation. Leaders communicate this direction to their teams and work to ensure that the team "gets it" as well. A leader spends time talking to people, attending team meetings and looking for opportunities to motivate the staff. A manager talks to people about being more efficient and effective. At the vision level, a leader talks to people about being the best they can be and moves people toward higher level goals and vision. A manager is able to achieve concrete objectives.

The prior characteristics should apply to all leaders. In addition to the outwardly-focused characteristics of setting a vision and leading people, leaders should have a number of internal qualities that govern their behavior. These are the types of characteristics that might separate a good leader from a bad one. A good leader should:

- **Be confident.** Leaders are confident in their ability and will typically take on challenges. This confidence does not have to be shouted out loud. In many cases, this is a quiet confidence. Many leaders are modest; they make sure their people are recognized for their contributions, while they take no credit themselves.

- **"Walk the walk."** Good leaders hold themselves up as an example of model behavior. They ask you to use certain principles to govern your behavior and they follow these same principles themselves. Leaders who do not model their own principles usually are disrespected and find that people are unwilling to follow them.

- **Set the bar high.** A good leader challenges himself or herself and the staff. Again, this relates to moving people toward a vision – not to where you were last year.

- **Recognize true achievements.** A good leader recognizes that when people reach the high bar, they should be recognized. This includes awarding them with promotions and higher performance-based salary increases. When the staff sees that rewards are consistently tied to high performance, they will understand the cause and effect nature. Setting the bar high and then rewarding people for not reaching it sets a bad example and will not get the team to follow the vision.

Story 20: "Lead!"

- **Let the staff determine how to reach the vision.** Most leaders are not dictatorial in nature and realize they do not need to make all the decisions. Good leaders involve their staff in many of the decisions that affect them. After the leader is satisfied that the vision is correct, he or she will let the staff help determine how to get there. People have much more motivation to move toward the vision when they are involved in determining how they will get there.

- **Be flexible and lead change.** One not-so-obvious characteristic of good leaders is that they are flexible to change. Businesses change; marketplaces change; strategies change. Your company may have a perfectly good vision today, but that vision may not be right in five years. Many people roll their eyes when change hits, and their tendency is to continue moving in the old direction. Good leaders accept change, internalize it and then lead again in the new direction.

- **Help make more leaders.** Good leaders try to develop other good leaders because they know that this is the way the organization is going to win in the end. Good leaders look for opportunities for others to lead and to develop leadership skills. These leaders also make sure that there is at least one person (if not more) that could take the place of the leader.

One area that "experts" disagree on is whether you can train someone to be a leader. Some say you can learn to be a leader while others insist that leaders are born and not made. This is an important question in my discussion with Al since it is vital that he be both a manager and a leader. He seems to have good management skills. He plans the work, assigns it, sets deadlines and has processes in place to handle managing risk, scope, problems, quality, etc. However, it appears his ability to lead is lacking.

Perhaps the question should not be framed in terms of whether you can teach people to be leaders as much as whether you can teach people leadership skills. On this question, I think the answer is "yes" – you can teach people many of the skills associated with being a leader. In my coaching to Al, for instance, we discussed the need for him to be a more proactive communicator with the rest of the team. This does not mean sending out more e-mails. This means getting around and talking to people. He needs to communicate the overall objectives of the project and why it is important. Each team member should have a personal vision for how their contribution helps the entire project be successful. Al can enlist others in this communication effort as well, including the sponsor.

I am also coaching Al on other skills that good leader's exhibit. This includes telling people when they do a good job, listening to their concerns, working the same hours as the rest of the staff, and giving the team members opportunities to lead in certain aspects of the project.

Al is probably never going to be a company executive. I don't think he has the ability to set a vision and drive an organization toward it. So, from that perspective perhaps it is true that you cannot totally "make" a leader. Most successful leaders show natural leadership signs when they are young. However, even a "born" leader needs to have the right environment to succeed and that environment should include skill building, training and mentoring.

Story 20: "Lead!"

In Al's case, the vision has already been set. He should be able to learn to positively influence and lead the handful of people on the project team. Those leadership skills, tied with his current management and organizational skills, should allow him to be successful on this project and on similar ones in the future.

Story 21:

Mort is Getting Involved in Politics, But He is Not Running for Office

My yearly golf trip with my son Tim was scheduled for the third week of April, and as such my calendar was very busy leading up to my one-week vacation. Tim and I would be heading to Arizona for a stay at a very nice resort hotel with two 18-hole golf courses on the property, and several more within easy shuttle distance. My wife Pam had decided to join us for this trip, as the resort had a full spa and several other activities that caught her attention. We normally only do our golf trip over the course of 3-4 days, but since we were traveling by plane, and since we were going to a fancy hotel, we decided to stay for a week. Besides, our tax return was slightly larger than it was last year, so we decided to live a little.

As the days went by, I found myself more and more excited about the trip, and I would say my morale was at an all-time high. I had been thinking about morale a lot because I had a meeting with Annette Venezuela scheduled for the end of the week and the topic was morale. I noticed this meeting as I stared at my calendar for the rest of the week. Annette was the new department head in the IT division, and that department always holds a special place in my heart as it is where I got my start at Mega. I was saddened to learn that morale had become a problem and was anxious to hear more from Annette when we met.

In the meantime, I had arranged for a meeting with Mort Blackwell at his office in another wing of the building. It was a good 20-minute walk involving several escalators and two elevators to get there. I knew if I was going to be prompt I needed to wrap up my calendar and get on my way.

Mort was a project manager working on a database overhaul. He had been with Mega for five years and was both competent and organized. I knew from working with him that he was a no-nonsense kind of a guy who believed in working hard and getting the job done right the first time. He was often known for being outspoken, although I never found him to be rude or arrogant.

When I arrived at his office door, Mort waved me in as he wrapped up a telephone conversation. I heard him saying "goodbye" as I closed the door, and then I heard him give out a long exhale and what I thought was a growl.

"Everything OK Mort?" I asked as I found a place to put my bag.

"Is it ever, Tom?" he said, trying to smile. "I'm up to my ears in office politics right now, and I am getting extremely frustrated. I really don't know what to do."

"You are way ahead of me, Mort. Let's back up a few steps and tell me what is going on."

Mort apologized and told me that he was having some difficulty delivering a fairly major project on time and within budget. He confided in me that many of the delays were, in his opinion, caused by office politics.

Story 21: Mort is Getting Involved in Politics, But He is Not Running for Office

"For instance, I recently received a major scope change request from one of the senior client managers," Mort said. "The senior manager insisted that the project needed to include the new scope. However, the sponsor disagreed. The two of them spent two weeks going back and forth before deciding on a resolution and that uncertainty caused some related work on the project to be delayed."

Mort went on to say that there was some political friction between the two senior managers in the client organization. "Whenever they are in the room together, it seems that nothing productive can get done. They are both vying for a promotion and are trying to make the biggest splash for themselves while holding the other person back."

"Sounds like a case of office politics to me, that's for sure," I said.

"I know politics in the office is a part of life, and I am stupid for thinking it won't happen, but the result of this is impacting my ability to deliver this project successfully. I am just not very good at this political game. Is there a class on office politics I can take? Can you teach me how to play the political game?"

Lesson #21 - Learn to Influence Others Without Moving to the "Dark Side" of Office Politics

All of us know that the idea of office politics has a bad connotation. The term "politics" is typically used with a negative connotation and implies backstabbing, making you look good at the expense of others, swapping favors on questionable transactions, etc. The implication is that office politics takes place in the shadows and results in behaviors and decisions that would not be justified if they were made in an open, transparent process. That totally negative view of office politics is too extreme.

When we talk about politics, we should first try to set a common definition. Generally speaking, politics is all about interacting with people and influencing them to get things done. This can be a good thing, a bad thing, or a neutral thing, depending on the tactics people use. The behavior of people can make office politics good or bad.

Since people are involved, you also need to take perceptions into account. One person may see an action as totally devoid of political intent, while a second person perceives it as the worst sort of deception. This can happen with something as simple as giving your opinion. If your opinion is in conflict with another person, he or she may think that you are playing politics.

Think about some of the good things that happen when you have the ability to successfully interact with people and influence their behavior.

- You are able to move your ideas forward in the organization and get people to act on them.
- You have an ability to reach consensus on complex matters with a number of different stakeholders.
- You receive funding for projects that are important to you and to your organization.
- You develop a reputation as someone who can get things done.

Story 21: Mort is Getting Involved in Politics, But He is Not Running for Office

Based on these traits, you can start to get recognized and ultimately promoted upward in your organization. Notice that all of these areas appear to be good. If you heard these comments used to describe a manager, you probably would not think in terms of office politics.

Now let's consider some of these same traits with a more sinister view of office politics.

- You are able to move your ideas forward in the organization and get people to act on them *by currying favor, suppressing other opposing ideas and taking credit for the ideas of your staff.*
- You have an ability to reach consensus on complex matters with a number of different stakeholders *by working behind the scenes with people in power, making deals and destroying people who don't get on board.*
- You receive funding for projects that are important to you and to your organization *by misrepresenting the costs and benefits, and by going around the existing funding processes.*
- You develop a reputation as someone who can get things done *by using legitimate and illegitimate tactics and by walking over people that get in your way.*

If you heard those words used to describe a manager, you would not have a very good impression of the person. Your first thoughts would be that he or she was good at playing office politics.

The first examples show that influencing people and getting things done in a company bureaucracy can be a good thing. The general term of "office politics" can have good or bad connotations. However, the typical use of the term is used to describe the shady methods that are used to get things done in the company bureaucracy, as shown by the second set of examples.

My discussion with Mort started off with the perception of office politics. In this case, his project experienced delays because of a disagreement on a scope item between two senior managers. Is office politics at work? It's hard to say when you are looking at people's motivations. It's very possible the delay was caused by an honest difference of opinion between two people who both think they are representing the best interest of the company. Actions that are in the best interest of the company are open to opinion and interpretation.

Of course, it is also possible that the delay was caused by infighting, turf control, and who knows what else. Perhaps one of the managers is in disagreement not because of the merits of the scope change request but because he or she does not want the other manager to get credit for a good idea. We have no way to know. They may both think they are acting in the "best interest of the company," but that standard is weak.

The other scenario in which the two client managers are vying for a promotion might be a little closer to the truth. Perhaps the negative side of office politics is at work here since neither one of the managers wants the other manager to get an edge.

Mort asked if he could "learn" the office politics game. Well, there aren't many classes designed to show you how to handle and practice office politics. I think it is a skill that must be learned and the amount of learning that is required depends on your communication and general

Story 21: Mort is Getting Involved in Politics, But He is Not Running for Office

people skills. Some people are better at it than others and that is one of the reasons that some people move up in an organization while others do not.

Many people are more comfortable working with "things," and they find it much harder to handle the politics. Engineering and Information Technology workers are typical examples of people who like to work with technology, computers, diagrams and equations. They like to work with people as well, but they enjoy working together on the tasks at hand. Many people, in these fields and others, are less comfortable working in jobs that require them to communicate and influence people on a daily basis. Therefore, they do not excel in roles like project manager, supervisor and team leader. Since they have a hard time reaching these first stepping stone management positions, they typically don't make middle and senior management positions.

Mort knows that office politics is not a standard project management process. You can define a procedure for managing issues and scope. You won't find a similar procedure for how to handle office politics when it impacts your project. Politics is people related and situational. What works for one person in one situation may not work for another person in the same situation because people, and their reactions, are different.

On the other hand, office politics is definitely an area that can be coached or mentored. If you have someone who can explain the nuances of how the political art is played within your organization, you can learn the process more quickly. Having a mentor also allows you to role-play how you would respond and react in certain situations where people-influencing skills are required.

My advice to Mort is that if he wants to be a successful project manager in the long-term, he is going to have to strengthen his communication skills and increase his ability to influence others. He can read books and find training on the subject of influencing others. Then Mort needs to apply these skills as best he can to get things done. As he gets more skilled, he should keep the following three points in mind:

1. Try to recognize situations and events where politics are most likely to be involved. This could include decision points, competition for budget and resources, and setting project direction and priorities.
2. In general, deal with people openly and honestly. When you provide an opinion or recommendation, express the pros and cons to provide a balanced view to other parties. Make sure you distinguish the facts from your opinions so the other parties know the difference. You should always try to communicate proactively with all stakeholders.
3. If you feel uncomfortable with what you are asked to do, get your sponsor or your functional manager involved. They tend to have more political savvy and positional authority, and they should be able to provide advice and cover for you.

As he learns to work better with people and influence their behavior more effectively, Mort will have plenty of opportunities to pick a course of action to get done what he thinks is necessary. Ultimately he will find many tools and techniques at his disposal. How will he know if he has entered the dark side of office politics? He first needs to make sure that he abides by all government and organization laws, rules, policies and standards. This is usually not hard unless

Story 21: Mort is Getting Involved in Politics, But He is Not Running for Office

your moral compass is really broken. Second, Mort needs to take the course of action that will allow him to look himself in the mirror and feel good about himself. If he can feel good about what he is doing, how he is influencing and how he is getting things done, then I think he is handling office politics the right way. If he feels guilty about how he is treating people and if he has second thoughts about the methods he is using to get things done, he is probably practicing the dark side of office politics.

Of course, Mort's particular problem is that he is getting in the middle of some politics between a sponsor and another senior manager. I told Mort that he had a couple choices. One option is to go ahead and take direction from the sponsor. In a project situation, the sponsor is the person with ultimate responsibility and authority. Another option is for Mort to discuss the problem with his manager and try to elicit the help of his own organization managers to intervene. It is possible that his managers can arbitrate this dispute with the sponsor and client manager and get them to resolve the problems.

Story 22:

Doing the Expected is not the Way to be Promoted

On my way out of Mort's office I bumped into Perry Williams, the manager of a four-person financial forecasting group. With only four direct reports, Perry was a very hands-on manager.

"Tom, I am so glad I bumped into you. I really wanted to schedule a meeting with you, but someone said you were heading out on vacation. I don't suppose I could trouble you for 30 minutes of your time?"

"I'm actually on my way back to a meeting at my office, Perry. But, if you would be willing to walk with me, it will take me about 20 minutes to get there and we can talk along the way. As long as what you have to discuss is not confidential."

"It's not confidential at all, and I would be very grateful for your time. I am happy to walk with you, too, as I am actually going that direction."

Knowing we didn't have too much time, Perry got right down to business. He wanted to talk about how to discuss career opportunities with his group. A couple people on his staff had made it clear they would like to be promoted and move into management ranks – at least into a hands-on management job like Perry's.

Perry, however, was wrestling with a common dilemma. He said he felt the people seeking promotion were capable of doing more, but neither of them showed a willingness to do anything out of the ordinary. They were both good people, but also basically 8 a.m. - 5 p.m. types.

"I don't want to tell people they are probably not going to be promoted because I want to keep their spirits up. But at the same time, I feel like people should not expect to be promoted when they only work normal office hours. It's like they think if they do a good job they will one day get tapped on the shoulder and handed a big promotion."

"If doing a good job was enough to get promoted, we'd all be running the company by now," I said as I pushed the down button on the elevator.

"That's precisely my point. When I got promoted, it was because I was constantly looking for more work and more challenges. I made sure my superiors knew that I would work however long it took to get a job done. These guys think just showing up and working normal hours is enough to move up the chain. How do I tell my people that they need to take on additional challenges if they ultimately want to get ahead?"

Lesson #22 - Encourage Staff to Take on New Challenges to Get Ahead

I have coached many managers that much of what happens to you in your career is within your control. Perhaps not everything, but most important aspects are. Many people, especially successful ones, already recognize this. Some people, especially those who are frustrated in their careers, have not bought into this idea fully.

Story 22: Doing the Expected is not the Way to be Promoted

There are a number of areas where you can exert control. An important one is in your flexibility to take on new challenges. Most managers can look back on certain times in their careers when small decisions ended up influencing future opportunities. For instance, you may have been asked to help out on a project that was in trouble. You may have been asked to work late to help resolve a critical problem. You may have been asked about working in a new area or picking up new responsibilities. You might find it interesting to think back over the past year, or even six months, and see how many times you had an opportunity for change or an opportunity to pick up something new.

The challenge for Perry was to get this message out to his people without sounding too negative. People who do more and show more initiative are typically the people that stand out over their peers. These standouts tend to be promoted and given even more responsibility. I think this is a very logical argument and it would be hard for most people to argue with those basic facts. So, I asked Perry to think about framing the discussion in three areas. First, people need to recognize when opportunities present themselves. Second, they need to be willing to take on those opportunities and third, they need to complete the opportunity successfully.

Let's look first at recognizing opportunities. The problem with many people is that they do not recognize when opportunities are presented. Sometimes the events are obvious. For instance, let's say you are minding your own business when your boss comes in and offers you a great new position along with a promotion and a salary increase. You might think to yourself "Hey, this is a pretty good deal. Maybe I'll take it."

Of course, the problem is that this type of event rarely takes place. In most instances, the requests are not that obvious and they are not so one-sidedly beneficial. I asked Perry if he could think back over the past five years and come up with some examples of when he may have had opportunities to grow. He thought for a minute and quickly came up with a couple. For instance:

- He took on the role of a mentor to a new co-op student from outside the U.S.
- He was the finance representative on the Vendor Management Committee for a year.
- He took on the temporary management of five people when their prior manager quit suddenly.
- He has been a regular member of the finance interview team for new hires, even though some of these interviews occur at night.

There is one thing that opportunities have in common. They typically require more work. The opportunity may require fitting more into your day, working some extra hours or at least stretching out of your comfort zone.

You might think that you don't really have a chance to accept or decline these types of opportunities and sometimes you are right. Your manager might ask if you will do something, but the implication is that you don't really have a choice. However, look at some of these examples above. In fact, Perry did have a choice in most of these situations.

Story 22: Doing the Expected is not the Way to be Promoted

The second area of coaching for Perry is to inform his staff that they should accept new opportunities. This requires them to have a flexible nature. If you want to work in a box with a narrow set of job requirements, you will probably find that you will stay in the box. On the other hand, if you are willing to stretch and take on new responsibilities, you will become more and more valuable to the organization, and develop a reputation as someone who is multi-faceted and can be counted on. It would not surprise you that these types of people tend to be presented with even more opportunities. Not all of these opportunities are glamorous. You will enjoy some work more than others. However, each opportunity is a small way to further your career and become more valuable to the company.

Perry reminisced about the time he was asked to take on temporary management of the second financial group. It was close to the financial quarter end and he knew he was going to be very busy with the work of his own team. He could have easily passed, given the critical nature of the quarterly close. However, he took on the extra work and extra responsibility. That may be one reason why his department seems to feel he is close to being ready to take on a larger group and more responsibility.

Two months ago, Perry was the runner-up on a promotion that would have quadrupled the size of the group reporting to him. The next time, it may be his turn. If Perry had not taken on the extra work, as well as the other extra opportunities, it is doubtful he would be considered for a promotion. He could have had a great career as a working manager. However, he would probably not have had the opportunity for the advancement he is seeing today.

I come back to flexibility because in many cases you have some control over how you respond to these potential career-building events. Most times they don't come with extra pay or extra perks. However, when you get involved in new areas you have an opportunity to learn new things, pick up new skills and meet new people.

Of course, performance is still very important and it is the third area I asked Perry to talk about. If you volunteer to help in a new area or if you accept new responsibilities and then you don't do a good job, you are not going to get any credit. As a manager, I have seen this happen many times. The typical example is when you ask a staff member to take on a new assignment or area of responsibility. The employee says yes, but the work does not get done right or responsibilities are not followed up on. This will frustrate a manager. If the person was not going to complete the request successfully, he or she should never have accepted the challenge.

Of course, I recognize that everyone is very busy. If you have an opportunity to contribute in a new area, sometimes you simply are not able to accept any additional time commitments. In that case, you may be able to negotiate your workload. For instance, you may tell your manager that you can help out in another area if you are allowed to stretch a current deadline out to a later date. You might also be able to pick up new responsibilities by negotiating with your manager to reassign some less important responsibilities you already have.

Perry needs to be careful when having this type of discussion with his staff. It would also be presumptuous to think that this advice is right for everyone. Perry should first validate each employee's goals and what they want to get out of their careers. Many people are happy to

Story 22: Doing the Expected is not the Way to be Promoted

apply their expertise in a narrow window, and they are not interested in moving much outside of that window. These people typically put limits on what they want to do and they do this in a conscious and proactive manner.

The problem, however, is when there is a gap between people's perceptions of where they want their career to go, and their actions. This can lead to frustration and despair. Remember the old physical law of cause and effect. If team members decline new opportunities, they may not be offered similar opportunities again. If they tell people they are too busy to work on a committee or help to plan an event, then people may get the perception that they are not interested in working in areas outside the basic expectations of their job.

On the other hand, if your staff members are flexible enough to accept new opportunities when they are offered, they will typically get more opportunities in the future. If they are involved in a lot of things, a lot of people get to know their capabilities. If the team member helps out others, those people will remember it when other opportunities arrive. Additional responsibilities tend to gravitate to people who are flexible in what they will do and have shown that they can take on additional responsibility successfully.

Perry should give this advice to his team members - match your expectations with your actions. If they want new opportunities, especially in the management ranks, they need to be flexible in the work they will do, and they need to accept new challenges when they are presented. If they want to work in a box, they should not have high expectations in terms of moving into the management ranks.

Story 23:

You Can Let an Employee Go – and Feel Okay About It

I shook hands with Perry Williams outside of my office and noticed that Penny Williams, no relation to Perry, was already waiting for me inside. I looked at my watch thinking I was running late, but it turned out Penny was about 15 minutes early for our meeting. Penny was an attractive brunette with green eyes and a white smile. She was married to a coach at the university where Pam worked, but I had never met him. Actually, I had never formally met with Penny, either, as she was a fairly new manager in the Accounting Department.

"Looks like I get to go from Perry to Penny," I said walking into my office. Penny turned around but never saw Perry leaving and did not get the joke. She smiled anyway and stood up to shake my hand. I tend to work more with newer managers in my role as people management coach and Penny was no exception. She was promoted to manager six months ago.

"How are you adapting to your new role as a manager?" I asked, gesturing for Penny to have a seat.

"So far it is OK," she replied, returning to her seat and straightening her pant leg.

"But you must have a challenge, or you wouldn't be here today. How can I assist you?"

Penny said she was very frustrated with Nancy Maravich, an employee who had been in the group for three years. Penny and Nancy worked together for two-and-a-half years as teammates before Penny's recent promotion.

"Nancy is very nice and will typically help out in any way she can," Penny explained. "But she is not a good senior accountant. She completes her work late and it is often incomplete. She made mistakes on a number of client financial audits and there are at least two departments that specifically request that she not be assigned to their work."

"Wow, that is not good. Do you think these behaviors are a result of your promotion? Are you concerned there is a conflict there?"

"Not exactly," she replied. "Let me explain further." Penny went on to say that she saw these flaws in Nancy when they were co-workers and Nancy had done nothing to change her performance in the last six months.

Penny was asking for my advice now, and I could tell she felt bad about the situation. She recognized that she needed to deal with Nancy's performance, but she was very concerned that the performance plan would ultimately lead to Nancy's dismissal. Penny had seen that happen to another employee a few years ago.

"Nancy is a nice woman and I know she has two kids," Penny said. "When we were co-workers, I would often try to help her with her workload and try to help her catch up. I can't do that now, though, as I have too many other responsibilities. I need her to do the work she gets paid to do."

Story 23: You Can Let an Employee Go – and Feel Okay About It

"How are her co-workers coping?"

"That's the other problem. I know it's not fair for everyone else if I keep a poor performer in the group. This situation is causing increased workload for everyone, especially if there are requests by the departments that will not work with Nancy."

"It sounds like you are going to have to make some tough choices Penny. Welcome to being a manager."

Lesson #23 – Be Open and Fair with Poor Performers – Including Parting Ways if Necessary

Hiring and firing are two of the classic responsibilities of managers. In large companies like Mega, managers cannot hire and fire people on their own, but they are responsible for the processes that ultimately result in people being hired and fired. In smaller companies, it is possible that some managers have sole discretion to hire and fire.

This is a large responsibility and it can be a burden as well. I can tell that Penny considers herself a people-person, and she prides herself on having a good, personal relationship with her staff members. There is nothing wrong with this. However, Penny really feels badly about having to take action against one of her staff. Penny considers Nancy a friend, and I guess there is an informal rule that friends don't fire friends.

Of course, the place I will start is to remind Penny that she may be very loyal to her staff, but as a manager, her first loyalty must be to Mega, and she should always act with the best interests of Mega in mind. Fortunately, in most cases, what is good for her staff is also good for Mega. However, this may end up being a case where there is some divergence – especially in Nancy's opinion.

Some managers can make the hard, cold calculation that an employee is not cutting it, and they have no problem letting that person go. At Mega there are performance processes to follow, so Penny needs to understand the process and then execute it. If she does, then the situation should work itself out in a manner that is fair to everyone. This process will give Nancy every opportunity to save her job. The general approach is as follows:

1. **Provide honest performance feedback.** It is not clear that anyone has sat down with Nancy and really laid her performance weaknesses out for her. Nancy has had some vague discussions, but it is not clear to me that the full gravity of the situation has been made clear. It is doubtful, for instance, that Nancy realizes that two departments do not want to work with her based on past mistakes she has made. Penny should document this formal discussion, as well as the specific action items that are agreed to. Penny should also be clear that if Nancy's performance is not improved, the next step will be to ask the formal advice of the Human Resources group. Even though Nancy has had performance problems for awhile, Penny should start with this internal coaching session first to make doubly sure

Story 23: You Can Let an Employee Go – and Feel Okay About It

that Nancy has the benefit of the doubt moving forward. Penny should also set a time limit for Nancy to show improvement.

2. **Provide timely performance feedback.** Penny should monitor Nancy's work and make sure that she is meeting Penny's expectations and the requirements of her position. Unlike in the past, Penny needs to make sure she is clear and timely in her performance feedback. If Nancy misses a deadline date, for instance, the feedback should be immediate, not saved for the next performance review.

3. **Evaluate whether the expectations were met.** At the end of the time period set at the first meeting, Penny needs to decide on next steps. If Nancy's performance has now turned acceptable, Penny can perhaps pat herself on the back for the turnaround. If the performance is not where it needs to be, Penny will need to get the Human Resources Department involved.

4. **Escalate to Human Resources if necessary.** If Human Resources becomes involved, they will probably recommend that Nancy be placed on a formal performance plan (this would not be their first choice, but Penny will have already done the first and second activities they would recommend). Penny should not feel bad about this. The performance plan is designed to provide every incentive and every opportunity for Nancy to turn her performance around.

5. **Monitor the performance plan.** Penny then needs to monitor the plan and document the accomplishments against the plan. Penny also needs to have ongoing performance feedback sessions with Nancy to ensure she is aware of how she is performing against the plan.

They key thing for Penny to understand is that this process gives Nancy control over her situation. Remember, if Mega was really a callous company, Nancy would have been fired long ago. Instead, a formal performance plan provides all of the criteria for Nancy to keep her job. If, at the end of the plan, Nancy has not fulfilled the clear expectations of the plan, she will be terminated – as called for in the performance plan itself.

This type of process is fair to the employee and to the rest of the team. It is fair to Nancy since it clearly lays out the expectations required to hold on to her job. It is fair to Mega and the rest of her team since Nancy will either fulfill the expectations or be terminated.

It is important to realize that the current situation is not fair to the rest of the team. The team has to work harder to make up for the shortcomings of Nancy. The rest of the team has already noticed, for example, that when work comes in from certain areas, they have to work more since Nancy is not allowed to participate. Penny should know this first-hand. She told me she knew of Nancy's shortcomings even when they were team members. As a co-worker, Penny may have felt her options were limited in dealing with this problem. However, as manager, Penny now has an obligation to address the situation. The truth is that she has already waited too long since she has been the manager for six months.

Some companies have a more drastic approach to proactively cutting out the poorest performers. For instance, in some organizations, the managers have to rank all of their people on a yearly

Story 23: You Can Let an Employee Go – and Feel Okay About It

basis. The managers are then asked to grow the lowest ranked people into higher performers or else terminate them. This may be viewed as harsh, but it is a direct organizational response aimed at managers who defer making the tough performance decisions on their own.

Under this "forced-ranking" approach, Nancy would have been seen as a weak link long ago and probably would have been terminated. Perhaps this should have been done long ago; however, at Mega, the culture does not force the weakest performers out. I think the truly poor performers are dealt with over time, but unfortunately the marginal-to-weak performers are allowed to hang around for too long. This can have detrimental effects on the entire team.

What most managers don't realize is that the rest of the team knows about the poor performers and if these poor performers are terminated, most of the remaining team members would understand. Many team members might even wonder why the weak performers were there for so long. Tackling the performance problem can be hard for a manager, but it is absolutely necessary for the good of the person and the good of the team. The manager can assist by providing coaching, training or restructuring the work if appropriate. However, the manager cannot do the work of the team member and so it is ultimately up to the team member to meet the expectations of their position or else go away.

I think Penny felt good about our discussion when it was over. I have given her a non-threatening place to start by having an initial coaching session with Nancy. This could escalate into a performance plan. If it does, the performance plan will have a clearly defined path for Nancy to keep her job. If she is able to stay on the path, Nancy will be fine. If she is not able to meet the expectations, Nancy will be terminated. However, since the plan is within Nancy's control, it is not like Penny would be arbitrarily firing Nancy. Instead, Nancy will have fired herself.

Story 24:

Morale Problems are Everyone's Problems

My last meeting on Friday was with Annette Venezuela, the new department head in the IT division. She had called me a week back to request a meeting on the topic of morale. From the brief conversation I had with her, it sounded like morale was low among IT employees. I did not know much about Annette, so I was looking forward to working with her more. I knew she had worked her way up the ladder at Mega, and I remember my friend Jerry Ackerman mentioning her on a few occasions, but he only said she was smart and eager to learn.

To prepare for my meeting, I called Jerry on my cell phone while driving home from work and asked him how things were going in the IT Department. He mentioned that he had not been working directly on IT projects for the last three weeks because he had been asked to participate in a project in the Human Resources Department.

"I haven't been too involved with specific IT projects, but I know things are crazy over there right now. I hear a lot of complaining."

"Can you discuss further? What is the problem?"

Jerry mentioned that systems problems were playing havoc on everyone's schedule. It seemed that systems were down off-and-on during the day, which forced many people to have to work long hours to catch up. Jerry knew several of his colleagues were working past 9 p.m. and coming in on the weekends.

Jerry's input gave me an overview of the problem, and I was anxious to talk with Annette to see if she would confirm what Jerry had said. She arrived at my door wearing blue jeans and a white buttoned-down shirt. Mega allowed for casual dress on Fridays, but I was somewhat surprised to see a department head dressed so casually. She explained right away that she, too, had been working long hours and needed a break from the routine, even if it was just wearing jeans.

"I've got a big mess on my hands, Tom," she said, plopping down emphatically in the chair across from my desk.

"You mentioned on the phone that your problem had to do with morale. Is that still the case?"

"Indeed. I am afraid the problem has only gotten worse since I spoke to you originally."

Annette began talking, and she confirmed that systems failures and server troubles were at the heart of the problem. When we spoke initially, Annette thought the problems would be resolved and life would be back to normal. She knew, however, that she was not doing a good enough job with morale, and wanted to talk after the fact about how she could improve.

"Maybe I am wrong, but I thought my supervisor-level employees would deal with morale. After all, they work much more closely with our techs and the rest of our employees. I know morale is down, but I just figured my supervisors would deal with it."

"And have they been?"

Story 24: Morale Problems are Everyone's Problems

"I know they are trying, but I also know they are looking for some leadership and direction from me. Just yesterday, in fact, one of my supervisors came to me and said he almost had to break up a fight between two of his employees. Apparently there was a miscommunication and the two were ready to throw punches. Thank God it didn't escalate to that, but this supervisor asked me if I could do something about morale. I did not know what to tell him."

"Honestly Annette, it sounds like you AND your supervisors could learn a thing or two about recognizing and responding to the issue of poor morale."

Lesson #24 – Don't Ignore Morale Problems – Turn Them Around

Morale refers to how well people feel about their company and their job. It is inevitable that different people have different perceptions of the company and their job, based on their own experiences and the things that are important to them. It would be nice if everyone felt good about their situations. In fact, some managers act as if morale should not come into play on the job at all. These are the managers who say "we pay you to do a job. So, as long as we are paying you, just do the job."

As most of you know, however, it is not that simple. Morale needs to be watched for the simple reason that people with poor morale are not as productive as those with good morale. Staffs with poor morale are not as productive and they don't generally feel like working as hard as others. Instead of spending time on their work routine, people spend time talking about how bad things are, or how bad the manager is, or how screwed up the company is. If people with poor morale find common ground with like-minded people, the discontent is reinforced and multiplied.

When business is good and everything is going well, morale is much easier to manage. It is harder to manage when the company is on hard times, when layoffs are occurring and when uncertainty is evident. Events at the company level can trigger morale problems, as can the situation on specific teams. Team morale problems can be caused by heavy overtime, a lack of recognition, poor communication with the team manager, etc.

Many managers find themselves in a situation where they need to battle morale problems. People's morale normally changes incrementally over time, so it is not easy for a manager to know the precise day morale turned the wrong way. You might think things are fine, and then one day it hits you that there is a problem.

Once morale problems are recognized, they should be addressed. It is possible that morale may turn around on its own, but you can't count on it. Bad morale causes productivity declines, quality-related problems, excess absenteeism and turnover. Therefore, a poor morale problem cannot be left alone, but must be addressed quickly and usually with a multi-faceted approach. The following process should help.

1. **Validate that you have a problem and determine the extent of that problem**. You may pick up anecdotal evidence that morale is poor or on the decline. In fact, one of your staff may even tell you that morale is poor (as was the case with Annette). However, you need to do more analysis to determine whether this is an organizational concern or just a problem with a few people. Hopefully you won't discover that morale is terrible.

Story 24: Morale Problems are Everyone's Problems

You should be able to detect the problem before it gets to that point. However, before you solve a problem, you should first validate that a problem exists and determine how extreme the problem is.

Of course, people rarely come right out and say there is a morale problem. However, you can usually spot the signs. People may point fingers at others on the team for having a lack of motivation. They may sound tired or they may not want to talk. They may sound negative or defeatist. All of these could point to poor morale.

2. **Determine whether morale is causing problems, and if so, what the problems are.** Don't assume blindly that all problems are caused by poor team motivation. There are many other potential factors in play as well. Let's also not assume that a morale slide has started to affect the normal work of the group. Morale problems usually lead to other workload problems, but you have to find out for sure. If you caught the problem early, the negative impact on work might be negligible. Knowing the impact to the expected workload will help you determine how urgent and dramatic the response needs to be.

3. **Look for the causes of poor morale.** Let's assume you have validated you have problems and that they are morale related. Morale problems are always a symptom of some other causes. In other words, people don't come to work one day and decide they are going to have poor morale. Poor morale is caused by something else.

You may find the cause or causes of the problem to be rather straightforward. For instance, if your department is experiencing layoffs or if people are working heavy overtime, you may have an obvious morale problem. If the cause is not obvious, it will take more questions and probing to figure it out. It is important to understand the cause or causes as best you can, even if some or all of the causes are outside your control.

4. **Turn things around - take care of the basics first.** Next you will need to try to turn things around. Some of the root causes may be beyond your control to fix. For instance, you may not be able to cause stock prices to rise. However, there are things within your control. The first rule is to take care of the basics. Encourage open communication on the team. Also make sure you are available to talk and to listen to concerns. Make sure that training needs are met. Make sure your working environment is clean. Do all you can to make sure people are leading a balanced life and are not working overtime over extensive periods. Taking care of basics is a way to make sure that people don't have reasons to complain. Industrial psychologist Frederick Herzberg found that when the basics were missing, motivation was reduced. You are not going to have high morale just by doing the basics, but you need to start there.

5. **Be creative to work on the extras.** In addition to the basics, look for other opportunities to increase morale and motivation. Herzberg found that things like achievement, recognition, responsibility and advancement provide positive benefits. Consider ideas such as paid time off, pizza parties and lunches with the boss. Look for any extra opportunity to talk with people.

Story 24: Morale Problems are Everyone's Problems

In Annette's case, low morale is most likely being caused by technical malfunctions that she cannot control. However, she can control how she responds to these glitches, and she can do more to impact morale on the positive side. When you work in the IT Department, networks crash, and servers and systems go down all the time. No one in IT should be surprised when these things happen. However, IT professionals are people, too, and they get just as stressed as anyone else when they have to work long hours and weekends.

Annette recognized the problem, but she assumed other people on her staff, namely her supervisors, would address it and deal with it. This did not happen, and it has caused morale to slip even further. Annette needs to immediately take care of the basics. She needs to communicate with her supervisors, perhaps even sending e-mails to everyone in the department recognizing their hard work and thanking them for it. She should also make sure people know they can talk with her openly about any challenges they are dealing with.

Next, she should get creative and do things to boost people's morale. She could, for example, order pizza on Saturday for the people who have to work, or bring in coffee and donuts for the Sunday shift. She may also need to discuss scheduling with her supervisors, to see if a schedule can be created which will allow employees to take a day off during the week, until the technical issues can be resolved. At the very least, these things will show her team that Annette recognizes their sacrifice and hard work and appreciates it. Sometimes just showing that you recognize a problem exists goes a long way.

Morale problems don't appear by themselves all at once. Morale usually declines slowly over a period of time. In the same respect, you are not going to bring morale back up all at once or with one large event. The key is to take a multifaceted approach and to keep it up over time. This approach should involve all of the managers in the organization, even the ones that might have some morale problems themselves. It may be surprising how a little focus, applied for a period of time, can have a measurable effect on improving morale.

Story 25:

High-Performance Teams are a Hole-in-One

After a very challenging week at Mega, I was finally ready to relax in the warmth of the Arizona sun. Temperatures in the state did not disappoint. When we left Dickens in the early morning for the short car ride to Chicago, temperatures were in the upper 30s. When we arrived in Phoenix, it was a warm 80 degrees, with an expected high of 87 for the day. When we arrived at the hotel, we all decided to put on our swimsuits and relax by the pool for the afternoon.

The next day, Pam booked herself a half-day at the spa and I booked a reservation for Tim and me to play golf at one of the hotel's two courses. When we arrived at the clubhouse, the attendant informed us that we would be paired up with a single for the day, and that he was already on the grounds and was putting on the practice green. Tim and I headed out to loosen up and I noticed our playing partner for the day on the practice green. He was an older gentleman, in this late 50s or early 60s, and he was wearing khaki shorts and a polo shirt.

Tim and I were taking practice swings when we heard our name called out for the first tee, along with Jimmy Purdue. I shook Jimmy's hand as he walked over toward us and introduced him to my son. The first hole on the course was a fairly easy 420-yard par four with only one major obstruction – a sand trap on the right side of the fairway about 250 yards out. I took out my driver and sailed one about twenty yards past the trap in the middle of the fairway. Tim played next and hit a solid shot straight down the center of the fairway. It rolled to a stop after about 175 yards.

"Your son has quite a swing there," Jimmy said, holding his hand over his eyes to see how far the ball would go before stopping. After Jimmy teed off, the three of us gathered up our clubs and walked down the cart path toward our balls.

By the third hole, I had found out that Jimmy was in his late 50s and worked for an automobile company in Detroit. He and his wife were also out on vacation and staying at our hotel. Jimmy asked what I did for a living, and I told him about Mega Manufacturing and my role as project management coach.

After we hit our drives on the 6th hole, a long par 5, Jimmy mentioned a problem he was having on his team before he left Detroit. He said he was frustrated with regard to his team's performance.

"When I was a regular team member, our team was super productive," he said, trying to figure out which iron to use for his second shot. "Our team knew what to do and the best way to do it. We got along well and everyone helped each other as needed. It was a great experience for everyone involved."

Jimmy said he still remembers how it felt to work on that team even though he left the group three years ago. As a manager, Jimmy is frustrated that his current team does not seem to be working at nearly that high a level of achievement. The team members seem to be always looking for Jimmy to make decisions and tell them what to do. Once in a while, they get to bickering and their work is unproductive.

Story 25: High-Performance Teams are a Hole-in-One

"Nice shot Tim!" I shouted as Tim's third shot landed on the green.

"Way to go Tim!" Jimmy shouted, waving his 9-iron in the air before flopping his shot onto the green.

"So you were saying your current team is not as high-performing as a previous team you were on?"

"Exactly, Tom. How do I go about recapturing that old magic from my former group? It seemed like my old group just 'gelled' naturally, without much work from our supervisors. I want that same dynamic in my current group, but I am at a loss for how to do it."

Lesson #25 – Strive to Create High-Performance Teams

Have you ever been on a project team that had everything going right? The team members all got along; they all had the right skills; everyone worked hard and pulled together to get the project done.

Those are just some of the characteristics of a high-performing team. High-performing teams can sometimes form by themselves, perhaps even in spite of a manager that gets in the way. However, it is more typical that a manager helps a team become high-performing and facilitates them through a process that leads to the team becoming as effective and efficient as possible.

For some managers, this journey is extremely difficult if not impossible. They may be very organized, technically strong, and masters of organizational politics, but they may not be very good people managers and not very effective at building a team. In some respects, it is also hard for a manager to guide a team toward high-performance if he or she was never part of a high-performing team. Reaching toward high-performance is almost a vision, and if you do not have a vision based on experience, it may be very difficult to guide a team of people there.

You cannot start with a new team and expect them to be high performing in a day, a week or a month. There are many aspects of building a high-performance team that require a long period of time to bring to fruition. You will find that teams that have not worked together before usually go through four stages of team development, as defined in the Tuckman model. They are:

- **Forming.** The team is first meeting and getting to know each other. They can't rely on others totally because they are not sure what everyone's skills, strengths and weaknesses are.
- **Storming.** The team struggles through understanding roles and responsibilities. Usually personality conflicts start to arise. Team members feel good enough to complain, but not always confident or knowledgeable enough to propose solutions. Team members know each other well enough that they can start to argue. Generally, the team is in flux and people are not exactly sure what they are supposed to be doing. Some immature teams never make it past this stage.

Story 25: High-Performance Teams are a Hole-in-One

- **Norming**. The team starts getting used to each other's strengths and weaknesses. Team members start to compensate for one another and a feeling of camaraderie starts to take shape. Team members accept each other as people and enjoy being around each other. The team may begin realizing that as a whole, they are stronger than they were as just a group of individual contributors.
- **Performing**. This is the last stage of a high-performance team. At this stage the team strives toward common objectives – written or unwritten. They rely on each other. When trouble arises, they ask how they can help. The team members can generally work without a lot of management supervision. The overall productivity is especially high and is recognized as such by others outside the team.

Team members of a high-performing team have trust and confidence in the other members of the team. They cannot build this level of trust overnight, which is another reason why these teams take some time to form. This sounds like the type of team that Jimmy was a member of a few years ago. Some of his comments point this out. Jimmy says that the team was very productive, but he also talked about the team relying on each other. He said that they knew what they needed to do and the best way to do it, which implies they required little supervision. These types of teams are rare, which is a major reason why people who have been on one remember the feeling even years later.

However, as Jimmy noted, they are not easily formed. Given a vision of the end result, a manager can try to put the pieces in place that will help a team get through the four-stage model described earlier. Jimmy's team is probably stuck between the second and third stage. They may, in fact, be stuck there permanently. However, there are some things that Jimmy can do to facilitate their growth.

- **Set common objectives.** Teams will have a hard time performing at a high level unless they are all striving toward a common set of objectives. Even if members of your team do different jobs, a set of objectives can usually be written that will encompass all of them. If possible, the team should also be rewarded based on achieving this common set of objectives. This will assist in getting everyone pulling in the same direction.
- **Establish good internal work processes.** It is true that you cannot build consistently good products, or deliver good services, with poor work processes. The high-performing team has a set of internal processes that guide how members act and react in particular circumstances. For instance, if problems arise, they know how to invoke problem-solving techniques. If a customer makes a request for a change to specifications, they know to invoke scope change procedures. In this way, they maintain as little uncertainty as possible. Another aspect of these teams is that they constantly look for ways to improve their current processes. If a process was perfect a year ago, it may not be perfect today. The team constantly challenges the current state and recommends changes for improvement.
- **Instill good work ethic.** This probably goes without saying. High-performing teams rarely form in an environment where people complain about their workload or where team members complain about the work habits of other team members. High-performing teams find the challenges associated with their work and work hard to complete their assignments within expectations. Sometimes hard work gets confused with working a lot

Story 25: High-Performance Teams are a Hole-in-One

of hours. These are not the same things. A high-performance team works efficiently and works smart. Members get more work done in a typical day than their counterparts (in fact, a team that must pull late hours all the time probably has some problems with focus that might need to be addressed to get them out of that rut). On the other hand, the high-performing team understands when members need to pull together to achieve the project objectives, and sometimes that does require working many extra hours.

- **Keep everyone focused.** The high-performance team is focused on the objectives and the deliverables, and understands how to achieve them. They don't get sidetracked by rumors or politics. They don't get absorbed in gossip. They don't spend more time complaining than working. They know what is expected of them and do the best they can to meet those expectations.

- **Maintain a high level of motivation.** The high-performance team identifies the challenges associated with meeting its objectives and completing its deliverables. This is both a self-motivation on the part of each team member as well as a reinforced motivation through the entire team.

- **Keep organized.** Team members understand what their role on the team is and what everyone else's role is as well. People understand the work they have on their plate today, as well as what the remainder of their work is. They understand the processes and procedures needed to run the team, including scope change management, risk management, issues management, quality management, and status reporting. If unusual events occur, they know how to manage the process and how to escalate when appropriate.

- **Strive toward a balanced set of key skills.** A high-performance team has all of the skills needed to complete the work on its plate. Team members have the skills needed from a technical standpoint, as well as the right set of role-based skills. For instance, it is hard to be a high-performance team when everyone wants to be the Team Leader. If some of these "leaders" are asked to build deliverables instead, they may not have the right skills or the right motivation for the team to be successful. If short-term skill sets are missing, then the appropriate skills are brought in from outside resources if needed. If the skill will be needed on the team in the long-term, team members receive the training necessary to perform the work in the future. In a high-performing team, people understand their strengths and weaknesses, but they also are willing to work outside their comfort area when needed.

- **Foster mutual respect.** Members of high-performance teams typically get along with each other. They have mutual respect for each other and trust that the others are working as hard as they are. They assist other team members when they are in need and understand that team members will do the same for them if needed. In general, team members are even-tempered and not prone to high ecstasy or depression. The team members respect each other's abilities as well as help compensate for any weaknesses, since they know others are compensating for their weaknesses as well.

Story 25: High-Performance Teams are a Hole-in-One

In the right circumstances, a manager can take the lead to move a team toward high-performance status. It takes time and in many cases the results will be disappointing. If it were easy, every team would be high performing, instead of the one or two that you may have worked on in your entire career. Jimmy is motivated to move down that path, so I have the following suggestions for him:

- **Empower the team.** Teams, like individuals, will mature over time if they are allowed to make more and more of the decisions that impact them. If the team is kept on a short leash and must always ask for direction from the manager, they will have little incentive or desire to mature toward high performance. It is possible that a high-performing team does not need a formal manager at all. To reach this stage, however, the manager must allow the team to make as many of its own decisions as is practical. As the team gets more mature, they should be given even more discretion. On a high-performing team, the manager acts more like a coach offering advice, rather than as a formal manager that tells everyone what to do.

- **Establish team processes.** The team needs to have good processes to follow for handling issues, change requests, status reporting, etc. Team members need to understand how things get approved, how to surface potential risks and what deliverables should look like. Some of these processes should exist already, but many probably are not formally defined. If possible, these processes should be consistent throughout the organization. However, if no consistent processes are available for the entire organization, then the entire team can work and agree on them when the project is starting.

- **Invest in training.** In a perfect world, the manager and the entire team would have experience in the technology being utilized and in the subject matter being delivered. Members would know the organization and the politics. In the real world, however, the manager and the team rarely have all the right skills needed. They need to understand what they do not know and try to get to the right level of expertise as quickly as possible. This usually implies being as liberal with training as possible while you are guiding a team down this path. This includes technical, professional, and business training. Also, consider specific team building and other training designed to show a team how to work effectively together. This can compress the time required to reach the higher levels of team performance.

- **Be flexible.** It is hard to know and plan everything. One of the key characteristics of a successful manager is to be comfortable working in an environment where change is a constant. If the manager works effectively in this environment, the workload will be updated on a continual basis and will accurately reflect what needs to be done to complete the project. The manager is also able to effectively deal with changing team dynamics over time.

- **Monitor team dynamics and progress.** Once the team is in place and well trained, it should be monitored to make sure the team members are progressing well and moving toward a state of higher efficiency and effectiveness. The manager should constantly reinforce good behaviors and deal with problems when they occur. When the team is really high performing, it tends to deal with its own problems before they are surfaced outside the team.

Story 25: High-Performance Teams are a Hole-in-One

Jimmy's desire to replicate the success of his prior high-performing team is admirable. High-performing teams sometimes come about by the accidental meeting of the right people with the right motivation. However, the right combination of circumstances cannot be counted on in every case. Jimmy has been waiting for this spark to arrive on its own and it has not happened.

Jimmy can go a long way toward building a high-performing team with some proactive coaching and guidance. If he steps back, he can define the characteristics of a high-performing team in his organization and make an effort to foster those traits on his current team. Jimmy knows this is not an overnight process. Even if the team is motivated, many of the characteristics of a high-performing team need to evolve as people become comfortable working with each other. However, Jimmy can guide his team through the various stages of team dynamics and help them reach the final state more quickly than if they were left on their own. Like most things in life, there is no guarantee of success. However, the odds are more in his favor than if he continues to do nothing proactive at all.

Story 26:

Manager – Heal Thyself

It didn't take me long to get snapped back into reality at Mega after my week-long vacation in Arizona. I had scheduled my first meeting back with Bert Zucker, an obnoxious man who worked as a manger in the manufacturing department. Bert was a divorced father of two with a big, round face and a small, stout body. His hair was turning gray, but was still sandy blonde on the top. He wore it short and spiked, which was not a great look on him.

Bert called me the week before my vacation and asked if I had time to meet with him before I left. Fortunately for me, my schedule was already booked solid and I told him we would have to meet when I got back. He insisted that we meet first thing Monday morning, and even though I wasn't looking forward to it, I obliged. At the time, I thought perhaps the jubilance of my vacation would carry over into Monday and it would help me deal with Bert. I was correct in that I will still in a happy mood from my trip, but I should have known better regarding Bert – nothing can help me deal with him.

When he arrived at my office, he was wearing a blue suit that fit him a bit too snug and a white shirt with a blue tie. I could tell he was trying to look professional for our meeting.

"You like nice and tan, Tom. Must be nice to have the time to get away."

I knew from his tone that he was implying he did not have the time to take a vacation, but I did not much feel like arguing so I just changed the topic to business right away.

"I'm sorry I could not visit with you before I left. What seems to be the trouble?"

"My boss actually told me I had to see you, so I am following his wishes. My boss and I are concerned about the morale in our group, as well as productivity."

So far, I was not too surprised by what Bert had to say. Bert's team was always toward the bottom of the manufacturing statistics. They generally produced fewer products than average, had a higher error rate, took more sick time, etc. I asked Bert if he had any perceptions as to why his group was lagging and he had a prepared list of reasons ready.

1. His people were not motivated.
2. He tried to train them but they only wanted to do things the old way.
3. Sick time was high, which reduced group productivity. He thought much of the sick time was faked.

4. Team members have more errors because they are not as smart as other groups.
5. His group was generally lazier than other groups.

Bert then gave me his management philosophy, which was to "tell it like it is."

"I'm not sure what else I can do," he said. "I have challenged the group to become better. They know where they stand with me. I have told them they are lazy and unmotivated and need to be better. I have explained to them that jobs are on the line – including mine. But like I said, they are not the sharpest knives in the drawer and I just don't think they get it."

Story 26: Manager – Heal Thyself

Lesson #26 – Understand That Your Attitude Rubs Off On the Entire Team – For Good or Bad

All managers have different work styles and I would not have it any other way. There are effective managers with strong dominant personalities and some with great people skills. Some get things done through a directive style, some are more collaborative. Different styles can be effective depending on the circumstances and different styles can be effective depending on the personality of the subordinates.

Then there is Bert. I did not ask Bert what his background was, but my guess is that he used to be a worker on the shop floor that was promoted into management. In fact, his management style may directly mirror the style of his old manager – the person that likely promoted him.

Where do you even start with a guy like Bert? I wish I could point out some techniques that he could use to improve the performance of his team. However, there is probably going to be more than a few tweaks required for Bert. I am reminded of the saying "physician heal thyself," which basically means that doctors need to address their own problems before they can be fully effective addressing the problems of others.

Bert fits this same philosophy. He is looking for answers on team morale and productivity problems while not realizing that he is probably the cause for much of the problems (if not all of the problems). Even in the short meeting he and I had, a couple obvious things come out.

- Bert perceives there is a problem with morale and productivity, but he doesn't perceive that he has a proactive role to play to make things better. All of his potential causes have to do with the team members, not his role as a manager.

- He does not have a sense of urgency and has not proactively tried to address these problems, even though the numbers have been clear for quite some time. Even my meeting with him is a result of his manager, not a proactive step that Bert took.

- He does not realize that a manager sets the tone for the group. If his team lacks motivation, Bert needs to address it. In this case, it is even worse since Bert is probably the cause of this motivation gap. This also comes out in the high sick time for the group.

- He attributes a high error rate to a belief that his group is just not as smart and that they refuse to follow new processes. This is really a poor observation. Organizations that focus on quality understand that when quality suffers it is because of processes, not people. Bert does not realize that processes are a management responsibility. It is his responsibility to make sure good processes are in place and that they are followed. When people have poor processes to follow, they will make poor products with many errors.

- Bert's management philosophy of "telling it like it is" might work in some instances. However, it is vital that he knows when this philosophy is appropriate. Bert is way off in his perception of how managers and subordinates relate and is probably causing most of the problems in morale and productivity. In fact, Bert probably doesn't know that if the manager has high expectations and constantly builds the team up, they will tend to

Story 26: Manager – Heal Thyself

respond accordingly. If the manager tells them that they are lazy, unmotivated and dumb, the team will tend to meet those expectations as well.

The place to start is to make sure you are doing all you can as a manager and a leader. Unfortunately, if you are a poor manager, you will have a difficult time being introspective and taking a good, hard look at yourself. If you are really bad, you may have difficulty taking suggestions and feedback from others as well. There are some basics that every good manager should have when it comes to managing people. These are core skills and it is difficult to be effective without them. They include:

- **Proactive communication skills** - make sure people know what is going on and what is expected of them. You need to be positive and you need to know how to give constructive performance feedback.
- **Good interpersonal skills** - the ability to show empathy and concern about individual team members and an ability to let people know you care about them and their concerns.
- **Good listening skills** – the ability to understand what people are saying to you. For instance, when team members come to see you, don't also be working on your computer or answering phone messages.

I left my meeting with Bert not knowing exactly what to do. I told him that I would consider his situation and provide him with some coaching advice in a day or two after I had a chance to reflect. As I said earlier, this is not a situation that is going to change with a few coaching suggestions. If Bert is going to grow as a manager, he is going to have to be prepared to change his entire managerial style, and I am not sure I am the right person to give him that feedback. I also feel bad going to Bert's manager, since that would seem like going behind Bert's back.

After thinking about this for a while, I met with Bert again and told him in very general terms that some of the problems he is describing might be the result of how he is interacting with the team. I told him about management's role in establishing good processes, and tried to provide him with enough feedback to improve his role as a manager. I then offered to meet with him on a separate occasion to start a series of coaching meetings that might lead to becoming a more effective manager, which in turn should lead to his team being more effective. If he takes me up on the offer, then I think some real progress can be made.

Story 27:

"Coach" Arnie Needs Some Coaching

After dealing with the issues of sexual harassment and diversity in the workplace earlier in the year, I decided to conduct new training classes on both subjects for all manager-level employees at Mega. The training class was required for all managers.

On the first Thursday in May I gave the training class to a group of managers in the finance division. I was happy to see Arnie Appleby, a tall, commanding figure, in the class. Arnie was in his late 50s and had spent much of his career in the military, advancing to the title of Major. He was a neat character who loved telling old war stories and other stories from "the good old days." I served on a hiring committee for the Finance Department two years ago when Arnie was hired, and got to know him well during the interview process for his current management job. He was disciplined and tough, but always fair and level-headed.

"How are you doing Arnie?" I asked as he approached me after the training session had ended.

"I'm doing great, Tom. You gave a very interesting presentation today and I wanted to thank you for the information."

"I appreciate the feedback Arnie. How are things down here in Finance?"

"Ship-shape. The troops are working hard and we've got a few tough projects coming up in the third quarter that we are preparing for."

Arnie talked a bit more about some of the projects currently underway, and mentioned that he was teaching the team some of the newer techniques for financial audits. In this discussion, Arnie said something that I felt I should follow-up on.

"You know, I really see myself as a coach for our team," he said. He used an analogy of a football team. "The coach is the one person everyone listens to, and as the coach, I will make sure everyone uses these new auditing techniques. If they don't, they will have 'Coach Arnie' to answer to."

"That's an interesting way to look at it, Arnie, although I am not quite sure your coaching analogy applies in this context," I said carefully so I could measure Arnie's reaction.

"Why not?" Arnie asked in a puzzled manner. He was proud of his coaching analogy.

"Well, let me try to explain."

Lesson #27 - Coach Your Staff So That They Can Mature and Grow

My initial discussion with Arnie got me thinking about the differences between coaching and training. I had just finished a formal training class for the managers in the Finance group. I used a certain set of skills and techniques for this class in my role as an instructor. On the other hand, I often step into a coaching role. When I wear that hat, I utilize a much different set of skills and techniques.

Story 27: "Coach" Arnie Needs Some Coaching

Training generally uses a delivery method that will allow you to teach similar content on a repetitive basis. For instance, the class on discrimination and harassment is one that I have given many times to different audiences of managers. I deliver the same basic class content to each audience. Computer-based training (CBT) is the same way. A CBT class content is more or less delivered in a similar way to different people. Training implies a formal teacher-pupil relationship and the formal instruction of material.

Coaching is different from training. Coaching is less structured, and usually involves talking about real situations that the person being coached is facing. Rather than talking to the trainee (person being coached) in general terms that would apply to anyone, the coach applies his or her knowledge of the subject in a way that can be applied directly to the problem at hand.

The whole purpose of coaching is to transfer information and expertise from the coach to the trainee. The coach must possess the knowledge and also the ability to transfer the knowledge to another person or group. When the subject is familiar, the coach can rely on a similar set of coaching points. When the discussion gets ad-hoc, the coach must respond with ad-hoc advice. However, the ad-hoc advice would all be within the context of the policies, standards and culture of the company. The coach has the ability to provide this information based on his or her experience and coaching skills.

I wanted to talk to Arnie further because it sounded like he has not necessarily gotten the full meaning of the term "coach." All managers should be able to perform in the role of a coach, but a coach does more than just tell people what to do. Let's look at Arnie's comparison of his role with that of a football coach. On game day, the coach provides the overall plan and asks the team to execute the plan. As the game progresses, the coach reacts to different situations such as a change in the weather or an injury to a key team member. The coach is the person in control. That is the coaching model that Arnie is using. However, Arnie has forgotten that the football coach does much more during the rest of the week.

Perhaps the most important thing a football coach does is teach. This includes teaching players how to execute the plays, where to position themselves, how to play each position, etc. All of this goes into the preparation before a team steps onto the field on game day. Likewise, Arnie should be coaching his staff and helping them to grow professionally. If there are new audit requirements, Arnie should explain them to his staff, answer questions and role-play how the new requirements might play out on an audit.

When people ask questions about specific situations they are dealing with, Arnie should apply his experience and knowledge to help the person come up with a solution. In fact, in many cases, there are no absolutely perfect solutions. Instead, there are "best" solutions, where "best" is based on experience.

A coach also helps determine how each person best fits on the team to give the team the best chance of success. Like a football coach, Arnie is probably doing this as well. Arnie understands the responsibilities of his group. He then makes sure that everyone has a role to play and that the combination of all of the roles will allow the entire team to be successful.

I am sure Arnie does some true coaching today, even though he seems to think a coach is

Story 27: "Coach" Arnie Needs Some Coaching

strictly a leader that everyone follows. However, the role of coach requires a different set of skills and techniques. Some of these skills are as follows:

- **Validate understanding.** You cannot coach people if you do not understand the situations they are facing. This is one way that coaching is different from training. Training is more generic. Coaching is typically applied to a particular situation or event.

- **Talk and listen.** Make sure you do not spend too much time talking without validating that the person being coached understands what you are saying. If the person repeats back to you what you are saying, then the chances are he or she is still mentally engaged. If he or she doesn't say anything for a while, then it could mean that he or she has lost interest or else has lost your message. If you find yourself talking a lot, stop at various times and ask the person to repeat back the information in his or her own words, or perhaps ask him or her how the information you are providing would apply to his or her situation.

- **Ask probing questions.** The coach needs to be careful not to dominate the coaching session by doing all of the talking. The coaching experience should be give and take. The coach should ask probing questions to find out additional information and draw out the participants.

- **Leverage personal experiences.** The coach should use personal examples, including experience from coaching previous people, during the coaching sessions. People coming directly out of college probably cannot be good coaches. They just don't have the experience necessary to give meaningful advice to others.

- **Be conscious of the person's body language.** It takes concentration and energy to provide coaching, but it also takes energy and focus to receive coaching. If you see the person is starting to drag or his energy level is getting low, you should probably take a break. Also keep in mind that if the coach starts to drag, then the person being coached will likewise start to drag.

Sometimes the body language or facial expression of the person being coached can lead you to believe that he is not receptive to your message or that he doesn't find the value in it. If you perceive this, make sure you also do a reality check. Ask the person if he understands what you are saying and whether he thinks there will be value in the processes on his project. If he has any objections, discuss them now so that they can be addressed as soon as possible.

Coaching is all about building skills and capabilities in others. However, it is done in a personalized manner so that it is relevant to the person(s) being coached. If the coaching is successful, the person being coached will be able to apply his new knowledge to the situation at hand. He will also have enough context and guidance to be able to resolve similar situations in the future – without having to go back to the coach for every permutation. All managers should consider coaching to be one of their core skills.

117

Story 28:

Contractors are People Too?

The second week of May brought some exciting business headlines to Dickens, as a news story broke that Mega was in discussions to buy Acme Manufacturing, the fourth largest manufacturing company in the United States. No one at Mega had any knowledge of the story, but the newspapers were reporting that our CEO had met with the CEO at Acme and that discussions were taking place. I called Barbara Peterson, a very good friend of mine and the head of our Public Relations and Public Affairs Departments to see if she knew more to the story.

"I knew the story was coming because I have been talking to the reporter for the past three days," she said. "This is obviously a major story that can have ramifications on things like stock prices and the like, so we are trying to keep a tight lid on it."

"So the story is true then?"

"It is true in that the two CEOs met. Acme has made great strides in several foreign markets, but is basically weak in the United States. Those foreign strengths are appealing to Mega, and would allow us to compete more significantly in markets outside the states, but as of right now I don't think anything is happening. Again, the two CEOs met, but a merger is not imminent as far as I can tell. Of course, I doubt I would be the first to know. I didn't know anything about the meeting until the reporter called me."

"Have you seen our stock price today?"

"I have been monitoring it for most of the day, as well as Acme's. We are up almost $5 and Acme is up $7. Again, that is why we are trying to keep a lid on this thing."

I was about to ask another question when I noticed Laura Adamson standing outside my door. Laura was here for her 9 a.m. meeting and was a few minutes early. I politely ended my conversation with Barbara and greeted Laura at my door. Laura wore black pants with a bright red turtleneck and was carrying today's newspaper into my office.

"Have you heard the news?" she said as soon as she sat down.

"Indeed. I was just reading about it before you walked in. Exciting stuff, to say the least."

"I wonder how much of it is true. Do you think there will be a lot of consolidation when we buy Acme? I have family on the East coast, you know, and I was thinking on the way over here that it would be neat to move out to Baltimore where Acme's headquarters are."

"Don't get too far ahead of the game, Laura. Deals like this don't just happen overnight and there is no guarantee anything will even happen. Even if Mega decides today to move forward, it would probably take the better part of a year, maybe even two, before a merger was approved by the government and before any changes came down."

"I guess that's true, although it is exciting, that's for sure."

We spoke about the article for a few minutes more before getting down to business. Laura

Story 28: Contractors are People Too?

was having trouble with one of her contractors, and was hoping to get some advice from me on how best to proceed. She mentioned that she had utilized contractors in the past without much trouble, but was now having performance problems dealing with one of her experienced contractors, Jane. If the contractor was brand new, Laura likely would have just let the person go and looked for a replacement. However, Jane has been on the staff for nine months. For most of that time Jane's performance has been admirable.

However, for the past few weeks something has been wrong. Jane has not been focused and has missed a couple important deadlines. She has also been late to work, which is unlike her. Jane has been apologetic, since she knows she is not performing up to expectations, but Laura has a project to finish.

"If Jane were an employee, I would just sit down with her to see what the problem was. But I am not sure whether that would be appropriate for a contractor."

"Your instincts are correct Laura. You really need to be careful here because you don't want to treat Jane like an employee."

Lesson #28 - Manage Contractors Effectively, But Differently Than Your Employee Staff

The use of contractors is a fact of life for many organizations. Many companies today have made a conscious decision to hire only a core staff of employees. When there is more work than the core group can handle, the company does not increase the employee count. Instead they hire contract resources to fill in the gaps. When the additional work is gone, the contractors go away.

At Mega Manufacturing, we use the terms "contractor" and "consultant." Here, a consultant is someone used for a specific skill set and in most cases they are responsible for completing one or more specific deliverables. A contractor, on the other hand, is used as a supplemental resource to help absorb additional workload, and they go away when the workload is completed. However, even if you have enough employees to staff your workload, you might still utilize consultants to work in areas where you do not have the right skill level. For instance, you might contract a marketing company to help with a web advertising campaign. Or, if your company purchases a specific third-party computer package, you may need consultant help to install the software.

On the other hand, a contractor would typically come in on a time-and-material basis to work on whatever needed to be done at the time. You might have a specific area they need to work in, and so you would hire a contractor with a specific skill set. However, once they were contracted, the contractor would do whatever you required, for as long as you needed them. In other words (and no disrespect intended), we typically hire consultants for "brainpower" and we hire contractors for "horsepower." Again, this is how we use the terms at Mega. Other companies have different ways to look at the two roles.

Let's look more closely at contractors, since that is the role Jane has on Laura's team. Jane is on the team as a supplemental resource, and works under the direction of Laura. Laura originally interviewed Jane and thought she had the right skills to complete a major set of work

Story 28: Contractors are People Too?

on Laura's project. For most of the past nine months, that has been the case. However, now Jane's performance is starting to deteriorate. If Jane were an employee, I would coach Laura to work though a process of trying to determine the cause of the performance problem, further monitoring, getting very specific on deliverables and due dates, documenting the performance problems, etc.

However, Jane is not an employee of Mega Manufacturing, so this level of performance monitoring is not appropriate. In fact, it can be dangerous. There used to be an informal barrier that separated employees and contractors, but in many instances managers treated contractors the same as employees. Contractors were invited to employee meetings, they went to employee training, they attended employee parties and lunches and they were generally treated the same as employees. The staff knew that the people were contractors, but in most ways they were treated just like another employee.

Now companies need to be more diligent in keeping a wall between employees and contractors. The problem arose because contractors started to sue their former clients for employee benefits. The contractors argued, successfully, that they were, in fact, actually employees of the company where they worked on contract. For proof, they showed that they worked the same hours as the employees, worked in the same space as the employees, attended the same meetings as employees, and in all aspects of their jobs were treated as employees.

This is where Laura's situation becomes trickier. Ten years ago, my advice to Laura might have been to just take the direct route and sit down with Jane to see what was going on. However, as you can see by the last discussion, this approach could cause problems today. Dealing with performance is one aspect of a manager-subordinate relationship. If Laura is not careful, this type of discussion might be used against Mega to show that Jane should really be classified as an employee.

On the other hand, we cannot erect a solid wall between a manager and a contractor either. A manager needs to communicate with all team members, and this communication by itself cannot be viewed as being part of a manager-subordinate relationship. Likewise, Laura needs to assign work, receive status information and hold people accountable for deadlines. These are not all aspects of a simple manager-subordinate relationship either.

So, where do you draw the line? Generally speaking, Mega Manufacturing has a policy to make sure that employees treat contractors fairly and with respect, but that we do not get into any situations that would logically be considered a part of a functional manager-subordinate relationship.

For example, one of the responsibilities of a project manager is to assign work and gather feedback on status. This is a relationship between a project manager and a team member. It is not a sign that there is a functional manager-subordinate relationship. On the other hand, if we provide a performance review for a contractor, that would seem to be a situation between a functional manager and an employee subordinate.

Story 28: Contractors are People Too?

In Laura's situation, then, she needs to be clear that she is assigning work and gathering feedback on the status of that work. If the work is not completed on time, Laura has every right to question Jane as to the cause. There could be a myriad of reasons. The work could have simply been overestimated. Perhaps Jane was pulled into other work that Laura did not realize. Therefore, there should not be a problem with Laura sitting down with Jane first to determine if there is a simple cause that Laura can understand.

What happens after this meeting will help determine whether Laura will need to get Jane's contracting company involved. If Jane's performance gets back to acceptable, the situation will have worked itself out. On the other hand, if the situation is not resolved, Laura has a performance problem she needs to address. Since Jane is a contractor, Laura cannot deal with her performance problems strictly on her own.

The more appropriate course of action will be to call Jane's contracting company and get them involved. Laura can explain to the appropriate person at the contract company that she is starting to have performance problems with Jane. Laura can describe the situation and her observations. She can then request that the contracting company get involved. Jane's manager at the contracting company can then talk to her in a more formal manager-subordinate relationship. Jane's manager can then get back to Laura with the results of the meeting.

This process may seem cumbersome, but it is the nature of contractor relationships. To do much more may invite further scrutiny down the road if there is a question about whether a person like Jane was a contractor, or an employee.

In summary, I explained to Laura that she should feel free to communicate and interact with Jane (and any of her contract staff) in any way that is appropriate for workload management. However, Laura has much less flexibility when it comes to any situation that is more appropriate for a formal manager-subordinate relationship. In these types of situations, we need to get the contracting company involved so that they can take on the formal functional management relationship that is appropriate.

Story 29:

Take Time Out for Time Management Skills

The proposed merger between Mega and Acme Manufacturing seemed to be the topic of conversation at all my meetings for the first part of May. As the weeks passed, several more articles were written, one even in the *Wall Street Journal*, which seemed to indicate a merger agreement was close. On May 12th, we even got an e-mail from our CEO admitting that talks were taking place and that we should not be worried about any implications of a merger. The e-mail asked everyone to be patient and not to believe everything they read in the papers. Of course, the day after the e-mail was sent out, a transcript of it appeared in the papers.

The major concern for people internally was one of redundancy. Clearly, Acme had its own Marketing Department and its own Finance Department, for example, so people in those departments worried for their jobs if and when the merger was announced. It seemed clear that Mega would basically be buying Acme, but it was not clear whether that meant our people were safe.

In the midst of the uncertainty, I still had meetings to keep, and today was no different. My first meeting of the afternoon was with Judy Masterson. Judy was the head of the inventory management team and she had five direct reports under her.

"How are you doing today Judy?"

"I am OK. Thanks for meeting with me. It's a crazy time around here, huh?"

"Indeed it is. It's nothing that we can control, though, so it is better to just wait and see what happens and continue doing our jobs."

Judy agreed and started talking about her problem. One of her staff members, Greg Bartlett, had been struggling lately meeting his deadlines and commitments. Judy did not think this was a major problem at first, but it was becoming more and more of an issue. Judy said she thought the problems started when Greg was asked to take on extra responsibility in the inventory analysis sub-team.

"All of my team had to take on a little more responsibility when one of the previous team members resigned," Judy said. "I was not allowed to hire a replacement for his position."

"Have you spoken with Greg about his missed deadlines?"

"In fact, I have. Yesterday, we sat down to discuss his performance, and the meeting went surprising well. Greg understood that he was not consistently meeting expectations, and he seemed to think his biggest problem was related to time management."

Judy said that before the increased responsibility, Greg had one primary area of focus. Now he has two diverse sets of responsibilities and he finds that he is not able to give either one the focus it needs. Worse, the new responsibilities also include daily support of the manufacturing financial managers. These people call at all times of the day asking questions and wanting information, and it is really causing havoc with Greg's ability to plan his time well.

Story 29: Take Time Out for Time Management Skills

Greg was looking for some tips from Judy on how to manage his time better. Unfortunately, Judy didn't feel comfortable with her time management skills either - hence her call to me for further coaching. This is the kind of opportunity I like. I can help both the manager and the team member with one set of coaching tips.

Lesson #29 - Increase Your Effectiveness with Strong Time Management Skills

Time management allows you to have a higher degree of control over what you do in a day, in a week and in a month. You may not have *total* control, but you have a much *greater* degree of control. Time management skills help you control your day instead of allowing the events of the day to control you. Time management skills can't give you more hours in a day, but they can help you spend the hours you have on the things that are most important to you.

Time management skills are easier for some people than for others. For instance, all time management advice is going to include some aspect of writing down what you want to accomplish. For many people this is easy and natural. Other people have difficulty creating lists and following through on them. It is a left-brain/right-brain issue and has to do with whether your brain prefers logic and structure (left brain), or whether your preference is on the creative and unstructured side (right brain). In fact, it sometimes seems that coaching people in time management is an exercise in futility. People that take the structured techniques to heart are probably already more structured in their jobs and in their lives. On the other hand, the people that really need the skills generally rebel against the structure that it takes to be better at time management to begin with.

But, you can never pre-judge people. When people see they have room for improvement in a certain area, they are more likely to be open to new ideas. I have a two-for-one opportunity at hand right now, since both Greg and Judy seem open to learning some new techniques. If you feel like you are not very good at time management, you need to be doing some of these things to take control. Time management requires discipline. If you are not prepared to be disciplined, then you are not going to be a very good manager of your own time.

Here is my top 10 list of time management techniques. Notice I did not call them "best practices." However, they do work for me and others who tend to be good time managers. There are many other techniques as well, but this will be a great place for Judy and Greg to start. If they can even adopt half of these tips, they can become much better at managing their own time.

1. **Create a list of things to do each morning.** Start with this basic activity. At the beginning of each day (or the end of the prior day) make a list of what you want to accomplish for the day (or next day). The list can include business and personal items. This can be a paper list or it could be on your workstation, PDA, etc. Keep referring to the list off and on during the day to remind you what is there. For example, if you have 10 minutes before a meeting, glance at your list. There might be an e-mail you wanted to send that would only take a few minutes. When you complete each item, check it off. Most "left-brainers" like nothing better than to check-off items from their "things-to-do" list.

Story 29: Take Time Out for Time Management Skills

2. **Write down all follow-up items on your list.** You start your day off with a list of things you want to complete. However, new things will come up during the day. How do you keep track of them? You got it – place them on your daily list. If your list is full and the activity can be completed tomorrow (or the next day) place it on your list for a day or two out.

   Have you ever wondered why many people tell you they will do something and then 50% (or more) of the time they don't follow through? It is because they don't write it down. Judy and Greg can use this technique for themselves and others. For instance, if Judy talks to a team member about some work the team member needs to complete, she should not have to trust the team member's memory. Ask the team member to write it down.

3. **Carry forward unfinished work and follow-up.** Now that you have a list of work for the day, and you have added new items for follow-up during the day, what do you do with the things that you have not completed at the end of the day? Just blow them off? No, you carry them forward and add them on to your list for tomorrow. Don't be a procrastinator. You don't want to be carrying an expanding list of activities from day to day. If the activity is important, get it done. If it is not important, follow-up with the person who is expecting you to do something and tell them you are not going to do the work.

4. **Keep track of due dates.** Use your list to keep track of due dates. This includes commitments from work colleagues and friends. My experience is that people miss their due dates more often than they hit them. Part of the problem is that people don't write things down. However, even when they write something down, they do not understand the due date. Then, even if they do the follow-up, they are still missing expectations in terms of when the activity was due. If you are not clear, ask when an activity needs to be completed, write it down, and then use time management skills to make sure the work is done on time. If you cannot meet the commitment, communicate proactively ahead of time.

5. **Create a list of priorities for this month and next.** I know many people make lists for today. However, how many make high-level lists of the things they need to do this month and next? Unless you have a transactional job where your timeframes are always short-term, you need to stop at the beginning of each month and determine what you want to accomplish. These are obviously at a high level, but, again, they keep you focused on what you want to accomplish. As the month progresses, start adding items to your list for next month. Judy should definitely keep her one-month priorities in mind throughout the month. This technique is probably less important to Greg, since much of his work is the same from month-to-month, and his focus is probably more week-to-week and day-to-day.

6. **Keep track of longer-term reminders.** Your "things-to-do" list is not going to help you for follow-up on items far into the future. For instance, you may tell a colleague that you

Story 29: Take Time Out for Time Management Skills

will follow-up with her to check progress in two months. You need to have a way to keep track of this follow-up and to remind you two months in the future. Many people use an online calendar to keep track of reminders. Place a reminder out for the date you want to follow-up. In fact, you can place multiple reminders over multiple days, so that if you miss one, you will catch the reminder the next day.

7. **Keep a clean desk.** Few good time management people work in a pigsty. In fact, people who have cluttered offices or cubicles tend to not be very good time organizers either. I don't think you can be a good time manager when you spend a lot of time looking for stuff in a cluttered work environment.

8. **Keep all of your current work in one area.** Over time, you may work on many separate activities and initiatives. However, keep your things organized. I always keep my current work papers in one area where I can get at them easily. When I am done with a project or an initiative, I move the folder elsewhere (see tip 9).

9. **Purge files and documents you no longer need.** Here is one that I mentioned to Judy that startled her – purge historical papers from long-completed work assignments. One person at Mega Manufacturing keeps adding new work folders to the front of one desk drawer. When the drawer gets full, he throws out folders from the back end. In other words, this person never keeps more historical files than can fit in one desk drawer. I contrasted that to Judy's system of keeping endless years of paperwork that no one cares about any more and no one will ever care about again. Of course, I am not talking about user's manuals or reference material that you need. I'm talking about the work files you accumulate every day. And yes, once a year, you might wish you could go back and find something that you threw out. However, usually you have the original documents backed up online anyway.

10. **Backup online files and then purge.** I have a similar philosophy about online documents. I would guess that 95% of what you have online in your work files probably has a shelf life of three months or less. So, periodically back up your files to CD and then go through and quickly delete all the older files you don't need anymore.

You cannot be a good time manager if you don't follow a fair amount of personal structure and discipline. Of course, you need to be flexible to deal with the unknown. You can't be a slave to your list. However, as you deal with the unknown as it pops up, you will at least have the perspective of knowing the things that are not getting done.

In my opinion, personal time management boils down to two things. First, keeping track of what you need to do and then doing it. Second, reducing the clutter. Keep your work environment clean and organized. There are many other techniques for this, including delegating and saying "no" to distractions. However, the 10 items described above provide the fundamentals to control your day and to make sure you are focused on the activities you need to accomplish. I hope Judy can take some of these techniques to heart. If so, she can then be a good role model to help Greg similarly improve his own time management skills.

Story 30:

Can't We All Just Get Along?

My son Tim and I hit the links again over the weekend, playing 18 holes on Saturday at a course about five miles from our house. I liked this course because it was fairly straight, easy to walk and did not have a lot of obstacles. As my son grew older, I would take him to more challenging golf courses, but for now I did not wish to discourage him by taking him to an extremely difficult course. He shot a 95 for 18 holes, which was pretty good for a 10-year old I thought. He would have scored much better than that had he not posted a 10 on the final hole. He was pretty tired by then and ended up hitting two balls into the water hazard.

Monday morning, I was recounting the story of the golf outing to Doug McDonald prior to our 10 a.m. meeting. Doug's son Benjamin was also a golfer, although he was 14 and was not good enough to break 100 most days.

"Sounds like your son might be pretty good when he is older," Doug said. "My boy enjoys playing, but he is not real competitive and he doesn't take the game seriously. I tried encouraging him like you do your son, but he is just not into it. He never was really."

"Tim loves playing right now, and would go every day if we let him. But he is young, and his interests may change as he gets older. For now, we are content to just keep encouraging him. He plays real well for his age, though, I must admit. He's got a sweet swing!"

"That's great. I wish my parents would have encouraged me more when I was a young kid. Maybe I would be on the professional tour right now instead of dealing with my dysfunctional project team."

With Doug providing an easy transition, I asked him to talk in greater detail about his team and the problem they were having. Doug was the manager of a project team of eight people designing and building a new manufacturing sub-process. The project was not going well, and there was a history of poor communication, confusion and missed deadlines.

"I'm just not real sure what to do," Doug said. "I am familiar with the standard project management processes of managing scope, risk, issues, quality, etc. But I am not as comfortable dealing with the people management side."

Doug asked me to talk to the rest of his team members to get a sense of the problems relating to team morale and cohesion.

"I'm afraid there are personality conflicts on the team that are keeping team members from working effectively with each other," he said

"Why don't I schedule some time – maybe 30 minutes or so – with each team member to get their sense as to what is going on?" I suggested.

"That sounds great."

Story 30: Can't We All Just Get Along?

When I met up with Doug again at the end of the week, I told him I had some interesting results in terms of team dynamics.

Lesson #30 – Proactively Resolve the Personality Problems of a Dysfunctional Team

Team effectiveness and cohesion is an area that can sometimes sink a project. Many people have heard of high-performing teams and some people have been fortunate enough to have worked on one. There are also some situations where the opposite occurs. You have a group of people who are each good performers in their own right, but when they get together on a team, the whole is not as effective and productive as the sum of its parts. There are a lot of factors that can cause this. There could be personality conflicts, a lack of project manager leadership or poor work processes.

I usually start by making sure the project team has effective work processes in place, since it is difficult to be a high-performing team on a project with poor work processes. The following aspects of project management have a direct bearing on team effectiveness.

- **Communicate clear objectives and deliverables.** It is frustrating to work on a team that does not have a clear idea of what it is doing and why. So, the place to start is to make sure that team members understand the purpose of the project, the benefits to the company and the work that is being produced. All this information should have been agreed to in advance with the Project Sponsor and documented in a Project Definition (also called a Project Charter). It is important that the information be shared with the entire team to give them a common sense of purpose.

- **Set clear work expectations.** The project should also start with a clear workplan (or schedule) that describes how the work will be performed. A small project of one or two people may not need a formal workplan, but Doug's project has eight people and he must make sure that they keep busy working on the right activities in the right order. Doug needs to be clear on the expectations of the work assignments, including when the work is due and how the team members will validate the work is complete and correct. If he does not set clear work expectations, people will be unfocused and that will lead to confusion and anxiety.

- **Communicate effectively.** Perhaps the biggest problem associated with teams that do not perform well is a general lack of communication. This includes poor communication from the project manager to the team members as well as from the team members to the project manager. As morale drops, communication tends to suffer even more.

- **Other aspects.** Make sure you have other good processes in place as well. This includes scope management, risk management, quality management, etc. Again, teams are not going to be highly effective if there is scope creep or if you are producing poor quality products. As the project manager, Doug needs to validate that there are effective project management processes in place because the lack of processes will hurt the team's effort to be the best it can be.

Story 30: Can't We All Just Get Along?

After you make sure you have good work processes in place, you should deal with the people side of the equation. This requires that you try to understand the particular problems on your particular team.

There are a number of approaches you can take. One approach that I already took was to talk to each team member for a few minutes. This initial discussion allowed me to determine that there were not major personality problems on the team. If there were, the team would probably have a limited ability for self-correction, since the same personality conflicts would keep the team members from actively engaging in a solution.

In the case of Doug's team, a group exercise might help. The value of this exercise is that it allows the team to critique itself in a safe environment and come up with some potential solutions. One of the big problems with dysfunctional teams is that much of the trouble lies just under the surface. This type of group exercise helps bring those trouble areas to the surface where they can be discussed and addressed.

I offered to moderate the group exercise as an independent facilitator. Having an independent facilitator is not mandatory, but it may get people to open up more. If the manager takes a lead role, the discussion might be more inhibited, especially if the team views the project manager as a part of the problem.

The group exercise has the following flow. These particular steps can be modified to meet the needs of your team.

1. Participants take sticky note cards and write down the top five problem areas that they think make the team less than fully effective. This is somewhat of a brainstorming effort, so there are no right or wrong answers. Everyone is presenting ideas from their perspective. You want team members to be open and honest. They should feel safe that any comments made will stay inside the room.
2. The facilitator gathers the notes and posts them on the wall. Problem areas that are related should be grouped together. You should end up with some general buckets like lack of leadership, poor planning, personality conflicts, etc.
3. Next, rank the general problem areas in terms of importance. Since the original list was built through a brainstorming process, now is the time to try to identify those areas that are most important. You will also find that some problems are really symptoms, and they will go away if more fundamental problems are addressed. One way to prioritize is to give everyone five sticky dots that they can place by the problem groups they think are the most important. Then count the total dots by each problem to see its relative ranking compared with the other problem areas.
4. Look at each problem area individually, starting with the most important. The facilitator asks each person to write down a few ways that the problem could be remedied. All of these potential solutions should be constructive and as practical as possible. When

Story 30: Can't We All Just Get Along?

possible, they should also be detailed. These solutions are again posted on the wall by the facilitator.

5. The group should discuss the pros and cons of each solution so that everyone understands what is involved. Many solutions may be similar and can be grouped together. Sometimes the solution requires people to think and act differently. Other times, a solution may require getting others involved outside of the immediate team.

6. After everyone understands the various solutions, the team again votes on which recommendation(s) make the most sense to implement.

7. After the recommendations are voted on and accepted, the team should be very specific in terms of the action plan required to solve the problem. There should be a set of activities, people assigned and end dates. It might make sense to create a section on the project workplan to account for this time, if necessary. Depending on the time involved you can also create the action plan after the meeting.

8. The team should continue with this process until all important problem areas are discussed and solutions are put into place. Normally, the project manager is responsible for assigning and following up on the work assignments, unless some other process or person is made accountable (the project manager does not do all of the work, but follows-up to make sure the assignments are completed). Again, the team may feel that the project manager needs to be more hands-off for this effort.

9. The team should set up one or more subsequent meetings to evaluate whether the work is being completed, and whether the team is performing more effectively.

When you have a team that is not as effective as it needs to be, this type of approach can be used to address the problems and resolve them. You will also find that once you start to address the problems in a safe and respectful manner, the team will feel more and more comfortable addressing the fundamental problems they see. To a certain degree, the exercise is therapeutic. It helps because it allows people to talk about what is on their minds.

Of course, there are other techniques and approaches that can be utilized as well. You can sponsor pure team-building events such as after work dinners, group lunches, outdoor team challenges, etc. You can get the team together for interesting tests and assessments, such as Myers-Briggs. These sessions help in team building by making people aware of why they behave as they do and why others behave as they do. Having this information allows team members to better interact with each other based on the knowledge of how differently everyone deals with information and with people.

When the first session is over, you should have come a long way toward getting people to work more effectively with each other, which will lead to higher overall team performance. However, don't leave it to chance. Make sure the team follows up on any action items and executes any action plans. The manager should also schedule follow-up meetings to make sure the team is moving toward the performance level it is capable of achieving. All of these meetings take time, but if your team is struggling because of interpersonal problems, the time invested should be more than made up by the increase in overall productivity.

Story 31:

In Praise of Technical Nerds

June 2nd brought the news everyone had been anticipating for the better part of a month. An e-mail was sent out to all employees from the PR Department that contained the press release announcing the proposed merger between Mega Manufacturing and Acme Manufacturing of Baltimore, Maryland. Several of the senior vice presidents attended a meeting with the CEO and CFO in the morning, and the press release was sent out shortly after the meeting ended. The name of the proposed new company would be M-A Manufacturing, a combination of Mega and Acme. The merger still needed the approval of the board of directors of each company, as well as from a federal oversight committee. Neither of these "hurdles" was seen as a major obstacle, as both boards had approved the deal long ago, and the government was not expected to interfere.

Executive managers at each company had spent a great deal of time discussing the financial impact of the deal, as well as the strategies for how best to merge the two companies. With all this thought, though, I was ultimately surprised by the lack of communication shared with employees. There was general confusion as to what the merger would mean to the common worker, and what impact it would have on their jobs. Rumors started to run rampant as people speculated on everything from where the new company would be headquartered to what the company's new strategy would be.

One of the unexpected results of the merger for me was a spike in the number of people seeking time on my calendar. It seemed clear to me that people wanted to do everything they could to show their superiors how valuable they were to the company, and how willing they were to improve their individual groups. Whatever was to happen next, I knew it would take time and I was not one to panic.

When I looked at my schedule for the day, I was glad to see Meg Roberson at the top of the list. Meg was a new manager in the IT Division having recently been promoted from the ranks of a senior systems analyst. Meg had 12 years of experience in positions of increasing responsibility, and came up "through the trenches" in the IT organization.

I was happy to be helping an IT person first this day because, even though I did not know Meg too well, I knew she would be calm and rationale. Like me, I was sure she would still be processing the news of the merger and would not come in frantic and emotional.

She showed up at my door in a navy blue business suit and an ambivalent look on her face.

"I take it you have seen the e-mail, Meg? Looks like we are officially merging with Acme."

"I saw the e-mail, Tom, but I am not too concerned about it. I am sure there will be implications for our division, but we probably won't find out about them for several months. In the meantime, there is work to be done."

Just as I suspected, she was still processing the information and was reacting in a very logical way.

Story 31: In Praise of Technical Nerds

"Well then, what can I do to help you today?"

Meg said she was having difficulty transitioning from being a staff member to staff manager. Many of the people she used to work with now report to her. This was awkward at first, but the group has seemed to accept her in her new role.

"You are not the first person to have difficulty adjusting to your new role as manager, Meg. I know it can sometimes feel weird to be someone's colleague one day, and boss the next."

"I don't mind so much being the boss. I guess I just really want to be seen as an effective leader of our group."

Meg said that in her 12 years of work experience, she has had only four managers, and she only considered one of those "exceptional." Her other three managers were like her – onetime technicians who moved up through the ranks. She said she was determined to be viewed as an exceptional manager.

Meg wanted to know how best to manage technical staff. She had seen many examples of how not to manage these people, but she wanted some insight into what makes a manager exceptional.

Lesson #31 - Understand Your Technical Staff and Manage Them Accordingly

I give Meg a lot of credit. She is fairly new to the manager ranks and already she realizes her current limitations. She also "knows what she doesn't know." In other words, she realizes she does not yet have the answers for how to effectively manage technical staff. Yet she knows it is important. She knows from her own experience that many Information Technology (IT) managers don't rise to the level of exceptional.

Perhaps that is not surprising. In many instances, management promotions are not based on the best possible candidate. They are based on the best person available at the time. Promotions also provide people an opportunity to grow and it is hard to tell if an individual will thrive in the management ranks or if they will end up just filling a position. Meg sounds like she wants to be a person that thrives – not one that is just filling a box in the management hierarchy.

So what about her question? Meg wants to get some insight into what it takes to manage her IT staff. This is a great question to ask. In this particular case, Meg is asking about her IT technical staff, but I think the lesson generally applies to many other "technical" disciplines as well, including engineering and even finance.

One important thing to remember first is that it is impossible to categorize everyone within a profession. We can make some general assumptions about IT people, but this does not mean that the assumptions apply to everyone. As a manager, you must ultimately have multiple techniques that you can apply to different people in different circumstances. One technique will not work for all people at all times.

That being said, let's make some generalizations about managing technical staff.

Story 31: In Praise of Technical Nerds

- **They tend to be introverts**. Generally speaking, the definition of an introvert is one who is primarily more comfortable with an inward focus in life while an extrovert is generally more comfortable with an outward focus. For example, when introverts receive a lot of new information, they tend to want to think for a while before speaking or drawing conclusions. Extroverts, on the other hand, are more comfortable expressing ideas to others. If they jump to the wrong conclusions, they just change their minds. Basically extroverts are comfortable thinking out loud. Introverts would rather think through the "rough drafts" in their minds and then talk when they think they have a coherent and logical position.

- **They tend to think more logically than emotionally**. This tendency should be obvious. Technical staffers typically are not motivated by a lot of "rah-rah" speeches. In fact, they tend to be cynical of this type of motivation. They will usually listen politely (perhaps even snickering to themselves), but the effects are short-term. On the other hand, they can be persuaded and motivated by a logical argument. If the logical argument can be combined with some motivational techniques, you might have a chance to actually get them excited.

- **They tend to be problem solvers**. This is a great strength of technical staff as well as one of their weaknesses. Most technical people love nothing better than to be confronted with a problem. They get excited and they immediately start to apply their problem-solving skills. The weakness comes in because there is a tendency to jump on a problem without fully understanding it first. This often can lead to being less than optimal in the use of resources. In many cases, the technical person will attack a problem immediately, and then have to regroup when they realize they didn't really have a full understanding of the problem to begin with.

- **They tend to be technically creative**. This may seem like a contradiction. Your first thought might be that the sales and marketing staffs are the creative people. In fact they are – in the sales and marketing areas. They will also be the first to tell you so – because they are extroverts. However, the technical discipline requires a fair degree of creativity as well. This is especially true in the IT world. In many cases, there is not one best solution to a business problem. In the development (programming) field, for instance, analysts need creativity when they are defining a solution with the business clients. Designers need to be creative applying technology in the best manner. Programmers need to be creative as well in trying to apply the best techniques to build the most elegant solution.

Understanding these general characteristics is the place to start if you are a manager of technical staff. Once you begin to understand how people work and how they are motivated, you can start to think of the best way to manage them. In my discussion with Meg, I pointed out a number of areas for her to think about. Not all of these ideas will be applicable to her staff, and even if they were, she might not be able to move on all fronts at the same time.

Story 31: In Praise of Technical Nerds

First, I asked Meg to make sure she created an environment conducive to performing well. For her IT staff, this includes making sure they have the tools to do their job, and removing any organizational roadblocks. For example, the staff should have good equipment. It does not necessarily need to be state of the art, but it should be of acceptable quality. Because they are in the IT field, IT people get frustrated when they don't have the right hardware to do their jobs effectively. Creating the right environment also means removing organizational roadblocks and shielding the team from organizational politics. IT people will tend to get cynical fast if they feel like politics is starting to become involved in their work or in decisions that affect them.

She should also make sure her people have the skills needed to do their jobs, but that they also receive opportunities to grow into new technical areas. IT people love to learn new things. Many people like to learn about new technology just for the sake of knowing it. Other people feel like they must get hands-on experience in new technology. Meg should look for options to keep the staff learning. This does not have to be third-party training classes. It can include computer-based training, seminars, webinars, books, magazines, etc.

In most instances, people don't have the option of getting hands-on experience in new technology – simply because their company does not have it, or because the person is valuable where they are. One potential option in many teams is to rotate assignments. People working in the support/maintenance area can get a chance to rotate responsibilities, allowing them to learn new things. Project team members may be able to cross-train in different areas to allow them to learn new skills as well.

Meg should strive to be a proactive communicator. Remember, many IT people are introverts who like to process information internally. They may or may not come up to you and ask you what is going on all of the time. Nevertheless, technical people spend a lot of time in internal reflection, so make sure they have enough information to keep their mental models in tune. Meg should make sure that she communicates as much as she can about what is going on in the company, her organization and her group. At a lower level, she needs to make sure that people understand what they are doing and why. Her staff needs to know how the work they are doing provides value to the company. If she has staff working on projects, she needs to make sure that the project managers are communicating the project status, what they are doing and why, and how each person is contributing to the final solution.

Meg also needs to make sure that the team continues to think of itself as a cohesive group. Much of what I said before about IT people being introverts might lead you to think they prefer to work alone. In some cases that is actually true, but usually that is not the case. IT staff may prefer to work independently, but they also like being a part of the team. Meg should nurture this need as well. For instance, she should have regular team meetings. If her team is not used to these meetings, they may first view them as a waste of time. But soon the team will enjoy them for the chance to get back together with the rest of the group. She should also make sure they have opportunities to do fun stuff as a group – even if it is just going to lunch together once in a while.

Story 31: In Praise of Technical Nerds

You might note that many of these management techniques are not unique to technical staff in general or IT staff in particular. It is true that many of the techniques can be used in other areas as well. However, they are particularly applicable to the IT staff. After sharing many ideas with Meg, I tried to summarize some of the general points to consider as she manages her staff.

- Try to establish an environment where people feel they have what they need to do their jobs. This includes having appropriate hardware, software, policies, procedures, etc.

- Technical people like to understand the work processes in the group, and then they like to be creative in working within that structure. So, set the high-level rules, but don't micromanage the details.

- Give people as much information as they need to do their jobs. Technical staff tends to reflect on this information. Ask for their ideas and opinions, but give them time and ample opportunities. Don't expect them to react immediately.

- Shield the team from office politics and all of the distractions that can abound in a large company. Tell people what they need to know (see prior point), but don't get them bogged down in the organization muck.

- Give people continuous opportunities to learn. This includes encouraging people to invest the time to learn, but also helping with some opportunities. There are many creative ways to learn new things. Once someone has mastered a certain skill or aspect of their job and they start to become bored, look for ways they can cross-train and learn new areas of the group.

- Be there when needed and respond to problems and concerns. Not all problems can be fixed, but many times the simple act of listening and trying is enough. People will give you credit for trying, even if the ultimate resolution to a problem is not available.

Meg left our meeting with enough ideas to keep her busy for a while. Given her own motivation, I feel good that she will grow to be the kind of manager her team members will consider to be exceptional.

Story 32:

Jorge is Losing Recognition to the Non-Participants

By the third week of June, I was beginning to notice an interesting divide shaping up at Mega Manufacturing among the managers I was coaching. About 80 percent of managers were excited about the merger with Acme Manufacturing, and saw it as a new opportunity for them and a chance to continue growing within the company. For this group, it was an exciting time and they wanted nothing more than to carve out their place in the new company. The other 20 percent were suffering from morale problems and were not excited about the merger. This group seemed paranoid that the future would bring termination for them and people in their group. They worried openly about their jobs and their roles and what responsibilities they would be asked to take on.

Jorge Herndon was a project manager in the "80 percent" group. He had recently been promoted from a position as lead financial analyst, and was excited about the possibilities a new company would bring him. In fact, the purpose for my meeting with Jorge was to discuss how he could better take credit for an impressive success he had on his first assignment as a manager.

As we talked in my office, Jorge spoke about his project. It was an assignment that had almost been abandoned prior to Jorge's promotion. The project team was constantly setting dates for reaching milestones, and then consistently missing the dates, perhaps because of the inexperience and the unrealistic dates set by the prior project manager. Jorge said that he put in a lot of time and sweat dealing with the client managers and the project team. Just as the project was on the verge of being canceled, the team performance started to turn around.

With the project on firm ground, and with Jorge's leadership, the company was actually beginning to get valuable business benefits from the work. By everyone's standards, this project was now a success. With success, however, came "hangers-on," which is why Jorge wanted to speak with me.

"I am really not sure what to do, Tom. Ever since the project turned around and became successful, people are coming out of the woodwork to take credit for it. I have never seen anything like this before. In fact, just yesterday I heard the prior project manager bragging to my sponsor that he had laid the groundwork for success prior to my coming on board. He said I was just growing what he had already planted!"

"Is there any truth to that?"

"Absolutely not. In fact, it took me a good two weeks just to undo what he had done so poorly. Part of me wants to take the high ground, but at the same time it bothers me. People are taking all sorts of credit and recognition for only marginal contributions."

Jorge went on to say that there was plenty of praise and credit to go around, and he would be the first to thank a long list of people who were involved. He was worried, though, that all the effort he and a few others put in could end up meaning nothing.

"How can I make sure that the right people get recognized for the hard work and sleepless nights they put in to make this project successful?" he asked.

Story 32: Jorge is Losing Recognition to the Non-Participants

Lesson #32 – Take Credit for Your Successes

Jorge has a concern that is common for managers and many staff members. The question is how to make sure that your contributions to the organization are recognized. Some people are very good at making sure they pat themselves on the back whenever they make any small accomplishment. Usually, these people are seen as egotistical and self-important. In general, most people are not as comfortable pointing out their own accomplishments. We love it when our manager congratulates us on a job well done. It really feels good if we are recognized in front of others. However, most people are opposed to obvious self-congratulating and self-promoting.

Some people would look at this situation and say that Jorge should not be worried about who gets credit for the project turnaround and success. After all, the company received value from an investment that was previously at-risk. All employees are trying to add value, right? While it is true the company came out a winner, is it also important for the people who contributed to the success to come out as winners as well?

Some people might say it doesn't matter whether Jorge gets formally recognized or not. Jorge knows the contributions he made on the project and as long as he knows, that is the most important thing. After all, the valuable experience Jorge gained will stay with him forever. He has learned how to take a project from the brink of cancellation and turn it around; he has learned how to deal with senior client management; and he has learned how to be a better project manager in general.

Helping the company be successful is a good thing. The fact that Jorge knows he contributed to this success is also great. Jorge should also appreciate the new experience and skills he has added to his resume and repertoire. But is that enough? I happen to think it is important to be recognized for your significant contributions. If nothing else, there is just a matter of fairness. It is only fair to recognize people who do good things, especially if you can identify the contribution. Normally you would expect your manager and sponsor to provide this recognition. However, all managers have strengths and weaknesses, and some managers don't do a very good job of recognizing the contributions of their people.

So, I think Jorge is right to be concerned about gaining some of the recognition and credit. But how can he gain the proper level of recognition for turning this project around without appearing self-important and turning people off? There is not necessarily just one answer. As with all situations dealing with people, it depends somewhat on the people and circumstances involved. Part of the challenge is to evaluate the people and circumstances that you find yourself in to see how best to proceed. Some of the things that work for Jorge might not work in another situation.

If you find yourself in this situation, first and perhaps most important, you have to start with an honest evaluation of your role and your contributions on the project. This is the part where people usually struggle. It's not uncommon for people to confuse hard work for

Story 32: Jorge is Losing Recognition to the Non-Participants

true accomplishments. People also have a tendency to overstate their contributions. In other words, it is common for people to think they deserve special recognition, when actually their contribution was not significant.

Everyone deserves to get credit where credit is earned. But do not take credit for other people's work and do not take credit for things other people perceive as failures. If you feel like you deserved special recognition, you must ask yourself what you specifically contributed to the effort that was over and above expectations.

In this specific case, Jorge was the project manager, so he had opportunities to influence the work more than most others. However, even he should start out by evaluating exactly what he did to turn the project around. There is more to this than just working long and hard. For instance, did Jorge provide more resources at critical times to hit the end-dates? Did he push the clients to take more active ownership? Did he have the entire project re-estimated so there was a clearer idea of effort and cost? Did he keep team morale high when the project was at its lowest? These are the types of questions that Jorge should ask himself in an honest self-evaluation. If possible, Jorge should seek feedback from others on his role as well.

While the project is still progressing, Jorge has an opportunity to set the record straight in a way that is perceived as factual and without appearing to be self-promoting. Here are a number of options:

- Once you have identified your major accomplishments, communication is a key ingredient to utilize in your favor. Fortunately, as the project manager, Jorge would be in a good position to exercise some control over the communication flow from the project. Jorge can leverage this to maximize his exposure. One idea is to communicate more often with his managers and stakeholders. Instead of the minimum monthly status report, for instance, Jorge could start communicating weekly. These status updates are a time to showcase the progress being made and the specific actions that Jorge is taking to keep the project on-track. Again, this is not a reason to take credit for the work of others, but a proactive status update can be used to point out the project accomplishments and Jorge's role in making them happen.

- The second area of communication is to make sure to bring the appropriate stakeholders into the decision-making process when possible. If Jorge keeps management and customer stakeholders in the loop on the major decisions, they will also remain engaged in terms of Jorge's role on the project.

- Jorge should also look for ways to stress his role on the project from a historical perspective. For instance, if he discusses team morale, he can point out how bad morale was earlier, and how much it has improved based on his specific actions. On the surface, this communication is meant to inform on current status. But under the surface he is trying to show the value he is providing today. Of course, from a political perspective he must be subtle. If the communication appears to be a forum for Jorge to pat himself on the back, it may backfire and turn people off.

Story 32: Jorge is Losing Recognition to the Non-Participants

- Jorge should also look for opportunities for personal dialog along these same lines with his manager and the sponsor. If he can't get regular meetings with them, he should try to catch them informally. Of course, he still needs to be subtle.

I have to be careful with my coaching so that Jorge does not take this too far. My advice is to be proactive in the communication of project status and accomplishments, which will also point out Jorge's role in the project. I am not coaching him to use communication for his own political purpose or for self-promotion. Jorge must also point out the accomplishments of all the other team members as well. However, being a proactive communicator will point out who is accomplishing what.

This proactive communication should also reduce the attempts by others to take credit for marginal contributions. If the managers and clients think they understand what is going on from Jorge's communication, they will question others who try to associate themselves with success if it is not deserved.

There is an old joke about the various stages of a project. One of the last stages is "praise and rewards to the non-participants." Sometimes it can actually happen that way. If you see that happening to you and your project, be proactive. Get your story out there, and remember to bring your team along with you. The best managers make sure that their teams get all the credit, while at the same time making sure people understand that none of it would have happened without their active involvement.

Story 33:

Fear and Loathing in the Purchasing Department

One of the first meetings I attended that seemed to be a direct result of the merger was with Abbey Smith, a department manager in the Purchasing Department who was trying to make some major changes. Her department underwent a series of changes in the 1980s to make several processes much more automated, but those changes were now 15 years old and more automated processes have been introduced into the marketplace. In talking with her prior to our meeting, she mentioned that her vendors and suppliers were asking for many of the changes. These companies use several new automated processes, but they cannot use them when working with Mega because our systems are so outdated.

When I showed up at her office Wednesday morning, she was wrapping up a team meeting in her office and several of her team members were standing around quietly talking. The mood of the room seemed somber and there was a tension in the air that was palpable.

"Let's get back to work people," Abbey shouted from behind her desk with a smile, waving her hands to "swoosh" people away. "My next meeting is here and I don't want to keep him waiting."

As the people filed past me, I could tell something major was happening.

"Seems like a somber group of people Abbey," I said after I had closed her door.

"Somber is a good word Tom. That's the reason I asked you for a meeting."

Abbey explained that several people on her team were not excited about the changes she was trying to implement.

"What exactly are the changes?" I asked.

She explained that the initiative would include the implementation of a new Purchasing software package that will result in much more automation of the Mega workflow. This new software should allow the Purchasing Department to provide better service while also allowing the size of her group to be reduced.

"The problem with the project is not the technology – it has been around for a number of years," she said. "The problem is the people on my staff. I thought that everyone would welcome automation, since it would make their jobs much easier. But people here are complaining and some are frankly worried about their jobs."

"From what you said earlier, it sounds like those fears are legitimate, Abbey. Did you really expect people to rally behind a project that would result in the loss of their jobs?"

"I guess I had not thought it all the way through. The bottom line, though, is that we are more than a decade behind in this department, and with the changes we are all about to undergo as a result of this merger, I cannot afford that kind of scrutiny. I want my department to be seen as innovative and up with the times. The project needs to go on, but I don't know how to get the team on board."

Story 33: Fear and Loathing in the Purchasing Department

Lesson #33 – Use a Multi-Faceted Approach to Implement Culture Change

Businesses run on processes. Many of these processes are automated, many are manual and many are a combination of the two. Managers must recognize that when they make changes that effect how people do their jobs, these changes have very large and very real repercussions.

The term "culture" refers to "how we do things around here." In other words, the processes a company uses, how managers and staff interact, the type of behavior allowed and how people treat each other all fall under a company culture. When you try to change how a person does his or her job, or when you change how people interact with each other, you are changing the culture. Hence these types of initiatives are known as "culture change initiatives."

One of the biggest problems with these types of culture change projects is not the process change itself. The biggest problem has to do with how people react to the changes. The people side of the equation is usually a lot trickier to deal with than the process side. Processes can be changed and processes can be automated. However, the needs of the people that are impacted by the changes are harder to anticipate and manage. When these types of projects have problems, it is usually on the people side where things go wrong – not the process or technology side.

The basic problem is that most people are creatures of habit. They understand their current role in a process and they become comfortable with it. In fact, their job may be boring and they may not even like it. However, people become comfortable. It doesn't take very much energy to do their jobs and it does not typically take much independent thinking.

Now, along comes change. Most people are naturally resistant to change. In some cases, they may recognize that change is for the better, but they are still resistant. It takes work to change. Change requires people to leave their comfort area and start to think again. Change requires people to learn new things. Change means that people may not be as comfortable as they were. Change is emotional. All of this makes it hard to change an organization and its processes.

The management team must recognize this when it tries to change the culture. Changing culture requires you to consider a more sophisticated and multi-faceted approach to ensure you will be successful. This more well-rounded approach needs to address not just organizational processes, but also the impact on people as well. This type of approach is called "organizational change management."

Driving culture change requires a lot more than simply changing processes or teaching new skills, although both of these certainly play a part. The manager (or project manager of the actual project) must evaluate various aspects of the organization that drive behaviors. Processes that drive good project management behaviors need to be reinforced. Processes that are barriers to good project management behaviors need to be changed or eliminated. Resistance to the change must be accounted for and expected. It must also be discouraged.

Story 33: Fear and Loathing in the Purchasing Department

Abbey certainly is sponsoring a project that will result in changes to the work processes. In fact, the work processes will probably be changed substantially. Therefore, she needs to think about this project much more broadly than just in terms of process improvement. She may be able to bring in new software and develop new processes for doing the work of the department, but that is only part of the battle she will need to fight to be successful.

As Abbey and I talked further, I gave her some ideas to consider on how to make the culture change successful in her department. These ideas included:

- **Build awareness.** Abbey should make sure she communicates to the group up-front about her vision and why she is moving in this direction. To Abbey, this seems obvious – better customer service, and more efficiency. However, people in her group have varying degrees of business acumen and many people do not have that obvious vision. Many people in the group don't think anything is wrong with the current processes and so they have no sense for how things can be improved.

- **Address concerns.** Many people in the Purchasing Department are concerned about these upcoming changes. The changes will require people to learn new skills and perhaps end up working in different ways. One of the challenges of implementing scope change requests is getting people to understand how a change will positively affect the group. Each person wrestles with whether or not the change is in his or her own best interest. If some people feel like the change is not in their best interest they will resist – either consciously or subconsciously.

- **Address the unspoken fears.** Abbey hopes her group can be much more efficient, but the rest of the group is wondering if that will mean layoffs. After all, doesn't increased productivity imply that you can do the same amount of work with less people? Abbey must have a way to address that concern. She may already know the answer on downsizing. In fact, Abbey said that part of the Return on Investment (ROI) for the project was that she could reduce her staff by 20 percent. This does not necessarily mean layoffs. Some people may be reassigned. A few may be offered early retirement packages. However, the group does not know anything right now and this is definitely an area of concern. Many of the people in the group would rather see the project fail than lose their jobs. Therefore, this concern must be addressed.

- **Communicate proactively.** In addition to addressing concerns and fears, Abbey should make sure that a steady stream of information is shared with the staff to make sure they know what is coming and when. The worst thing that can happen in a culture change initiative is that people are surprised. If people are aware of what is going on and are kept informed of progress they will have a lot less anxiety and less natural resistance to change.

- **Make everyone a part of the solution.** Part of the way to address people's natural apprehension to change is to ask them for their input in the changes. This gives the staff not only a chance to add their requirements to the new solution, but also allows them to have input into how the new solution is implemented. Abbey has already done this by asking her team members for their ideas. If people feel like they are part of the solution, they are much more likely to accept ownership of the changes and much less likely to resist the changes.

Story 33: Fear and Loathing in the Purchasing Department

- **Train the staff.** At some point close to implementation of the new software, Abbey needs to make sure all her staff is adequately trained. Again, this will help ease people's natural apprehension and it will ensure people are able to leverage the new processes as quickly as possible. After all, although there are many new changes coming, it is just a matter of time before the new processes become routine and a part of the normal work culture.

- **Align performance processes.** Ultimately, it is important for people in Abbey's group to buy into the changes associated with the new processes – even if it requires them to leave their comfort zones. One way to make this happen is to make sure that her department management and staff members have performance objectives tied to the successful implementation of the changes. This is a powerful motivator and one that is often ignored. All too often, managers have big plans for changes. The changes do not get implemented because of staff resistance and yet everyone gets normal performance reviews and merit salary increases. The much better approach is to make everyone responsible and accountable for making sure the new changes are implemented successfully. Part of this accountability is reflected in each person's performance objectives. If the staff understands they have a personal monetary stake in the outcome of the initiative, they are much more likely to get on board and make sure that the initiative is successful.

- **Committed leadership and governance.** Organizational processes are the responsibility of the organization management team. Ultimately, then, Abbey and her management team need to take responsibility for the successful implementation of the process changes. The entire department reports to Abbey. She has organizational power in the group to make things happen. This all falls under the concept of governance. Governance is basically the process associated with how the management hierarchy gets things done.

   In other words, if people are resistant to change, Abbey needs to make sure the supervisor in that area is addressing the problem. If the problems are not being addressed, then Abbey needs to deal with the performance failure of her supervisor, and the supervisor needs to deal with the performance problem of the staff member. My advice to Abbey is to rely as much as possible on carrying out organizational change through awareness setting, inviting team ownership, addressing concerns, etc. However, when push comes to shove, Abbey has to be prepared to enforce the changes through her organizational power. At the end of the day, people that don't get on board need to be dealt with as performance problems. If the performance behaviors do not improve, Abbey may have to replace people. If she is not prepared to enforce the changes using her management governance, then she will have much less chance to be successful.

The bottom line is that whenever you ask people to change how they do their work, you are getting into a culture change initiative. The way you implement culture change is with an organizational change management process that addresses change from both process and people perspectives. The activities I recommended to Abbey will be similar for all culture change initiatives. Depending on how much change is involved, you may well need to add many activities to successfully drive change in your organization. In fact, the activities associated

Story 33: Fear and Loathing in the Purchasing Department

with organizational change management might end up being a substantial, if not dominant, component of the project. The key, however, is to recognize and understand that there will be a natural human tendency to resist change. Your approach to overcoming this resistance must be comprehensive and thorough to have the best chance for success.

Story 34:

There's a "Good Old Girl" on the "Good Old Boy" Team

The July 4th holiday fell on a Thursday this year, and Mega's management team was kind enough to count July 5th as a holiday as well, giving everyone a four-day weekend. A fairly large military base was located about an hour outside Dickens, and as such people in the town took Independence Day seriously.

There were a few veterans at Mega, and one of them was Wes Foggerty, a manager in the facilities group. Wes served in the Marines right after his high school graduation, and participated in the first Gulf War. He was wounded in combat fighting to liberate Kuwait, and received a purple heart which he proudly displayed every Fourth of July. Wes was quite a leader, and he loved telling the story of how he took a bullet in his left shoulder returning to a combat zone to save the lives of two of his fellow Marines who had been shot.

Wes had booked my last meeting time in the afternoon on July 3, and I was not the least bit surprised when he showed up wearing a denim shirt and American-flag tie. He wore his purple heart on his chest, along with a medal he received for his efforts to save his comrades during the war.

"Great to see you Private Foggerty," I said with a smile as he walked in.

"Reporting for duty Colonel Mochal," he snapped back with a real salute.

"I am honored for the officer's title, Wes, although you might have the rank a bit high! Why don't you come in and talk to me about the facilities group. What's going on in your department these days?"

Wes had been a manager in the group for almost 10 years, taking a job at Mega right after the war. His group did the initial design work for office moves.

"Although it might seem like offices and cubicles are thrown together randomly, the location and integration of cubicles, walls, tables, cabinets, electrical outlets, etc. are all designed by me and members of my team." He said this with pride and I knew that he took his job seriously – a great trait for a manager.

Wes went on to say that he had always prided himself in his people management skills, but the newly hired Sarah Alderman was testing him recently. Until Sarah's hire, Wes said his entire department was made up of white men. The new department manager had made it a priority to hire a more diverse staff, and Sarah was the first on board.

"As soon as she started, there was friction," Wes admitted, talking matter-of-factly and not implying anything. "The team of 'good old boys' now had a 'good old girl' and the types of interaction and horse-play that went on before don't seem to go over as well with Sarah. In addition, Sarah has a hard time working on weekends because of her two children."

Wes said that many team members felt periodic Saturday design sessions were vital for the team to get their work done on time.

144

Story 34: There's a "Good Old Girl" on the "Good Old Boy" Team

"I give you Credit, Wes," I said as I adjusted my tie. "Clearly you are here to try to make things better. Instead of fighting the change in diversity, you are accepting it and trying to proactively make it better. Given your positive attitude, I think it might be possible to help get you and your team through this 'trauma,'" I said with a smile.

Lesson #34 – Be Sensitive to Differences When Managing a Diverse Staff

You have all heard the saying "it takes all kinds of people to (fill in the blank)." Yes, in fact it does take all kinds of people to make a team, a department, a company or even a country. Think about how boring life would be if we were all the same. Some people aren't so crazy about themselves to begin with. Just imagine if everyone was the same as them.

The best teams are usually made up of a diverse group of people that come together to make something work. Different people have different strengths and weaknesses and the puzzle is completed when the strengths of some people interlock with the weaknesses of others.

When we talk about diversity, however, we are usually talking about broader concepts than just having a diverse set of skills. We are usually referring to having a group of men and women with diverse cultures, ethnicity and racial backgrounds. These diverse groups of people need to come together for the purpose of working together on some set of common objectives.

There are a number of reasons why diversity is important to companies. First, a diverse workforce usually (but not always) implies that your company is not consciously or unconsciously discriminating against people. The thought here is that a company or organization that is made up of mostly men may be discriminating against women. Likewise, an organization made up entirely of Caucasians may be discriminating against Blacks. This discrimination may not be obvious. It may simply be a matter of managers tending to hire people that are more like them. However, this can result in many qualified applicants being passed over.

The other thing that diversity does is open up a broader range of ideas and points of view. For instance, men and women may have different ways of thinking about problems. When complex problems arise, wouldn't it be better to have four ideas to consider from a group of men and women, rather than only two solutions from a group of men that all think similarly? In some organizations, diversity is vital to being able to achieve success.

For instance, the marketing organization can better appeal to a broad spectrum of customers if the marketing team is made up of a broad spectrum of people. In other words, a team of five white males is going to have a hard time marketing effectively to Latinos, African-Americans and women. Hiring five more white males might help a little, but is not going to solve the basic problem. It seems obvious that a diverse marketing team made up of men, women, Latinos, etc. would have a greater chance of success.

Story 34: There's a "Good Old Girl" on the "Good Old Boy" Team

So the question for Wes is how best to manage a diverse workforce. Of course, Wes does not have a diverse group now that Sarah is on board – it's just more diverse. However, understanding the general aspects of managing diversity will help Wes in his particular case. As a manager, the first point to remember is the simple fact that all people are different. It is important to recognize the differences and to blend the individuals into a cohesive team. Managers should consider managing diversity from a number of angles.

- **Don't tolerate prejudice or harassment.** This is the vital starting point and if a manager cannot handle this requirement, he or she needs to be replaced. Before we get into some of the finer points of managing a diverse work force, a manager needs to be absolutely sure that the environment is safe and that the playing field is level. Harassment and hostile activities cannot be tolerated. At Mega, in fact, the first offense of this policy may be enough for an individual to be fired. If the manager knowingly failed to address the situation, he or she might be fired as well.

- **Be aware of the differences.** The thought here is that each person is different because of who they are, but they are also different because of the culture where they grew up. For example, a woman might be quiet because she has an introverted personality. She may also be quiet because she is from a culture where women do not find it as easy to push their opinions in front of men. The manager of the group should be aware of this and make it a point to seek out everyone's opinion.

- **Be supportive of the differences when possible.** This is a key aspect of managing a diverse workforce. The manager is responsible for figuring out how to make it all work out. If a manager looks for reasons why things won't work, the diversity of the team will be seen as an impediment, not a strength. There is another manager at Mega, for instance, who has an employee who cannot work on Friday evenings for religious reasons. Normally this would not be a problem except that his group does software installs, and the installations need to take place at off-hours when most of the company is not working. This installation window includes times from Friday evening through Sunday evening. How has the manager dealt with this? The manager purposely never schedules the employee for work on Friday night. However, this employee has no problem working on Sunday when other staff members would prefer to be off. Some managers might have seen these limitations as big problems, but this manager was able to make the situation work to the benefit of all team members.

- **Help everyone grow.** Look for reasons to give everyone responsibilities and opportunities. Again, don't look for reasons to limit people. Focus on their strengths instead. In Wes' case, he has hired his first woman and she finds it harder to work weekends because of her children. However, it turns out Sarah has no problem working from home on weekends. It also turns out that on the rare occasions when the team does need to work extra hours, the work can be done at home. And guess what? It turns out that many of the men would prefer to work at home during these periods as well. So, again, a win-win situation has worked out for everyone.

I am sure you are thinking that the examples given above happened to neatly work out to the benefit of all. Yes, it is true that in some limited cases, a cultural need may actually have an adverse and significant impact on an individual's ability to do a certain job. However, if you

Story 34: There's a "Good Old Girl" on the "Good Old Boy" Team

manage with diversity in mind, you will find these situations are few and far between. If a manager tries, he will find he can make the differences work in most instances. These situations will work out to the benefit of the individual and the benefit of the team.

Wes seems to understand that already. He first needs to overcome any obvious or subtle discrimination and harassment from his team toward Sarah. At the same time, he needs to determine how Sarah's strengths can be best leveraged to make the entire team more successful. My guess is that when team members reflect on their situation at some point in the future, they will realize they are actually much more successful with Sarah and others like her in the group.

Story 35:

Delayed Feedback Causes Delayed Problems

By the end of July, the proposed merger between Mega Manufacturing and Acme Manufacturing had been approved from all parties and the federal government. With those hurdles cleared, the time had come to actually merge the two companies together under one new banner – M-A Manufacturing. Ever since the merger was announced, tensions in the office had risen dramatically, and there was a real sense of nervous apprehension regarding how the merger would play itself out.

I, too, was nervous because I wasn't sure how the top-level management of the new company would view my current role at Mega. I knew our current CEO saw the value of my position, but there had been no real communication yet on who would be running this new company, let alone who would oversee all the major departments. I was thinking about what role I might play in the new company when a surprise visitor showed up at my door: Dennis Lucas, CEO of Mega Manufacturing.

"Got a minute young man?" Dennis said as he walked into my office. Dennis was in his mid-60s and was the opposite of intimidating. He looked more like a grandpa than a CEO, and he prided himself on being a "regular guy." I quickly sprang from my chair as he walked in and met him halfway to shake his hand.

"I can't stay long, Tom, but I wanted to come by and talk to you personally about something."

"Certainly, why don't you have a seat and we'll talk." I did not feel comfortable sitting behind my desk, so I offered Dennis a chair and I took the one next to it. What I heard next just about knocked me out of my chair.

"Tom, several members of my executive staff have spoken very favorably of you, and they have come to admire and respect your leadership ability. As you know, we've announced a pretty big merger recently, and the time has come to integrate two companies into one. To aide in this process, I am forming a team of very senior-level executives from both companies who will meet for a period of 5-8 weeks and make strategic recommendations on all aspects of the merger – from issues regarding facilities, to staffing alignments and everything in between. This committee will basically be preparing a roadmap for how best to merge these two companies."

"That sounds like a logical next step and a very big undertaking."

"It is a big challenge, that's for sure. That's why I am coming to speak with you. I hear you are an expert with challenges." We both smiled at his comment. "So what do you say? Do you want to be a part of it?"

At first I was speechless. On the one hand, I was extremely flattered by the offer and excited about the opportunity. At the same time, though, I was by no means a senior-level executive and I wondered if I was the right person for this task.

"I am extremely flattered by the opportunity Dennis, and of course I will accept if you really wish me to be a part of this team. I do wonder, though – why me?"

Story 35: Delayed Feedback Causes Delayed Problems

"Simple really. You know this company inside and out, and your role for the last few years has given you a chance to interact with just about every manager we have. You know the processes and you know the people. Your expertise will be invaluable in this regard."

With that, he stood up to leave. "I'll have my assistant e-mail you this afternoon with the pertinent information. I am glad to have you on board."

I had hardly gotten back to my desk to process what had just happened when Marcia White knocked on my door. I needed time to digest this new responsibility, but at the same time I had meetings to keep so I told myself I would not think about it until I had the time to do so.

"Come on in Marcia. How are you today?"

"I am fine, Tom. I hope I did not interrupt you. I wasn't expecting to find the CEO in your office."

"That makes two of us Marcia."

"Is everything OK?"

"Everything is fine, thanks. Let's talk about why you are here."

Although I could tell she was curious to know more about my meeting with the CEO, she let it go and got down to business. Marcia worked as a group manager in the IT Application Support Department and had 12 people reporting to her. One of her employees, Fred Wiley, was having sporadic performance problems. The problems had existed for a while, but Marcia had not addressed the problems head-on. Since the problems were sporadic, in each case she hoped the problem was isolated and would go away on its own.

Now, however, she was hearing complaints from other team members. It appeared the performance problems were affecting other people in her group as well. Marcia realized that she needed to do something, but she wasn't sure what. Her first thought was to call her Human Resources contact, but she felt that was premature.

Since the problems were reoccurring, Marcia thought Human Resources might want to initiate a formal performance plan. She didn't feel that was appropriate yet. Plus, bringing in Human Resources would put a spotlight on the fact that Marcia had not performed her job, since she had procrastinated in dealing with this problem.

"What do you think I should do Tom?"

Lesson #35 - Provide Clear Performance Feedback on a Timely Basis

There are many management responsibilities that can be delegated and there are many responsibilities that might be optional in your organization. Providing performance feedback is not one of them. Providing performance feedback is one of the key job responsibilities that separate managers from non-managers. Managers manage people. Non-managers do not. You cannot manage people without providing performance feedback.

Story 35: Delayed Feedback Causes Delayed Problems

Unfortunately, this is an area where many managers feel they are weak. Providing good performance feedback can be very difficult. It's not hard to tell someone they are doing a good job – something most managers still don't spend enough time doing. However, it is difficult telling someone they are not meeting your expectations. The discussion may be difficult, and it may be emotional. The person receiving the feedback may not accept it. There are a lot of things that can go wrong in the discussion, so managers hesitate.

Many managers end up in a situation like Marcia. She has an employee who is having trouble meeting expectations on a consistent basis. However, the problems are sporadic, so Marcia first convinces herself that the person will come around and that this performance problem might be an anomaly. However, problems have occurred off and on since. Each time they occur, Marcia hopes they are the last time.

But now there is a new dynamic. Other team members are starting to complain as well. The truth is the other team members have probably seen the performance problems from the start. They understand that performance feedback is one of the responsibilities of a manager and they have probably been wondering why Marcia has not intervened. If Marcia's people are like most, they are not going to complain about a fellow team member. Marcia should assume that since a few of them have started to voice their concerns about Fred, it means that Fred's performance is starting to affect them all.

Providing good, clear performance feedback should not be the cause of angst and anxiety on the part of a manager. Like most parts of management, there are techniques and best practices that can help. One of the first things you need to realize about performance feedback is that it cannot wait until the next performance review cycle. Good managers observe what is going on in the group and provide feedback on a timely basis.

What do we mean by a "timely basis?" A manager needs to determine the timeliness based on the context of the situation. For example, if the manager observes a situation where there is sexual harassment, discrimination or danger involved, the feedback should be immediate and by that I mean "now," not three days from now. On the other hand, if the work environment is focused on some short-term deliverable, the feedback might wait for a couple days until an appropriate time is available.

Remember that people can react negatively to performance feedback, no matter how hard the manager tries to be constructive. So in some cases, it may not make sense to disrupt forward momentum with performance feedback that can wait for a short period of time.

When you give performance feedback, keep these things in mind:

- **Be timely.** There is no question that timely feedback is the most beneficial, within the common-sense limits described earlier. If your feedback is timely, you can still relate what happened based on the circumstances that are fresh in everyone's minds. If you wait too long, it will be hard to remember the context of the situation and the feedback will not be nearly as powerful.

- **Be specific and clear.** There is nothing worse than going through the effort of providing performance feedback and then ending the meeting with confusion over exactly what

Story 35: Delayed Feedback Causes Delayed Problems

was meant. Some managers are so wishy-washy that good feedback comes out sounding bad, and bad feedback ends up coming out good. For instance, if you tell someone that "people are talking about you" it's not exactly clear what is meant. Many managers also pre-qualify their feedback, which makes a person uncertain whether they are getting praised or faulted. For instance, feedback such as "You are one of the stronger performers in a weak group," or "You have strong analysis skills but have not applied them effectively" leave the subordinate unclear on exactly what is intended. Many managers will try to balance good feedback with bad, and that is not a bad approach. However, don't mix the two in one sentence. Be clear on your feedback or it will be harder for the person receiving it to improve.

- **Describe the observed actions or behavior.** It is very hard to provide performance feedback if you cannot tie the feedback into actual observed behavior. If you don't have observed behaviors, the person receiving the feedback may challenge you and you will not have any base on which to stand. When you provide feedback, give the person examples of where the behavior was observed.

- **Describe your perception of how the behavior has impacted performance.** This last piece is what ties it all together. Generally speaking, it is hard to provide relevant feedback to people if the feedback does not reflect somehow on job performance. This applies to good feedback and constructive feedback.

Putting all the pieces together, the manager talks to the subordinate in a timely manner, clearly describing the observed actions and the manager's perceptions of how the behavior is impacting performance. If a manager can frame the performance discussion in this general model, there is no reason for procrastination or apprehension about proceeding.

Look at the four parts again. Notice that nowhere does it state to tell the person he or she is doing a bad job. In addition, nowhere does it state that you are telling someone they are a bad person. All the manager is doing is describing how an observed behavior has caused a performance problem. The discussion should be timely and clear.

With this in mind, what can go wrong? There are two areas where the manager might get challenged. First is on the observed behavior. The second area is the impact. The observed behavior is just that – observed behavior. If the person receiving the feedback has some relevant information that could change the context of the observed feedback, the manager should hear him or her out. However, usually there will be agreement on the observed behavior.

The second area is the impact. Notice I said here that the manager should share his or her *perceptions* of the impact. In some cases, there is a clear cause and effect relationship. However, in other cases, the cause – effect relationship is more complex and open to some interpretation. Again, listen to the other side of the story if there is one. You might agree that your perception of the impact was not correct. However, even if you do not agree, your performance feedback is still valid because you can still place it in the context of your perception – even if the manager and subordinate are not in agreement on this perception.

Story 35: Delayed Feedback Causes Delayed Problems

If possible, the manger should attempt to turn the performance feedback meeting into a coaching session by talking about some alternative behaviors that might have been more appropriate given the circumstances. Again, since the feedback is timely and both sides can relate to the observed event, the manager is in a position to describe how a similar situation could be handled in the future.

Usually when we think about performance feedback, we think about constructive criticism or "negative" feedback. However, this same performance model works for positive feedback as well. With positive feedback, we are trying to catch someone doing something good, and reinforcing the good behavior. The same general model applies – be timely, be clear, discuss the observed good behavior and describe the positive impact.

Marcia has really done a disservice to Fred. Rather than waiting and allowing performance problems to slide, Marcia should have had a performance discussion with Fred immediately after observing the missed expectations the first time. It is conceivable that Fred would have taken the feedback to heart and corrected the behavior at that time. Instead, he has continued to exhibit the bad behavior off and on until not only Marcia, but other team members have begun to notice. Marcia should not have waited for the team to complain. She should have met with Fred right away and been very clear about the behavior and the problems associated with the impact. This performance feedback cannot wait until the yearly performance review.

If managers do their job right, there should never be a surprise during a performance review. Instead, the performance review should just formalize the feedback the manager has been providing throughout the year.

Story 36:

Meet Bob, the "Can't Do" Manager

I called Pam over my lunch break to tell her the news of my new assignment. I had grabbed a quick lunch from the cafeteria and brought it back to my desk to process the news of the day and how it would impact me. I had already received the e-mail from Dennis' secretary, and it contained almost five pages worth of meeting times, agendas, topics for discussions, names and titles of every team members, etc. I was surprised initially with regard to how soon this group would meet. The first meetings would be held in Dickens on August 1, for a period of 3 days, before the group would fly to Baltimore for three more days worth of meetings. I knew my first task would be to rearrange some meetings, but I was unsure what to tell people who called seeking meetings for me in August and early September. From the looks of the schedule, I would be unavailable during this timeframe.

"I am sure Dennis will provide more direction," Pam said. "For now, you should feel proud of yourself for this opportunity. I think it says a lot about the work you have been doing for Mega."

"I do feel honored, that is for sure. There are several challenges in front of us, and I am looking forward to working through them with the group."

Pam had a meeting to run to, so we hung up and agreed we would discuss the merger team later over dinner. I finished my lunch just in time for my 1 o'clock meeting with Bob Drudge, a manager in the Finance Department. Bob arrived wearing a dark brown suit and dark-rimmed glasses. Bob wore contact lenses on most days, and his glasses made him look a few years older than he really was.

"Come on in Bob and have a seat. Let me just throw away my lunch mess."

When we had both taken our seats, Bob began sharing with me that he was encouraging his staff to give new ideas on how to make the projects in the Finance area more efficient and effective.

"I am actually disappointed in how this has turned out," he began. "I hear grumbling about how projects are staffed, managed and executed. But no one has any ideas for improvement."

"Gathering feedback from the troops is a neat idea," I agreed. "How did you communicate with everyone?"

"I made a point of going to all of the project status meetings," Bob explained. "I discussed the need to do things better, faster and cheaper. Those sessions seemed to go pretty well. I even received a few immediate suggestions."

"Great!" I said. "Is this a long-term initiative, or are you just trying to build focus for the short-term?"

"My initial thought was to put a short-term focus on this, but I thought that if people had some success with submitting ideas, this might be a behavior that they would use over the

153

Story 36: Meet Bob, the "Can't Do" Manager

long-term. However, in spite of all my encouragement, there hasn't been much feedback even in the short-term."

"Well, you said that you received some ideas when you first discussed this with the project teams," I recalled. "Were any of them worth considering?"

"Not really," Bob said quickly with a bit of a chuckle. "I heard the tired old idea about flextime, but I told them 'no way.' People asked about working from home for a day or two each week, but I don't even want to go there. Someone suggested that we shorten the Project Definition template, but I told them they just needed to get used to this format."

"I see. What else?"

"Two people suggested that we allow project teams to have a team lunch once a month, but with budgets as tight as they are, my manager would never go for that. I encouraged people to come up with more ideas, but no one has sent in anything for the past week."

"I've got an idea on what the problem might be." I said to Bob. "You keep saying you are encouraging suggestions and ideas, but are you really?"

Lesson #36 - Encourage and Embrace Process Improvement Suggestions

I think it is understood that no organization is perfect, no products are perfect and no processes are perfect. Some are pretty good, but in the business world, as in life, everything can be improved.

In some cases, improvement comes through a significant departure from the current state. These significant or even radical changes can result in very large improvements over a short period of time. Sometimes they can transform companies and transform entire industries. However, these major transformations are rare.

Continuous improvement, on the other hand, should be a focus of every person and every organization. Continuous improvements are all about the small changes that can be made to processes on an ongoing basis. Each of these small changes can result in a process becoming more efficient and more effective over time. The Japanese pioneered the formal emphasis on continuous improvement. They even have a word for it called "Kaizen," which roughly translates into three concepts:

- Gradual and continuous improvement
- Sustained focus over time until it is a daily part of everyone's job
- Seeking improvements through minimal investment

Sometimes people have a hard time understanding the generic term of "process improvement." Many people only have a vague concept of what the term "process" means. So, it is important to break the term down into components that might make it easier for everyone to participate. Generally, when you are explaining process improvements to staff, you are looking to become more efficient and effective through the following activities:

Story 36: Meet Bob, the "Can't Do" Manager

- Eliminating waste, such as wasted time, spillage, scrap and spoilage
- Completing the same work as today with fewer steps
- Completing the same work as today with fewer people involved so there are less handoffs of work from person to person
- Completing the same work as today for less cost – either through the use of less labor or by reducing the material components
- Changing the process to produce more with the same amount of effort and material
- Improving the general work environment with the thought that people can be more productive in a more conducive work environment. This might include ideas like better lighting or a quieter work environment. These ideas don't directly impact a process but can make people more productive.
- Improving the capability of equipment and machinery, including reducing maintenance and repairs
- Providing better information to decision makers
- Providing information in a more timely manner to decision makers
- Improvements in product or service quality

Managers should encourage people to submit process-improvement ideas. In my discussion with Bob, it appeared that he had taken part of this philosophy to heart. He understands that every process can be improved, and that the people who work with the processes every day can provide a great deal of insight into how they can be improved.

Bob said a number of times that he was encouraging his people to submit ideas. However, you heard how he responded to the four ideas. He is doing a classic doublespeak. He says he is encouraging suggestions, but his actions show that he is discouraging them.

How would you feel if you were one of the people on Bob's team? Your first thought might be that this is just another of Bob's crazy ideas. But then, after hearing more, you realize that this process improvement stuff might have some merit. You decide to give it the benefit of the doubt. So you come up with an idea that would be appealing to you, and could result in increased efficiencies. Let's say you were the team member that suggested people be allowed to telework (work from home) once or twice a week. You heard Bob's response of "don't even go there."

How would you feel after that exchange? No words of thanks for the suggestion. No offer to consider it offline. No effort to see if it might make sense on a limited basis - only a quick "no." I guess you would be hard-pressed to offer another suggestion. People on the team who heard the exchange probably were de-motivated as well.

In addition, it appears that the negativity was reinforced. Based on Bob's feedback, it did not seem he was very encouraging on any of the initial ideas. There are much better ways to encourage people to submit ideas. These include:

Story 36: Meet Bob, the "Can't Do" Manager

1. **Always thank people for their ideas.** Even if you don't think the idea is a good one, you can still recognize that the person made an effort to contribute.

2. **Don't say "no" right away.** Think about the implication of the idea and if a variation on the idea would work. In many cases, the original idea is impractical, but the line of reasoning will lead to another, related improvement.

3. **Don't pre-judge.** In Bob's case, he should take the idea of team building lunches to his manager. The answer might still be "no," but Bob doesn't know that for sure. Perhaps a spin-off of this idea would work. For instance, perhaps the team-building lunches are used as "lunch & learns" or opportunities to receive training that will be beneficial to everyone.

4. **Remember that things change.** Just because an idea did not work before, doesn't mean it may not work now. Things change. Maybe now is a great time to move forward on telecommuting or flextime.

5. **Be open-minded and creative.** This is the most important point. Don't just think of why an idea won't work. Instead, think of what it would take to make it work. You will be surprised how many good ideas there are, if you are willing to think outside the box.

All that being said, many ideas still are not practical. However, when people submit an idea, thank them for their contribution and let them know you take all suggestions seriously. If you decide not to accept the suggestion, let the person know the reason. If you treat people and their ideas with respect, you are more likely to receive additional tries.

A process improvement program is a culture change initiative. It makes people change how they think about their job. Now you are asking the staff not only to execute a process, but to improve it as well. The management team, or in the case above, Bob, needs to reinforce a positive message about this initiative over a long period of time. Bob also needs to find some good ideas and implement them. If people are encouraged to contribute and if they see the positive results of prior improvement ideas, they are much more likely to respond positively. Once people get comfortable with submitting suggestions and seeing results, it can gradually come to be seen as a normal part of their jobs, and one that they think about on an ongoing basis.

Story 37:

Jack the New Guy is Shaking Things Up

About a week after I was asked to participate in a special "executive task force" assigned to facilitate the merger of Mega and Acme Manufacturing, a memo went out from the CEO informing all employees of the task force and who was participating in it. The memo indicated that the people involved in the task force were, in essence, being temporarily reassigned and would be focusing solely on task force issues for the better part of two months.

It didn't take long for the phone calls and e-mails to come in after that memo was sent out. Most people were calling to offer their support and congratulations, while some people were calling trying to get the latest "gossip" about the merger, and others still were hoping to sneak in time for consultation before my reassignment. One such call for a "last-second" meeting came from Jack Brewer, a new department manager for the company.

Jack's story was a little unusual in that he was hired from outside of Mega for a management position. Of course there are others like him, but I would guess that 80 percent or more of the managers at Mega were promoted from inside the company. Jack was specifically hired to shake his organization up. His boss was not happy with the group's performance and he didn't feel that replacing the manager with another Mega "clone" was going to get the job done.

Because Jack was still fairly new to the company, I thought it important to get together with him before my temporary reassignment. As it was, I had a cancellation in the afternoon and Jack was able to come by on short notice.

When we met in my office, Jack immediately began sharing with me his frustrations.

"I was brought in from the outside and given a clear mandate – make changes. But I cannot change the entire culture of my department overnight."

"Change takes times, Jack. I doubt your boss expects you to turn things around in one day."

"I know he doesn't, but it is still a struggle. I know I will be very unpopular for a while as I begin to implement new processes and discuss new strategies, but I want people to know that I appreciate their feedback and am open to suggestions. Right now, everyone seems afraid to even say 'hello' to me because they know my job is to turn their world upside-down."

"I doubt your team is that paranoid, to be honest with you. You seem to think people are frightened of you because they know you will be making changes. But change happens all the time and I doubt the majority of your team is fearful of change. I think you have forgotten that you are new to this company. People do not know you and probably do not know what your expectations are and what your personality is like."

Story 37: Jack the New Guy is Shaking Things Up

Lesson #37 - Make Sure People Know You and Your Expectations When You are New to an Organization

It is interesting to me how the management–staff dynamic works over time. To a certain degree it does not matter what your style is. A manager might be autocratic or a consensus builder. However, over time, management and staff make accommodations required to peacefully co-exist.

This peace is interrupted when managers get replaced. A manager might be replaced or a team member might get reassigned to a new manager. Over the course of a person's career, he or she will work for many managers. However, there is always a period of adjustment.

Perhaps the least adjustment is needed when a manager is promoted internally. The new manager is familiar with the group and their work processes. The remaining team members are familiar with the new manager. There is still a period of awkwardness as manager and ex-peers now get used to working in a manager-staff relationship, but the internal friction can be kept to a minimum.

On the other hand, some management transitions can be very traumatic. In some cases, it is just a matter of different management styles. In other cases, a new manager may come in with a mandate for change. If you are a new CEO or Division President, you might even replace all of your direct reports, which ripples more change throughout the organization.

The timeframe for dealing with the trauma can be very different as well. For instance, many new managers take their time to evaluate a situation before deciding to implement changes. An executive manager might wait three to six months or even up to a year before implementing changes. This can keep the organization in a state of flux while the evaluation is taking place and for months or years after the changes are introduced. If you are a first-level manager, you might want to wait a few weeks or a few months before implementing changes.

How about Jack? Jack is a Department Manager so the changes he will implement will affect a group of perhaps 75 people. Of course, there will also be changes having to do with relationships with peers and other stakeholders. The fact that Jack is coming in from outside Mega Manufacturing will present challenges as well. Not only will people need to get to know Jack, but Jack will also be in a new environment and he will have to learn and adjust to the Mega culture. On the other hand, the fact that he is new probably means he is not coming into the job with any excess baggage. In other words, he probably won't have any detractors or enemies - yet.

Because Jack is so new to our company, I advised him to take the following actions:
- **Understand the expectations of your manager.** Jack is not going to be successful unless he understands the expectations of the person who hired him. For instance, if his manager thinks things are going well in the group, he might ask Jack to keep things going as they are and only make incremental changes when needed. In this kind of a situation, introducing major change could be counterproductive and might get the manager in trouble. In Jack's case, it appears that his manager wants him to shake things up. Under

Story 37: Jack the New Guy is Shaking Things Up

these circumstances, if Jack only implements incremental changes, he might not meet the expectations of his manager.

- **Meet with the entire staff as a group.** Try to meet with the entire organization as quickly as possible. This might mean a team meeting with five people or the entire department of 75 people. Figure out the logistics, but it is important to get everyone together to hear the same message. If there are a large number of participants, the meeting will not be very interactive. However, you should make sure you introduce yourself and your management style. Talk about your vision for things and let people know what to expect at a high level in the coming months. Ask for questions. Usually you won't get any, but if you do, they may be pointed and might highlight problems that you need to overcome. Welcome all questions and answer them as honestly as you can. People should not expect full, detailed answers on all subjects. After all, you just started.

- **Meet with the entire staff individually.** This is practical if you have less that 20 or 25 people in your staff. If you have more than that, you might need to meet just your management team individually and then meet with a subset of the rest. During the meetings, ask questions about morale and about how people feel about their jobs. You will start to uncover problems that the previous manager may not have seen because he or she was too close. The prior manager may not have realized there were problems, but as a newcomer, you might be able to sense the situation quickly.

- **Look for short-term improvements**. Short-term improvements help to build credibility. Start with simple problems that you can solve with a minimum of effort. Here are some examples:

  - If people are tired of what they are doing, look for ways to rotate people into new roles.
  - Give people more responsibility - especially your direct reports. This is where you have the most control.
  - Increase the opportunities for training.
  - Make short-term, obvious changes in work processes. Remember, you are not married to the old processes. If something doesn't make sense, change it.

- **Create a vision for long-term changes and sell them to the staff.** Your staff wants to understand where you are going, and once they know, they may not want to go there with you. So, having a solid plan is critical, but it is also important to sell the plan to the staff. You may get there in any case, but it will be much easier if people are not fighting you every step of the way.

- **Make sure you have a group of direct reports who you respect and can count on.** A new manager needs to evaluate the direct reports as quickly as possible. As mentioned earlier, if the new manager is high enough, he or she might have the discretion to replace all of the direct management reports. This allows a new manager to make sure he or she has a management team that is aligned together and will support the new management

Story 37: Jack the New Guy is Shaking Things Up

philosophy. Managers at a lower level normally don't have that complete discretion. However, this does not mean you are stuck with the management staff that was in place when you got there. You will be required to work with your managers and get them on board with your style and philosophy. Ultimately, it does not make sense to be at cross-purposes with your direct reports. If you cannot work successfully with some of your managers, you should determine the best way to transition them out over time and replace them as appropriate.

- **Communicate proactively**. Communication does not stop after the first staff meeting. New managers should be especially diligent in communicating proactively with the staff and stakeholders. Look for opportunities on an ongoing basis, including regular e-mail updates, group voice messages, individual group meetings, periodic lunches, etc.
- **Be visible.** This is part of communicating proactively. It is easy to complain about a faceless manager who is never seen. It is harder to complain about a person that walks around the work area and stops by to say "hi." It will be harder for people to resist changes if they know you and like you.

A new manager has one big opportunity to shake things up. It is the one time when you can pick everything up and put it back down again. You can clean off the dust, take a fresh look and see what is lurking below the surface. Once your window of change comes and goes, you become a product of the new environment. It's not that you are incapable of change. However, it will be harder for you to spot the things that need changing, since everything is set up according to your vision. You might bring order to a chaotic environment, but one day you will be gone and the new manager might think the situation is just as chaotic as you did when you were new.

The bottom line for Jack is that he was brought in to shake things up, not keep them the same. So, it is likely that people will be apprehensive and nervous about what is going on. Jack can aggravate the situation by being autocratic and hiding behind his office walls. On the other hand, he can make the transition process go more smoothly by being open, communicating proactively, working with his management team and being visible throughout the change process. Given Jack's desire to meet with me in the first place, I am hopeful that he understands the difficulty of implementing organizational changes, and will opt for the shorter and less painful route.

Story 38:

What's Wrong Here? The Organization Failed, But Every Staff Member Was Successful

During the months of August and September I participated in what would turn out to be one of the most challenging and rewarding experiences of my career. I worked with a group of twelve senior-level executives – six from Mega and six from Acme. Our goal was to set the framework for how two powerful manufacturing companies would merge together under one roof. The sheer magnitude of the project was overwhelming at times, but I was fascinated by the process and learned a great deal about how decisions are made at the highest levels within a corporation.

I was also amazed at how thoughtful people were about every decision that was made. It was not an exaggeration to say that thousands of people would be impacted by the decisions and recommendations made by this relatively small group of people, and group members were always conscious of the fact that people's lives would be impacted. Still, decisions had to be made and the people in the room were not afraid to make the most difficult of decisions.

During a break in one of our first weeks on the job, I had a chance to communicate one-on-one with Owen Martin, the CIO of the IT Division at Mega. Owen was a quiet man who did not speak frequently during group discussions. He spent a great deal of time listening, though, and when he did speak his comments were extremely engaging and thoughtful.

Owen and I sat down together at a bench on the grounds outside Mega. Although we had just broke after an extremely intense session regarding the physical location of the new M-A Manufacturing, I was surprised to find out Owen wanted to talk about an issue he was having in his department, namely how to make the performance review process more effective. Although initially caught off guard, I was more than happy to offer my advice and opinions. It was actually a nice diversion for me to be able to talk about managing people again.

After exchanging some pleasantries, Owen talked about the review process as it existed today. We agreed that it did a reasonable job of allowing the manager and team member to engage in a discussion of the employee's performance over the past year. However, Owen made a great point about the effectiveness of the review process from an organizational perspective.

"I cannot help but wonder, Tom, how it is possible for the IT Division to miss its yearly organization objectives, while at the same time every employee in my division is judged to have done a good job on their performance reviews. When our division misses its objectives, my executive team feels the impact. But the same does not appear to be true for the rest of the organization."

Story 38: What's Wrong Here?

Lesson #38 - Unleash the Power of an Aligned Organization

Some divisions in Mega do a better job of assigning relevant performance objectives for their people than do other divisions. Some organizations, like the Sales Division, have very clear ties between compensation and performance, with the performance measured against a set of specific individual objectives. The personal objectives are based on the organizational objectives. In other words, each salesperson might be asked to deliver $10 million in revenue. If there are 10 salespeople in the department, then the department objective might be for revenue of $100 million. In sales, it is fairly straightforward. If the Sales Division misses its objectives, the chances are slim that people will meet their own personal objectives.

Alignment means that all the resources in your company are striving toward the same general purpose. Alignment comes from making sure people and organizations know what is important to the company. It also means that people have incentives to move the company in one direction and not in directions that are counter to the general themes.

You cannot align individual objectives to the air. Your organization needs to have a set of high-level statements that describe what is important and what the organization is trying to achieve. These high-level statements are mission, vision, goals and objectives.

A company's <u>mission statement</u> provides a concise description of the purpose for the company being in business, and usually speaks to the value the company is trying to deliver to its customers. In other words, the mission statement describes the reason for the existence of the company.

No matter how successful a company is today, it is always striving to improve. For example, companies want to exploit new markets, increase market share and provide more value to customers. The company's <u>vision statement</u> describes what the company would look like if it ever achieved a perfect state.

The company mission and vision are defined at a high level and typically do not change from year to year. They might get tweaked once in a while, but they are not substantially changed unless your company has a major change in business focus.

Each year, companies also create <u>goals</u>. Yearly goals are outcomes the company wants to reach to help it achieve its mission and move toward its vision. Goals are also written at a high-level, and may take more than one year to achieve. Company goals can change from year to year, although they are written at a high-enough level that they remain fairly consistent from one year to the next. Company goals provide more detail and guidance to the organization on what is important to achieve in the next one to three years.

If we assume for a minute that your company sets the high-level mission, vision and goals, then each division determines what they need to do to help the company meet its goals. This is part of the alignment process, and it takes place in two forms. First, each division creates

Story 38: What's Wrong Here?

goals and objectives to support the company goals. The division goals are also written at a high level, but are more relevant to the work of each division. <u>Objectives</u>, however, are more detailed and concrete statements that describe what the division will try to achieve in the coming year. Objectives are written at a very specific and low level. They are also measurable so that the organization can tell if objectives were successfully achieved or not.

Second, after setting more detailed and relevant goals and objectives to support the company goals, each division also creates a <u>strategy</u>. The goals and objectives tell you "what" needs to be achieved. The strategy tells you "how" the goals will be achieved. Organizational strategy is important because it provides a roadmap of how the goals and objectives will be met. For instance, if the Sales Division wants to increase sales by 10 percent, one of the strategies might be to focus on increasing the level of training for salespeople or implementing a new CRM package. These are not goals in themselves. They are ways to build capability in the organization so that sales can be increased. Ultimately, the measure of success in this example is not going to be all salespeople taking a training class. The measure of success will be to increase sales by 10 percent.

Some companies do have overall company and division goals, but they do not do a good job of keeping them all aligned. For example, let's say your company has an overall goal to reduce costs to become more efficient. However, the Sales Division might be focused on increasing revenue by implementing new products. These new products may cost the company more money in the short-term. Manufacturing may be focused on building more capacity to support increased sales, which again may increase costs in the short-term. The IT Department may be trying to be more client-focused by supporting major initiatives from many divisions, which will require them to hire more contract labor. You can see that each organization is striving for something good. However, it is doubtful that the company can achieve its cost-reduction goals since the division goals are not aligned, and in some cases actually require more money to meet their priorities.

Owen and the IT Division have a mission, vision, strategy, goals and objectives. In fact, Owen mentioned to me that if his division does not achieve its objectives, he and his executive team feel the pain. However, they have not done a good job of aligning the rest of the IT Division in a way that gets everyone focused on these same important areas.

As mentioned earlier, alignment means that all the resources in your organization are striving toward the same general purpose. In the case of the IT Division, the next step in alignment is ensuring that each department within the division has a set of goals and lower-level objectives that describe how the departments will support the division goals and objectives (each department can also have its own mission and vision aligned to the company mission and vision). The IT departments also need a strategy that specifies, at a high level, how the goals and objectives will be met.

Depending on how big your company is, the alignment process ripples down into each lower organizational level. Each organization looks at the goals, objectives and strategies of the organization above it, and then establishes a lower level set of goals, objectives and strategies to directly support the ones above it. Each organization also adds specific objectives that describe the items that are of most importance to it in the coming year. Of course, any new objectives

163

Story 38: What's Wrong Here?

must all support the higher-level goals and objectives – not conflict with them. Also, not all organizational objectives can be rolled down, but each group aligns to the higher-level objectives wherever they can.

Ultimately, people must execute all the work of the organization. Therefore, Owen needs to make sure that everyone also has specific individual objectives that support the organizations where they work. It is very difficult to tie individual objectives to a company goal, or a division objective. That is one reason why the higher-level goals and strategies must be broken down into lower level department, group and team objectives. In that way, managers and staff can establish personal objectives that align directly to the organizations where they work.

At the end of the alignment process, each person in the company works with their manager to create a set of realistic individual objectives. These individual objectives must support the organization where they work, but they must be written at a very low level so that the actions are within their control.

Let's look at a couple examples of personal alignment. We will use the easy example of an organization that is trying to reduce costs. Many people don't see how their jobs can contribute to this lofty company goal. They think that it is only the job of management to reduce costs.

However, first remember each person only needs to align to the organization to which they belong. This helps make alignment easier than it otherwise might be. Therefore, each lower level organization has more direct and targeted guidance as to what needs to be focused on.

- Let's say your group has seven members and one of them is retiring this year. Your team may have an objective to continue to operate without replacing the retiree, therefore saving the company the cost of the replacement. Each person in the group may have an objective to learn some aspect of the retiree's job, and effectively take on the new work.
- A team on the factory floor has an objective to look at their manufacturing process for ways to improve productivity. Their objective is to produce five percent more product, using the same resources as today. Each person within the team then has a similar personal objective. All of them now have an incentive to make suggestions on increasing efficiency and reducing waste.
- A marketing group realizes that it is inefficient to use five companies for their marketing campaigns. They set an objective to reduce the vendor list from five to two, in exchange for receiving volume discounts from the two remaining vendors. Each person on the team then has a personal objective to assist in the evaluation, and to help in the transition of work to these vendors.

The last part of the alignment process is to ensure that people are actually rewarded based on how well they achieve their personal objectives. There may be other performance criteria as well, but the achievement of objectives must be part of the equation. Companies that go through the trouble of achieving alignment, but then do not have the review and the rewards process aligned as well are just kidding themselves. In other words, if cutting costs is a company goal, then you can't give full rewards to people who don't contribute. This goes for the CEO, CIO, as well as each manager and employee. This does not mean people get no reward, since there may be a number of objectives that are important to each person. However, if a person

Story 38: What's Wrong Here?

does not reach their objectives around reducing costs, then they must get less of a reward than they would have if they had achieved this objective as well.

Owen and I had a great discussion on the power of an aligned IT Division. The vision is that his executive management team maps the overall direction of the IT Division (based on the direction of the company) and then count on every employee to do their part to help get there. The IT organization has close to 2,400 people. Wouldn't it be great to count on 2,400 people moving in the same direction and making decisions based on a common strategy and set of goals and objectives? For example, if the IT Division needs to cut costs, they can count on 2,400 people looking for ways to do it.

Alignment is a very powerful process. It is very difficult, especially at first, which is why few organizations achieve it. In fact, it will likely take a few years for the IT division to get there. Like all culture change initiatives, it takes management focus, perseverance and courage. Owen seemed excited to give it a serious try.

Story 39:

There's Nothing to Fear – Except Your Job!

By the end of August, having worked four solid weeks on merger details that were at times fascinating and at other times mundane, I was ready for a change of pace. I was also ready to return to my old job coaching people, and I missed being in an environment where I felt very knowledgeable and able to help. As part of the merger team, I felt like I was making good contributions and providing solid feedback and suggestions, but there were also times when I felt very much like a fish out of water and struggled to understand the problem, let alone how to solve it. The session on media strategy, for example, and how many point levels on television it takes to deliver a message effectively was difficult to grasp. Luckily, the Senior Vice Presidents of Marketing from Mega and Acme were both in the room to help walk everyone through it.

My good friend Sam Edmonds sensed my burnout and invited my wife Pam and I out to dinner with him and his wife Courtney. Sam and Courtney had been married for 11 years and we had known them for eight. Sam worked in the IT Department for a mid-sized software company, and much to my delight, he needed some advice on how to deal with cutbacks. When we arrived at the restaurant, our wives excused themselves to use the restroom to freshen up, and Sam and I discussed business.

"What's happening at work, Sam?"

"Well, we're being downsized – and pretty substantially."

Sam said his staff size was not out of line given the company's revenue a few years ago, but as revenue had fallen, his company decided it could no longer afford to invest as heavily in the internal projects, enhancements and support the team currently performed. As a result, his team of 13 was being cut down to five.

"Wow, that is significant. How will that impact your team's ability to support the other teams in the company?"

"That's a big issue, actually. Like any IT division for a company our size, we provide the day-to-day support for finance, sales and marketing. Our work is the typical work of IT people – we fix errors, answer user questions, respond to help desk tickets, etc. We also work on various internal projects to build new business capabilities or to support new business initiatives. And if we have extra time, we also deliver enhancements to current business applications. In general, we do anything and everything that is required."

"It sounds like your ability to handle all these responsibilities will be greatly impacted as a result of the cutbacks. How much time do you have to prepare for the loss of employees?"

"If there is any good news in all of this, that is it. We've been given two months to prepare before jobs are eliminated."

Story 39: There's Nothing to Fear – Except Your Job!

Sam said that if his staff stayed for the full two months, they would receive a modest incentive package. Keeping the staff on board for that period of time would allow for the completion of various projects in progress, as well as provide an opportunity for transitioning support from those who were leaving to those who would be staying.

Lesson #39 – Make Sure Your Organization Can Survive a Staff Reduction

Unfortunately, Sam's story is not unique in today's business climate. It's one thing to lose a few people to layoffs; however, it is much more devastating when a large percentage of the staff is let go. The first reflex from the team is one of shock and then a sense of sorrow. The people facing job elimination need to start thinking about their next job, insurance coverage, getting their resumes updated, etc. The people left on the team need to start thinking about how the work is going to get done with a reduced staff. There may also be a sense of uneasiness about working with people who are losing their jobs.

In many job eliminations, people are walked out the door when the cutbacks are announced. So, relatively speaking, Sam's group was lucky - their job eliminations would not occur for two months. This gives the people leaving some time to put resumes together and start looking for new jobs while they still have a job. From a company perspective, the buffer time allows remaining team members to have a smoother transition from the current team to the smaller team.

Sam is looking for my feedback on where he and his team should start. My advice to him was to proceed along the same lines as he would if one person was let go. This won't be the end of what has to happen, but it can provide some focus as to where to start.

I proposed that Sam initially get his team together and look at four areas:

1. **Determine the work that will be completed and the work that will need to be stopped.** The team is in the middle of a variety of projects and other activities. Given the future cutbacks, not everything can be completed and not everything should be completed. There are many other priorities to be completed before the job eliminations take place. This is going to force some current work to fall off the plate. The support of critical business processes needs to be placed first. The projects that are in progress need to be quickly evaluated to see which ones absolutely need to be completed, and which ones should be completed before the cutbacks occur. All other projects need to be quickly ramped down and stopped. The focus during the next two months is on support, completion of a few high-priority projects, and transition activities.

2. **Reduce the Applications Supported to the Critical Core.** If Sam's group lost one or two people, it could continue to support all of the internal business applications with a marginal decrease in service levels. That won't work with a cut of this magnitude. Like everything else, the business applications themselves must be scrutinized, and potentially reduced. When times are good, applications that seem important are built or purchased,

Story 39: There's Nothing to Fear – Except Your Job!

but these applications don't necessarily support the company's core business. Such is the case in Sam's group. Some web applications built in the past few years are nice, but not critical. They need to be turned off. Other applications that are not core to the business should be turned over to the clients to support for themselves (it is either that or retire the application). Sam feels his team can reduce the production applications they support from 17 to 8. These are the eight key business processes that the company must continue.

3. **Set New Expectations for the Group's Future Service Level.** Just as the current workload needed to be downsized, it is clear the group will not be able to do nearly as much work in the future as it did in the past. It is important that expectations be reset with each of their major client areas. This includes understanding that there is more chance for application errors and that errors might not be fixed as quickly as in the past. Questions and problems will take longer to be resolved. Enhancement requests that might have taken one month in the past will now never even be placed on the priority list. This requires a series of meetings with client managers to set up expectations on future service levels.

4. **Transition of Primary and Backup Support Roles.** This might be the area that benefits the most from having a two-month transition time. If jobs were eliminated immediately, there would be little time for cross-training. If production application experienced problems, there might literally be no one with the knowledge to fix them. However, the transition time allows the team to try to work through some of these knowledge gaps. Remember that the entire list of production applications is going to be reduced dramatically. So, even though there are fewer people, the remaining staff will be able to focus on a smaller set of responsibilities.

   The transition work begins by identifying new primary and backup people for each of the remaining production responsibilities. The current primary and backup resource should document all of their current responsibilities and all of the activities they perform today. That detailed list will be used as the basis for detailed cross-training between the current primary and backup staff members and the newly identified primary and backup people. Obviously, it takes a lot of time for new people to be proficient in an application. However, given two months of head start, at least Sam's team has a fighting chance to make sure the new support people have an idea of the direction to go when problems arise.

You might think it will be difficult to plan for completing the remaining strategic projects given the future cutbacks. In fact, you are right. So, how do you properly staff the projects and motivate people given this scenario?

Sometimes when there are cutbacks, the remaining staff has very few options. For instance, if the staff members who were terminated were walked off the site on the same day (which happens all the time), the remaining staff would just have to deal with the new reality. This would include dropping work, providing less responsive service levels and working more hours.

Story 39: There's Nothing to Fear – Except Your Job!

When staff cutbacks do not happen for a few months, you at least have some options to consider. But you must be smart. If the staff has been given notice, in all likelihood many of them will be out looking for new jobs. This is especially true for the younger people who do not qualify for as good a severance package. Of course, given the situation, it is entirely possible that one or more of the remaining team members will leave as well, which makes staffing even more risky.

There is no question that staffing will be risky, and what better way to deal with the risk than with a risk management plan? Here is an example of dealing with the staffing risk. On one project, the team currently includes a part-time project manager and three team members. To account for the staffing risk from this layoff, the project is instead staffed with one part-time project manager and four team members. In addition, a second project manager goes to all meetings and is aware of the project status. Even though the staffing is less efficient than it could be, this plan will allow the project to continue if one of the team members leaves. Also, because the extra person results in the work getting done sooner, it narrows the window where turnover could disrupt the project. Lastly, by assigning a second project manager to be somewhat involved, the project is protected in case the primary project manager leaves.

Sam also needs to make sure the team sees this situation as a case of a glass half-full, not as one that is half-empty. Although the laid off team members situation is not great, it is much better than being let go immediately. Given that a cutback was inevitable, receiving a few months notice is really a luxury.

That being said, every team member needs to plan for his or her own future. Some people will start looking for a new job right away and leave as soon as a good opportunity surfaces. Other team members will work for the entire two months to pick up the small severance package and then deal with their future after that. Given the personal uncertainty, it is important to help people from a human standpoint, as well as to make sure that people are motivated to complete all the work that is left on their plates. I told Sam that it might be nice if his company offered some help to the affected people. This includes:

1. Using an outside firm to help people put their resumes together so that they are accurate, presentable and professional.

2. Bringing in recruiters from local permanent and contract agencies to give people a sense for the marketplace and to receive advice on how best to search for and acquire a new job.

3. Providing flexibility, where possible, to give people time to talk to headhunters and to interview. Again, since everyone knows what is going on, there is no reason for secrecy. Being as open as possible allows Sam to make proper staffing decisions based on how close people are to finding new positions.

Story 39: There's Nothing to Fear – Except Your Job!

Sam has his work cut out for him during the next few months. He needs to focus on transitioning the group from its current state to its future state – downsizing not only the people, but also the group's responsibility. He also needs to make sure that he takes into account "unexpected" turnover and still gets the groups critical work done. Lastly, he should provide some benefits and support to the people being laid off to keep them engaged and focused on the work that must be completed before they leave. All these steps are designed to sustain the group's core responsibilities, keep people content while they are still here, and make the best of a bad situation.

Story 40:

Rose the Clerk Made a Mistake – Fire Her!

The month of September was practically non-existent for me at Mega. My merger team spent a great deal of time that month in Baltimore evaluating Acme's facility and people. In fact, for the final two weeks, we broke up into two smaller groups, with one group going to Baltimore to evaluate staff, and the other staying in Dickens to evaluate staff. I went to Baltimore.

While there, I had a great opportunity to meet and interact with several well-qualified managers. I knew many of them would survive the initial round of layoffs as the newly merged M-A Manufacturing eliminated redundancies, and many more would be reassigned to other departments. One of the managers who I really enjoyed was Murphy Martinson, a project manager in charge of a project to clean up the thousands of customer records that the Acme Sales organization had generated over the past year, since the last big yearly clean-up effort. He said the clean up involved analyzing inactive customer records to determine whether the customer was no longer valid (out of business, merged, etc.) or simply did not have a reason to place an order for more than 24 months.

Murphy was still fairly young, in his late 20s or early 30s, but he seemed bright and capable. I knew that the customer update process was a big deal in the Sales organization at Mega, so I asked Murphy about the progress being made. I expected a normal "everything's going fine" kind of response, but Murphy confided that there was a glitch.

"One of my team members, a clerk named Rose from the Accounts Receivable area, inadvertently deleted thousands of customer records," Murphy said with a sigh. "I guess she had run some type of query that pulled in a couple thousand names. Rose thought she was simply deleting one name on the list, but it turned out the entire list of customer names was deleted."

"That seems like a pretty costly mistake. Was the information stored in any backup system?"

"Unfortunately no one caught the problem for a few weeks and now it is uncertain whether the system backup tapes are still around. It is possible the records might be lost for good; although I doubt that will be the case ultimately."

Murphy admitted that in time they could probably recover the customer information, but it may not be enough to save Rose. He said he was already hearing word from his manager that the clerk should be fired.

"It's really too bad," Murphy said. "Rose is really a very good employee. It's too bad that the quality of her work on this sensitive project left something to be desired."

Lesson #40 - Look at Processes, Not People, to Solve Quality Problems

Seeing how organizations deal with quality and quality problems goes a long way toward evaluating the maturity of the organization. The same general question applies to individual managers as well.

Story 40: Rose the Clerk Made a Mistake – Fire Her!

The traditional view of quality is that it just comes down to the people. The thought is if you have good people and train them well, you will end up with good quality processes and products. By implication, then, problems with quality are all about people. The purpose of assigning blame when problems arise is not always to punish. Rather, the manager may simply want to know whether more training is required. The manager might also sit down with the person in question and give them a pep talk, or perhaps warn them that they will face more dire consequences if the problem happens again.

On the surface, that approach might seem reasonable. However, over the past 15 years, this approach has changed at companies that have a more mature philosophy on quality. Mature organizations realize that quality is mostly a matter of processes, not people. This is part of the approach of Total Quality Management (TQM) and it is part of what drove Japanese companies toward a cultural renaissance in the 1970s and 80s.

The new thinking is that companies cannot produce a high-quality product without having good processes in place, and the overall approach is to develop process-driven organizations. It turns out that 80 percent of the problems with quality have to do with faulty processes and only 20 percent have to do directly with people. Take the case of Murphy and the annual customer cleanup. Murphy has already implied that Rose was not a poorly-performing employee. In fact, Murphy said it was a shame that she might lose her job over this incident since she was really a good employee.

This is a great example of how managers deal with people and processes. They have a good person that is working with some poor processes. Even if they fire Rose, there is no guarantee that a similar problem might not happen again next year … or the year after. This is a case where the team needs to look further at the purging process to ensure that this type of thing does not inadvertently happen again.

When I spoke with Murphy we talked about people and processes, but it was apparent that Murphy needed some examples. So, he and I took a look at certain aspects of the customer purge process.

1. First, since we agreed that customer records are obviously very important to the organization, I asked why clerical members of the team had the ability to delete customers to begin with. Murphy thought a minute and agreed that this was a flaw in the current process. After all, he said, clerical staff cannot delete customers out of the system through any normal business process. That is one reason that the yearly cleanup is needed to begin with. So, we agreed that it probably made sense for the clerical staff to perform the original research on inactive customers, but that they should really be making recommendations for purging – not performing the actual purge process themselves.

2. Second, if the clerical person had the ability to delete customers, could they also get into other unauthorized system transactions? Murphy agreed that they could. Therefore, Murphy said the entire security access level for these clerical team members should be changed. That way, even if they accidentally deleted someone, the system would reject the request.

3. Third, I asked whether any audit reports exist that show the number of customer records

Story 40: Rose the Clerk Made a Mistake – Fire Her!

that were added, changed or deleted in a day. Murphy said that he has seen a report like that, but it may be turned off. We both agreed that this is a report that should be printed for someone to review. This could be a daily process, but it especially made sense during the yearly customer cleanup.

4. I asked whether it was really a good process to delete customers and actually purge them off the system. Might it make more sense to mark them as inactive first and then actually purge them at a later time? Murphy was not so sure on this one, but that is fine. We are just looking at examples of process changes.

5. The last question I had was why their system backups are not kept for longer than two weeks. Murphy quickly agreed that this was too short. He said his managers also saw this as a problem right away.

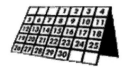

After looking at five examples, Murphy got the idea. High quality results are only partially the result of good people. They are also the results of having good quality processes. When quality problems surface, we should not blame people first. We should look at fixing our processes instead. This is all a part of quality management and of a process-driven organization.

If people always produced high-quality results, there would be no need for quality management. However, even the best people make mistakes, including managers! Therefore, we must get to the point where our processes are sound enough that mistakes are few and far between.

Quality results will come from having quality processes, and the management hierarchy is responsible for the work processes.

- Managers are responsible for having good processes in place.
- Managers are responsible for approving work processes.
- Managers are responsible for monitoring the work processes to ensure they are effective.
- Managers are responsible for revising and improving work processes to make them more effective and efficient.

Everyone in the organization can make suggestions and submit ideas for improvement, but the organization managers are responsible for the work processes. The key to having a high quality organization is to have processes in place that prevent errors from occurring to begin with. The second line of defense is to have processes to detect errors as soon as possible after they occur. It is cheaper to build good quality processes than to clean up quality problems at the end of the project.

Murphy was an interested student and was excited to make some changes after our meeting concluded.

Story 41:

Marcia Needs to Get Formal with Fred

With my assignment completed as a member of the merger team, I was greatly looking forward to a return to the world of people management and coaching. Our executive committee had put together a series of recommendations on a myriad of topics, and the next step was for the newly formed Board of Directors to be briefed on the proposal. At the beginning of the process, Dennis Lucas, the CEO of Mega, was named the new CEO of M-A Manufacturing, with Stanley Mack, CEO of Acme Manufacturing, agreeing to an early retirement package. Ultimately, Dennis would decide which recommendations to implement, although he was required to present the group's recommendations before the Board before proceeding.

Before I left for Baltimore for my last visit to the Acme plant, I had asked my assistant to begin scheduling appointments for me starting the first of October. I was not the least surprised, having been gone for two months, to find my entire month booked solid. Although happy to be back playing the people management game, I was sad to see that my first meeting was with Marcia White for the purpose of discussing how to escalate a performance problem. I had met with Marcia two months ago, prior to my reassignment, to discuss a performance problem she was having with Fred Wiley. Unfortunately, it looked like things were not improving.

"Come on in Marcia," I said as she knocked on my door.

"Thanks, Tom. I am so glad you are back in action. We've all missed you!"

"I appreciate the compliment Marcia, although I am somewhat sad to see you here today. Sounds like your performance feedback discussion with Fred did not work out."

"Unfortunately, it has not. As you suggested during our first meeting, I had a meeting with Fred and gave him some performance feedback based on specific, observed events. I created a 60-day action plan for Fred, but during that time his performance has not improved."

"That's really too bad Marcia. It sounds like we may need to take an unfortunate next step to something more formal."

"I think you are right. What do I need to do to escalate this into a more formal action plan?"

Lesson #41 - Escalate a Performance Problem with a Formal Plan

One of the hardest jobs of a manager is to take an employee down a path that may ultimately result in termination. It is hard enough for most managers to provide performance feedback to begin with – even when the employee performance is good. When the employee performance is not where it needs to be, it is even harder.

The first thing you need to do when you see a performance problem is sit down with the employee, discuss the performance observations, try to determine a cause and put a short-term action plan in place so that the employee has a chance to turn the situation around. In my last discussion with Marcia, this is the approach we took. This short-term approach (or something similar) should be performed with all employees who are in this situation.

Story 41: Marcia Needs to Get Formal with Fred

At this point, however, the initial performance feedback and short-term plan have not had the desired effect. Therefore, the manager needs to take additional actions. In some companies and in some positions, the next step might be a demotion or termination. This might also be the case at smaller companies where the management team needs to make personnel decisions quickly, and where the company is not under as many obligations from a Human Resources standpoint.

In larger companies, however, managers normally don't have the authority to fire employees on their own. The Human Resources Department normally has processes in place to make sure that people are treated fairly and within allowable legal guidelines. Since Marcia has tried to resolve this situation on her own and was unsuccessful, it is now time to bring a formal Human Resources process into play.

Marcia deserves credit for highlighting this performance problem and trying to deal with it. Many managers shy away from confronting these situations head-on – to the detriment of the entire organization. However, for the good of the person and the good of the organization, a performance problem should not be allowed to linger.

Managers sometimes hesitate to take personnel-related actions because of their concern for how the rest of the team will react. If the employee is a popular one, there is a tendency to believe that the team will react negatively. In fact, that might be the case if the manager acts arbitrarily. However, with Marcia and Fred, that should not be the case. Marcia provided ample opportunity for Fred to come around. If the situation ultimately leads to a termination, she should be able to explain to the rest of the team how every effort was made in Fred's favor. The rest of the team should understand first-hand that Fred's performance was weak. Also, they should understand that replacing Fred is in the best interest of the team, the entire organization and perhaps in Fred's best interest as well.

A team knows its weak links. In many situations, the rest of the team ends up working harder to compensate for the person with the weak performance. In the best cases, the team does so willingly (and perhaps subconsciously), but their actions mean that they cannot be effective. In the worst case, teammates start to turn against the poor performer, causing resentment, animosity and friction among team members.

Usually poor performers are uneasy in the situation as well. Sometimes a perceived performance problem hits them totally by surprise. However, in most cases, they already understand the situation. Poor performers should see that they are missing deadlines or that "completed" work requires a lot of rework. Once they get on a short-term improvement plan, they become keenly aware of whether or not their performance is meeting expectations. If they still cannot meet expectations, it will become increasingly obvious to them. This situation will cause them more anxiety, which can drive performance down even lower. The situation should be resolved as soon as possible for the sake of the employee as well as the organization.

Remember that putting a formal performance plan in place is not the same as termination. The performance plan is really a way to save the person from possible termination. A good performance plan puts everything into black and white, and it should precisely set expectations. Specifically, include the following items in your performance plan:

Story 41: Marcia Needs to Get Formal with Fred

- **The basics:** Employee name, manager name, date, organization, etc.
- **Length of the performance plan.** Specifically state the end date. Don't just say three months. Instead, say the 30th of June, 200X.
- **Expectations.** Set the specific expectations of the manager, along with interim due dates as appropriate. For instance, if the employee has a series of deliverables due over the next two months, place them into this performance plan, along with the due dates.
- **Employee reporting requirements.** Ask the employee to complete interim performance reports, in writing, every week or every other week. This must be completed and submitted to the manager on time.
- **Manager reporting requirements.** The performance plan spells out the commitment of the manager as well. One thing that the manager needs to do is provide ongoing written feedback to the employee on how he or she is progressing against the performance plan.

- **Approvals.** Signatures of the employee, manager and Human Resource manager. This confirms that the performance plan was read and understood.

Once the performance plan is signed, it is activated. The employee should strive to meet the expectations of the performance plan. The manager must provide ongoing feedback on the employee's performance and whether the employee is meeting expectations. This entire process is set up to manage expectations. If the employee is not meeting expectations, the manager must continue to say so in the ongoing written feedback. This ensures there are no surprises.

There are a number of ways performance situations can turn out.

1. **The employee completes the plan successfully.** This indicates that his performance is now meeting expectations. It does not mean he is excelling. It only means that he has met the requirements of the performance plan. If he can continue to perform at this level, he will probably be okay. If his performance slips again, more drastic measures may be needed, including having to take termination action without the benefit of another performance plan.

2. **The employee quits.** In many cases, when an employee finds himself on a performance plan, he takes the hint to start looking for another job. As a manager, you should be prepared for this situation. In fact, this may be the best solution for everyone. The employee ends up with an opportunity where he may have a better chance to succeed. The company gets to immediately look for a new person rather than continue with the performance plan that may or may not be successful.

3. **The employee fails the plan.** A performance plan is a serious attempt to turn around unacceptable performance. A performance plan is also the *last* attempt to turn around unacceptable performance. When you put a formal performance plan in place, there needs to be a stated timeframe for the plan and it must be clear what comes after the

Story 41: Marcia Needs to Get Formal with Fred

unsuccessful completion of a plan – termination. However, the company must feel good about how the situation was handled. The employee was given the benefits of a short-term informal plan. The employee was also given a chance to complete a formal performance plan. As part of the plan, the manager was providing ongoing feedback so that there were no surprises that the employee was still not meeting expectations. Therefore, termination would be the obvious and expected result. In fact, it could be said that the employee fired himself, since he was in direct control of the process leading to his termination.

The point at which you create a formal performance plan is a significant one. The performance plan must clearly contain the criteria for success and failure. Once in place, the manager is just executing a process and the process must be followed exactly according to the performance plan. Any deviations from Fred could result in his failing the plan at that point. Any deviations from Marcia might result in having to revalidate the plan. Marcia has decided to proceed with a performance plan for Fred. We hope that Fred is successful, but if he is not, he will be terminated. However, the outcome is directly within Fred's control, as it needs to be.

Story 42:

Everything's Personal with Marvin

Tonya Zucker was a middle-aged woman with brown hair and a pointy nose. She looked like the stereotype for a librarian, although she did not wear glasses. I met with her during the second week of October to discuss a re-occurring problem she was having on her team. When I met her for lunch in the cafeteria, she, like almost everyone else in the company it seemed, wanted to chat about the merger and, more specifically, what I knew about what was going to happen. As we sat in our booth, I had to tell her the same thing I have told everyone else.

"Unfortunately, I am not allowed to discuss the recommendations made by the merger team. I can tell you, though, that the next step is for the recommendations to be presented before the full Board of Directors, and that meeting is scheduled for Oct. 20th. After that meeting, I expect we'll all start hearing news of the changes. It's likely the goal will be to spend two months implementing the majority of changes, so that the new company can be ready to roll in the new year."

"But where will the new company be located? Surely you can answer that. I mean, how are we supposed to plan for our futures when we don't know if we have a future, or where that future might be?"

"I wish I could answer that Tonya, but I cannot. After all, what if the committee's recommendation with regard to facilities does not get approved? I could tell you one thing, you could plan for it, and then the exact opposite could happen."

"I'd be willing to take that chance. So why don't you tell me the recommendation and let me deal with the consequences?

"Nice try," I said, starting in on my tuna salad. "Instead, why don't we talk about the troubles you are having on your team?"

Tonya gave an exaggerated pouting look, but she quickly smiled and got down to business. As way of background, Tonya mentioned that she had 18 people in her group, reporting to four team leaders. The team leaders report directly to her. She told me she had a particularly difficult time providing feedback to one of the team leaders – Marvin.

"Marvin is nice enough," she said, twirling her pasta with her fork, "but there are times when he seems to do stupid things. I know he has a good heart, though, and I'd like to work through his shortcomings via some targeted coaching."

"That sounds like a good plan. So what is the problem?"

She said she was frustrated because every time she tried to give Marvin performance feedback, he would listen to what she had to say but would immediately get defensive. She said he would start to get nervous and make excuses that don't really seem applicable.

Tonya gave me an example. A few weeks ago, Marvin told a client that his team would have a problem resolved by the end of the day. However, he did not speak to the appropriate team member working on the problem to realize that it would take a good eight hours to get the problem resolved. Since Marvin had already given a target date to the client, he asked the team

Story 42: Everything's Personal with Marvin

member to work late to correct the problem. The client was happy, but the team member was unhappy.

When she spoke to Marvin, her coaching was that he should make sure he had the relevant facts before making commitments. However, Marvin didn't get that point. Instead, he got excited and talked about servicing the client. He talked about other problems he was having at the same time. Tonya said that he even got a little teary-eyed as he thought that he was in trouble.

This type of discussion makes Tonya frustrated and she is not quite sure how to respond. In her opinion, the point was logical enough. Why didn't Marvin get it?

Lesson #42 - Recognize the Difference Between Logical and Emotional Feedback

I would call Tonya a "good" people manager. I cannot vouch for how effective she is in her job, but in my dealings with her, she appears to be a good people manager. This story gives an indication of some of her management techniques. First of all, she tries to provide performance feedback as soon as possible after she observes an event. She doesn't wait a month and she doesn't keep a list of items to bring up at a formal performance review.

Second, she realizes she is struggling with one of her direct reports. However, she doesn't take the easy way out and have him replaced. Instead, she sees the value that Marvin provides to the team and tries to use her coaching ability to help him grow as a manager. Third, when she is having difficulty connecting with Marvin, she does not blame the employee, but instead looks at herself to see what she can do better.

The question of what she can do differently is not an easy one because of all the things she is doing right already. However, I do have some coaching that may help her in her current situation. The place to start is to recognize there are different ways people respond to performance feedback and all feedback in general. Some responses are based on logic and some are based on emotion. When you are talking to someone who is behaving logically, 1+2 always equals 3. When you are talking to someone who is responding emotionally, there are hundreds of reasons why 1+2 might not equal 3 in every circumstance.

Tonya's difficulty in relating to Marvin may be based on her misperception of how Marvin is reacting. In Tonya's mind, she has observed a behavior that she feels needs to be corrected. She is describing the behavior to Marvin, as well as providing a logical argument for how the situation might have been handled differently and more successfully. To Tonya, there is no reason for arguing and no reason to take offense.

But Tonya thinks Marvin is not reacting logically. He is reacting emotionally instead. This emotional response will drive the conversation a different way. Instead of a logical discussion based on the "facts," Marvin wants to get into an emotional discussion. He starts talking fast and getting excited. He might feel that Tonya is picking on him, or that Tonya is mad at him. Marvin starts to make excuses that don't really fit a cause-effect pattern. He is trying anything to deflect the feedback. Ultimately, he may start to cry or at least get teary-eyed, which is usually a sure giveaway that a person is responding emotionally and not logically.

Story 42: Everything's Personal with Marvin

It's easy to read this example and think that Marvin is just a baby who needs to grow up. You know – if you can't stand the heat, get out of the kitchen. However, none of us know the mind of Marvin and we do not know what is motivating his behavior. It could be that this is part of his basic behavior pattern and one that shows up in his personal life as well. This type of behavior could be masking a sense of insecurity. Again, this could be personal as well.

The work environment may also contribute to a person responding emotionally. For instance, if you are a manager in a department that is experiencing layoffs, you might find that people will tend to react emotionally – especially if they have families to support. It is possible that an employee could view any negative feedback as a pretense to a potential layoff.

Managers should not have to be trained psychologists, and they should not have to determine the inner workings of every employee who reports to them. However, there is no question that sometimes you need to put on the hat of a quasi-psychologist and ask a few questions to see what is motivating a person.

That is where Tonya needs to start when this situation happens again. Let's discuss how this might happen in a similar situation. First, let's assume the same type of performance and coaching meeting that Tonya discussed. Let's say Tonya describes the behavior Marvin displayed and that Marvin gets excited and starts to make excuses. At some point in that give-and-take Tonya should realize that Marvin is acting emotionally, not logically.

Once she realizes that Marvin is responding emotionally, Tonya needs to change her tact. All the logical arguments in the world probably won't sway someone who is reacting from an emotional stance. Tonya should start to ask different questions to get at the reason for the emotional response. Some techniques include:

- **Summarizing.** Summarize the discussion so far and make sure that you get agreement on the conversation. This will be the starting point for the rest of the discussion.
- **Ask "feeling" questions.** Instead of continuing along your logical path, take a few minutes and give the person a chance to tell you how he or she is feeling. This might be as simple as asking "How do you feel about the discussion so far?" or "Do you have any concerns about what I have described so far?" This also opens the door to letting the person know you are taking his feelings into account as well.
- **Start off with praise.** Since you are going to provide performance feedback, look for ways to start off with some good news. Think of something that the person has done well lately and praise him for it. This should help him feel more balanced when you then discuss an area of improvement. If you can think of two areas of praise, save one for the end of the discussion as well.
- **Empathize.** The person will typically feel more at ease if he thinks that you know how he feels. Empathizing means that you say things like "I can understand how you feel …" or "I know there is a lot of confusion going on around here …"

Story 42: Everything's Personal with Marvin

- **Reveal.** Look for opportunities to relate the circumstances of the situation with a similar situation in your life. The person you are talking to will feel much more at ease if he knows you have been down a similar path. For instance, in the example of Tonya and Marvin, Tonya might share a time when she may have mishandled a similar situation and had a similar discussion with her manager. This, in turn, will allow Marvin to safely reveal what he is thinking now as well.

The purpose of switching your management style to deal with the emotional side is that you are trying to establish a level of trust that will get you through the rest of the discussion. Let's recap how this will work for Tonya, who ultimately wants to provide performance feedback and coaching to Marvin.

1. She starts down the logical path and then realizes that she is receiving emotion-based responses.

2. She switches her management style to emotional, so that she can address Marvin's emotional concerns and fears.

3. Once she has successfully accomplished this and has Marvin back into a learning mode (and out of the emotional defensiveness) she can complete the logical discussion on performance feedback.

Of course, it doesn't always work 1-2-3. Sometimes you need to go back and forth throughout the discussion. This can be very challenging, but it is the best way to have a discussion like this and really make your point stick. You cannot have an effective coaching session, or an effective discussion of any kind, when one person is discussing from a logical standpoint and one person is discussing from an emotional standpoint.

Story 43:

Tricks or Treats for Isaac's Project Team

Halloween Day is always an interesting time at our corporate offices. Several years back, the company decided to allow people to dress up for the day and wear a costume to work. As the years went by, people got more and more competitive, and we started seeing some very "unusual" costumes. In response, the company created several award categories to recognize and reward people in categories like "scariest costume," "most creative costume," and "funniest" costume. A panel of judges was selected by the HR Department, and awards were handed out at the end of the day. Last year, the company offered two extra paid vacation days to the winner, so there was real competition. I had the pleasure of serving as a judge last year, and found the experience to be quite intense.

This year, Mega had upped the ante and was offering a trip for two to Hawaii for the winner of the contest. The trip was supplied by one of our media partners, as a bonus for the amount of advertising dollars we spent on their station for the year. Normally these trips are given to senior executives, but the CEO decided to give it to an employee this year. I was glad I was not a judge.

My last meeting of the afternoon was with Isaac Danielson, a manager in the IT group. He showed up at my office wearing a fake black mustache, white shirt with black bow-tie and a red lounge jacket.

"That's an interesting outfit. Who are you suppose to be?"

"See if you can guess now," he said, pointing his two index fingers at me with his thumbs pointing upwards. He also tilted his head and cracked a cheesy smile.

"Isaac the bartender from *The Love Boat*?" I asked.

"You are correct!"

I congratulated Isaac on an interesting and original costume. I had chosen to wear black pants, a black shirt and a long black trench coat for the day. Isaac looked me over but appeared puzzled.

"What are you suppose to be – a German artist?" he asked.

"No. I'm Neo from *The Matrix*."

"Oh, I see. I never saw those movies."

I was dumbfounded by his comment, but decided to let it go. Isaac grabbed a chair and sat down to discuss an issue he was having. He said that, due to a variety of circumstances, he had ended up managing a project team that was located off site from our main facility.

"Things started off normal enough," he said. "I had a team of two employees and three contractors. In addition, I had part of the project outsourced to a Canadian company that specializes in certain technology. Over the course of the first four months, I agreed to let the contractors work at home four days out of five."

Story 43: Tricks or Treats for Isaac's Project Team

"That doesn't seem too unusual for staff members who spend most of their time on programming," I offered.

"I agree. One of my employees, though, ended up getting moved to another building across town with her entire group. A second employee quit, but was allowed to complete work on the project from his new home in Atlanta. Topping it all off, my client is the European Marketing Unit, so they are typically scattered all over Europe."

All of this had Isaac a little nervous. He said he had control over whether the contractors worked on-site or not, but they appear to be more focused when working at home. Things are going okay now, but the lack of personal contact has him more nervous each day.

Lesson #43 - Proactively Manage to the Strengths and Risks of a Virtual Distributed Team

Most everyone works in a team environment. It has always been understood that the most effective teams are those located together. Being together allows people to interact and helps in the process of forming a team. Ultimately, it allows the team to become high performing. In fact, many managers have opted to spend the money to co-locate their team after every reorganization, even though the constant churn of people moving from place to place is seen by many as unproductive.

Against this backdrop is a global phenomenon that is driving team staffing in the other direction. The Internet, faster and more reliable communication, and collaborative tools are allowing people to come together on teams that are no longer co-located. In fact, the whole concept of "globalization" is pushing work all over the globe, with independent people and teams working anywhere and everywhere. These groups are sometimes referred to as "virtual" teams. In fact, they are real teams and they fit a classic definition of teams in terms of working together to achieve a common set of objectives. However, they are referred to as "virtual" mostly because they do not communicate and interact in a traditional face-to-face manner.

Isaac's team is probably more of a hybrid virtual team. He definitely has some virtual members, such as the ex-employee in Atlanta and the outsourced project team in Canada. The three contractors and the employee that moved across town are mostly virtual, but they can also show up in the office when needed.

Twenty years ago, Isaac's project staffing would have been very difficult to carry out successfully. Ten years ago it would have been unusual. Today, there are some aspects of virtual teams in almost every company. Maybe not on every project, but in some projects for sure.

Technology is a big factor in the change. The Internet, e-mail and collaborative tools make it more and more convenient to field a team of the best people available – regardless of their physical location. The appearance of virtual teams brings advantages and challenges. Some of the advantages are:

Story 43: Tricks or Treats for Isaac's Project Team

- **Using the right people.** It used to be that the best people for a project were those who were available and on-site. If you used contractors, the expectations were still that the person would be local and work on-site. This is no longer a hard-and-fast rule. Virtual teams have allowed organizations to staff projects with people who are local or half a world away. Entire chunks of projects can be outsourced to companies that are in different cities or different continents.

- **Saving office space and cost.** Many decisions on outsourcing work are made on the basis of not needing physical space for the team. This helps drive down fixed costs for buildings and facilities. This is one rationale for companies using virtual labor, and it is also a factor in allowing (or mandating) that certain employees work from home.

- **Increasing the quality of life.** Many employees think it is a benefit to be able to work outside of the office – usually at home. For many people, there is a lot of stress in getting ready for work, surviving the daily commute and dealing with the daily disruptions in the workplace. Many people would rather work out of their homes, and companies are finding that these people can be just as productive, if not more so, working at their homes. Employees also tend to find that the experience provides more job satisfaction and leads to more company loyalty.

Of course, the challenges are there as well. These include making sure people still feel like part of a team, that they understand the work they need to do and that they are, in fact, productive at home as they are in the office. These are all management challenges that must be understood and overcome.

This is the situation Isaac finds himself in. His project appears on-track, but he is nervous. He understands that virtual teams *can* work, but he must make sure the virtual team *does* work for his situation.

Isaac and I discussed how he can overcome the challenges of the virtual team. We started off by excluding the Canadian team in our discussion. While they are a virtual component of his team, Isaac does not have to worry about them in the same way. He is not their project manager or their functional manager. Isaac needs to follow the work progress of the Canadian team, but he does not need to be proactive in his management of the people on the team. That is the challenge of the Canadian project manager.

Isaac also does not need to be as worried about his virtual client. There are challenges with getting requirements and keeping virtual clients involved and engaged, but he is not their manager so he does not have the same set of concerns with them.

Isaac does need to be more concerned and proactive in dealing with the rest of his virtual team. Here are some of the areas where I recommended he focus:

- **Make sure team members understand why they are a team.** If the team members think they are all working independently, they will act independent. If they know they are part of a team working on common objectives and deliverables, they will tend to feel better about their work and be more active in their collaboration with other team members.

Story 43: Tricks or Treats for Isaac's Project Team

- **Look for opportunities to "socialize."** Team members located together have opportunities to socialize throughout the day. This socializing helps the team gel as a unit and typically makes them more effective. Virtual teams don't usually have this same opportunity to interact with each other, so it is more important for the project manager to look for ways they can bond. This might include getting everyone together one time in a face-to-face setting. The manager might also look for more opportunities to get the entire team together in teleconferences or web conferences.

- **Establish ground rules for the team.** This is actually very important. Even though the team members may be remote, they still need to exhibit a common and acceptable set of behaviors. In fact, it is probably more important for virtual teams. These ground rules include setting the hours when the team members are expected to be working, establishing lunch times, determining which meetings are mandatory (in-person, web or phone), setting expectations for communication turnaround times, etc.

- **Communicate, communicate, communicate.** Isaac needs to be extra proactive in his communication to make sure everyone understands what is expected. At the same time Isaac also needs to know how each team member is doing. It is hard enough to keep everyone informed on a "regular" project. The communication lines on a virtual team must be opened up especially wide.

- **Be extra diligent in workload management.** Isaac needs to be very precise in assigning work to the virtual team and he needs to ensure that work is completed on time. If the work is not done on time or not done correctly, Isaac needs to determine the cause and try to put a remedy in place. This is not the time to give people long assignments and hope that they are completed by the deadline. Instead of assigning a six-week activity, for instance, Isaac should assign the work in three two-week activities. In the former case, he would not know for sure if the work was done for six weeks. In the later case, he can tell every two weeks if the work is on track.

In spite of the current project status, Isaac has a virtual team and that makes him nervous. He actually does not know why he is nervous, since the project is currently pretty much on track. However, I think his apprehension is based on the fact that he cannot see and touch people like he is used to, and so he is afraid he is not in total control of the project resources.

Isaac is not afraid, but he is a little nervous about his virtual team. Hopefully, he will proactively manage the virtual aspects of the project team, while using his proven people management and project management skills, to make sure the work is completed successfully. Managing virtual teams is transitioning from an unusual event to a core competency in many companies. Managers who can be comfortable working in a virtual environment will get more and more opportunities in the future. I think Isaac will be one of those people.

Story 44:

The First Snow Won't Cover Up Joe's Mistake

The first week of November came with a preview of winter, as temperatures nose-dived into the low 20s. Several days of rain gave way to freezing temperatures and dangerous road conditions. As I arrived at work Monday morning, I was surprised to see so many cars in the parking lot. On a day like today, it would not be unusual for a good 10-20 percent of the office to be out or running late. All the area schools had been closed, and most people had to scramble to line up babysitters for their suddenly-at-home kids.

As I walked from my car to the building, it hit me why so many people were here bright and early – today was the day when an internal memo was expected regarding the merger of Mega Manufacturing and Acme Manufacturing. I was not as curious as most folks, since I knew what the majority of the recommendations were, but I was excited to have more news out in the open so that people would stop trying to pry information out of me.

Sure enough, the office was abuzz the second I stepped inside. I learned right away that the memo had gone out at 6 a.m., and an all-company mandatory meeting had been scheduled for the following Tuesday at an off-site location not too far from my house. I managed to sneak by most of the crowds of people discussing the various aspects of the memo, and got to my desk to read it for myself. To my surprise, I found a folder on my desk with a hand-written note from Dennis our CEO. "Thought you'd like to see the result of all your hard work. Not too many surprises. Thanks again."

As I sat back in my chair with the memo, there was really only one thing I was curious to find out. I scanned through the document until I found the number I was looking for. To my disappointment, it was bigger than I anticipated.

"Wow, 4,000," I mumbled to myself. It was the number of people expected to be laid off as part of the merger, as the new company eliminated redundant positions and consolidated several departments.

I was still thinking about the layoffs when a good office friend of mine, Joe Abernathy, a manager in the Finance Department, showed up for our morning meeting. Joe and I had known each other for 10 years, although we didn't really socialize outside of work.

"I see you are reading the memo," he said, sitting down in the chair in front of my desk.

"Just scanning it, really."

"I suppose there's not much in there that caught you by surprise," he said, cracking a small smile. He shifted his weight after he spoke and stared into the floor. I could tell from his body signals something was troubling him.

"Tell you what, this memo is going to be the topic of plenty of conversations today. Why don't we focus on you and the Finance group and tell me what's going on?"

Story 44: The First Snow Won't Cover Up Joe's Mistake

Joe took a long inhale and started his story. He said he had made a major error in balancing the monthly financial reports for the prior month. If the report was only for his group, no one would care. But this error was on the company financial numbers that are reported to the Division President.

The financial numbers were generated by automated reports from the IT organization, but it was Joe's job to validate the reports were correct and balanced. So, because of the mistake, the financial numbers were reported inaccurately to the Division President, and moved up into the company's consolidated financial reports. No one knew now, but they would find out soon enough when the reports ran again next month and the numbers were way off expectations. Joe was plenty worried – even to the point of worrying about his job.

Lesson #44 - Be Honest and Upfront When Dealing with a Mistake

We've all heard the saying "we all make mistakes" and "to err is human." However, these trite sayings don't provide much comfort to a 20-year employee who feels his job is potentially on the line. Yes, everyone makes mistakes – some people on a daily basis. But some mistakes can be career-threatening.

That's what makes Joe's problem more serious. Personally I think he is overly concerned about being terminated. However, I don't know how serious an error of this nature is, and I don't know for sure whether it is the first time something like this has happened. Joe is obviously concerned because he has made a very big mistake, but my coaching to him would be the same whether the mistake was major or minor.

The advice I will give to Joe does not depend on whether the mistake and the perpetrator of the mistake will be discovered. This is a key point. Do you handle a situation like this differently depending on whether you think you will be caught or not? I don't think so. If you do, then you are not being intellectually honest with yourself and that is a bad sign in a manager (or any employee).

So in Joe's case, he realizes that he has made a major mistake and that it will be discovered next month. However, I feel like Joe would be asking for my advice regardless of whether the error was discovered or not. My knowledge of Joe tells me that he is fundamentally an honest person.

In fact, Joe is not asking me whether he should own up to the problem. I think he knows that this is the place he needs to start. However, he would like some advice on how to best present the information. He is also looking for some advice on how best to recover from the mistake.

The first step in recovering from a mistake is to admit to the mistake and to take ownership and responsibility. Regardless of the consequences of the mistake, Joe will be much worse off if he tries to make excuses and blame others. Normally, people see right through this. The credit you get from coming forward gets lost quickly if you try to place the blame on others or implicate the innocent. In Joe's case, he could actually turn around and blame the computer system and the IT staff for the fundamental problem. However, Joe knows that the computer system may have made the initial error, but he also knows that it is his job to catch the error.

Story 44: The First Snow Won't Cover Up Joe's Mistake

The other thing that rarely works when admitting to a mistake is to make excuses and whine about all the problems you have or all of the work you have. That tact might deflect some of the responsibility for mistakes made by staff members, but it is not expected of managers. If there is a legitimate reason for the mistake, make sure that you explain it. However, being overworked is rarely a good cause for someone in middle management like Joe.

I was a young team member once on a project where a client made a major mistake that resulted in an important operational system being down for two days. A half-dozen departments were impacted. The client called a meeting and it included all affected organizations. I remember walking to the meeting with my manager and having him tell me that the client was going to get beat up badly. Everyone was upset. However, when the meeting started, a strange thing happened. The person who made the mistake started off by admitting the mistake and empathizing with the problems and disruptions the error caused.

As I looked around, I could tell the foul wind was instantly blown out of the room. Rather than take a negative tone, the rest of the meeting focused on minimizing the impact of the error and determining ways to keep the error from reoccurring. After all, what good would it do now to beat up the poor client for the mistake? The client had already acknowledged the error and the pain caused by the error. Continuing to play the blame game would simply be repeating the blame that the client had already accepted responsibility for.

So Joe needs to first admit to the mistake. He does not need to do this directly to the CEO. The first admission of a mistake is usually to your direct manager. After this discussion, you and your manager can determine the most appropriate communication process.

After the initial admission and acceptance of the error, the second thing Joe and his manager need to do is determine whether there is a solution to the problem. You don't want to be in the position of admitting an error and then throwing your hands up in surrender. When you communicate the error to the appropriate people in the organization, it is best to have one or more potential resolutions ready as well. If there are several, have them ready as possibilities, as well as a recommended course of action. In fact, sometimes there are no good resolutions, in which case you might need to look for the best solution amongst poor alternatives.

After you admit the error and attempt to come up with a list of potential solutions, it is time to communicate to all interested parties. This is the fun time. Hopefully you will find an initial sympathetic ear with your manager. However, once the communication starts, it is hard to control how everyone else will react. Of course, you don't need to publicize your error to the entire company, but you do need to let everyone who is impacted know.

Based on Joe's initial thinking, he is at least prepared to communicate the error, the impact of the error and some possible solutions. At this point, Joe should also solicit additional ideas for solutions. It is very possible that other people may think of different solutions to the problem.

Story 44: The First Snow Won't Cover Up Joe's Mistake

Joe also needs to make sure the problem does not happen again. This may include changes to his work processes or perhaps just a rededication and refocus to this balancing activity. Remember that step two involved alternatives to recover from the mistake. Step four involves figuring out ways to ensure that this problem does not reoccur.

I told Joe that if he does these four steps (admission, alternatives, communication, correction) he will have done all he can at the moment. This gets the error out in the open and allows the affected people to make the appropriate decisions. The next step might be out of Joe's hands. As I mentioned earlier, there are some factors that come into play that I do not have a good understanding of. For instance, I don't know whether the Division President is a person quick to punish or whether he is a person that prefers to learn from mistakes and to ensure they do not happen again.

I am also not clear on Joe's organization capital. By that I mean I am not sure whether this is an aberration that will be overlooked for a typical high performer or whether this is the latest in a history of problems for Joe. Without this knowledge, I cannot easily offer advice to the Division President if he were to ask for it. If this is an aberration, I would counsel the Division President to provide coaching and feedback to Joe, and I would think that would be enough to ensure it never happens again. However, if this is a pattern, then I would need to recommend stronger action.

Based on my personal knowledge of Joe, I assume and hope that this is an aberration. However, this is a personal observation and would not change my coaching one way or the other. Even if I thought that an error could mean that a person could be terminated, I would still give the same advice. Owning up and taking responsibility for our errors is advice that all people should follow – both in their careers and their personal life.

Story 45:

Use Multi-Tasking to Make Everything Take Longer

Most people were still on edge at Mega the week of Thanksgiving. An internal memo outlining merger changes had gone out at the beginning of the month, but the consequences of that memo, especially with regard to layoffs, were still being discussed. Acme Manufacturing had many bright employees, especially in the senior ranks, and as such no one at Mega felt safe in their jobs. Many people took it as a positive that Mega's facility in Dickens would remain as the new corporate headquarters for the new company, because they thought (or hoped) it meant more people from Acme would be let go than from Mega, but the reality was good people were going to be let go at both companies.

For my own part, I kept busy with several appointments right up until the holiday break. One such meeting was with Jay Bondermann, a manager in the Finance Department. I met with him on Tuesday in his office.

"How are you doing Jay?" I said as I shook his hand in his office.

"I am OK, Tom, how are you?"

"Just fine, thanks. I haven't been over to this part of the building in awhile. I almost got lost!"

"Well, I really do appreciate you coming to meet with me here. We're coming up to the end of the year, and that means busy days and nights for us financial guys."

"Not a problem. What exactly can I help you with?"

Jay mentioned that he managed six people in his department. His group was responsible for coordinating the financial reporting of all of Mega Manufacturing's regional and branch offices. Their job was important since they made sure financial reporting took place in a consistent manner and that everyone was on the same financial page as the corporate office.

I spoke with Jay for an hour, and it was clear he was frustrated with the productivity of his group. They used to have 10 people and now have six – but they still have the same workload as before. Because of the nature of their work, they were always getting little projects from the field offices. These projects were typically small – 10 hours here, 20 hours there, etc., but Mega had 26 field offices, so there were always three or four projects being worked on at any given time.

Jay told me that one of the most valuable skills people needed to work in his group was the ability to multi-task. However, this was also a concern of his. His group was not as effective as it should be since they frequently were not able to meet the deadlines of the field offices. Jay was looking for advice, since everyone was working harder and harder on more and more work, and yet they were missing more and more deadlines.

"We've got to get better at multi-tasking," Jay said. "We may have 20 things going on at the same time, but we have got to do a better job of getting all twenty of the jobs done on time."

Story 45: Use Multi-Tasking to Make Everything Take Longer

Lesson #45 - Minimize the Inherent Weaknesses of Multi-Tasking

Ah, multi-tasking. You have all seen the commercials of the super-productive worker who types on his computer while signing reports while giving an employee performance review. More realistically, multi-tasking means a person is working on a number of initiatives during the same timeframe.

One of the people in Jay's group is a five-year veteran named Juan. A typical scenario would be for Juan to have three projects assigned to him. The projects would all be scheduled to take one week, and they would all be of similar priority. Therefore, Juan would theoretically work on all three assignments at once. This translates into something like two hours on each assignment each day. Juan could also multi-task the three assignments on a daily basis – perhaps assignment "A" on Monday, assignment "B" on Tuesday, assignment "C" on Wednesday, etc.

So, what's wrong with multi-tasking? People do it every day and have been doing it forever. As Jay says, perhaps people just need to do a better job of multi-tasking and all the problems will go away.

It turns out there are a couple problems with multi-tasking. One of the problems is more obvious and has been recognized for a long time. This is the productivity hit you get when you ramp-down and ramp-up between different assignments. Let's look at our prior example of Juan and his three assignments. Let's say that Juan works two hours on assignment "A." He is going strong until an internal bell rings in his brain that says he has been on that assignment long enough. He then switches to assignment "B." It is not possible for him to re-focus on the new assignment all at once.

First, he has to reorganize his workspace, moving assignment "A" out of the way and bringing the papers for assignment "B" to the forefront. He also needs to close his prior computer files and open a new set of files for assignment "B." Now that his workspace is ready, Juan needs to quickly re-familiarize himself with where he left off the prior day. He then needs to ramp up his focus on assignment "B" and regain his full productivity. However, before the day gets too far gone, another alarm bell goes off in his head and he switches gears to begin work on assignment "C."

It's easy to see the productivity hit that takes place when you move from assignment to assignment in a multi-tasking environment. There is no way to get around the time to ramp one assignment down and pick up another one. This process is sometimes referred to as "thrashing." It is the unproductive time required to move from assignment to assignment. Some people are better at multi-tasking than others, and by implication this means they have less thrashing time when they move between tasks. In the example with Juan, this thrashing may take 20 minutes per assignment, or 60 minutes per day for the three assignments (in addition, there is always ramp-up time at the beginning of the first assignment and ramp-down time at the end of the last assignment).

One way to decrease this thrashing is to extend the amount of time you spend on each task. In Juan's case, for instance, he may be able to save some of this thrashing time by working a full day on each assignment. On Monday, Juan works on assignment "A" all day. This means that there is some ramp-up and ramp-down time, but only at the beginning and end of each day.

Story 45: Use Multi-Tasking to Make Everything Take Longer

Juan works on assignment "A" on Monday and ramps-down. He does not pick up assignment "A" again until Thursday. It will take him longer to ramp-up since he has more of a time gap. However, this once a day ramp-up is still probably less time than having to thrash multiple times in one day.

The process of thrashing is well known, but it is historically accepted as the price of multi-tasking. However, there is another simple and logical reason why multi-tasking is not a good practice in many environments – it ends up making most of the work take longer than it would normally take, while not getting anyone's work done sooner than expected.

The example with Jay and Juan is a great one to evaluate. Remember that Jay has three assignments, each estimated to take one week and each of similar priority. If he multi-tasks and works on all three at once, Juan should expect to complete all three in three weeks time. This assumes that he keeps thrashing to a minimum.

However, look at the alternative. If Juan works on assignment "A" from start to finish, he will actually finish the assignment in one week. Then he starts to work on assignment "B" and completes it in a week. He likewise moves on to assignment "C" and completes it in a week. He has just completed the same three-week cycle. In each case all three assignments were completed by the end of the three weeks.

However, look at the difference from a client perspective. Client "A" received their work after only a week, which was two weeks earlier than with multi-tasking. Client "B" received their work after two weeks, which was one week earlier than with multi-tasking. Juan completed the assignment from client "C" after three weeks. In other words, by working on the assignments sequentially instead of in parallel, Juan was able to deliver the work to two clients earlier. Even client "C" was not penalized. Client "C" received their work in the same timeframe that they would have received it under the multi-tasking approach.

This feature of "delayed completion" is actually why more and more organizations are starting to minimize multi-tasking. Assuming that priorities stay constant, many have come to the simple conclusion that handling the workload one assignment at a time allows work to be completed sooner, while not penalizing anyone. The time when work gets assigned is strictly a feature of the priority. This sequential assignment of work is easier on the employee, easier to manage, and ends up being more efficient from a work management perspective.

With that said, there are still times when some level of multi-tasking is required. One obvious instance is when there is downtime in your assignment. Let's look at Juan again. Let say he is at a stopping point in assignment "A" because he is waiting for a piece of information from a field rep that is out for three days. What should Juan do? Should he just sit on his hands for three days? Of course not. The prudent course is to assign Juan the next highest priority, assignment "B," so that he has something to work on while assignment "A" is on hold. Likewise, if assignment "B" has a delay or lag, Juan begins assignment "C."

Story 45: Use Multi-Tasking to Make Everything Take Longer

However, once Juan can resume work on "A," he should work on it until it is completed or until he hits another holding point. The moral of this multi-tasking exception is that it is better to take the productivity hit associated with multi-tasking than to have people sitting idle.

Another time when multi-tasking is required is in a job that requires you to handle many smaller tasks and problems. Typically, the smaller tasks and problems come up during the week and you don't have much choice other than to work on them and resolve them.

Jay has a person in his group, Nora, who works well in this manner. Nora typically takes problem calls from the field offices. In many cases, she can solve the problem and move on to other things. In other instances, she needs to take down the pertinent information and resolve the problem over the next day or two. This problem solving may require help from other members of the team. Nora uses a spreadsheet to keep track of the status of these problems. If you look at her spreadsheet at any given time, you might see five to 10 open problems and follow-up items. Is she multi-tasking? You bet. However, these short support issues, problems and questions don't take nearly the thrashing that occurs on longer assignments where a more focused train of thought is required.

Multi-tasking is also required for Nora because of the same reason as above – there are lag times associated with each of the tasks. For instance, she might have a problem that requires the IT staff to get involved. While the IT staff is working on the problem, she is not needed. She only needs to ensure that the problem is ultimately resolved and that she closes the loop by providing feedback to the originator.

When I spoke to Jay, he clearly had his mental model stuck on the inevitable nature of multi-tasking. However, Jay also said he finds more and more of the assignments from the field being completed late. I could tell up-front that Jay understood the thrashing involved with multi-tasking. His thinking was typical – the thrashing was inevitable but could be reduced by better work management techniques. Actually, the better idea is to stop the heavy multi-tasking and focus on sequential work assignments when possible. It may seem counterintuitive, but working on the assignments sequentially will actually result in most of them being completed earlier. This will make his staff happier as well as his clients. Seems like a great opportunity for a win-win situation for everyone.

Story 46:

Phyllis Fills in Nicely in the Mentor Role

November's early chill turned out to be more than just a subtle warning of the approaching winter. The cold season came early this year, with two inches of snow falling the day after Thanksgiving. The fresh powder wasn't enough to cancel our Christmas shopping, but it did remind me to purchase more antifreeze and a new snow brush for the car. By the time I got back to work Monday morning, more than 6-inches of snow had fallen over the weekend, with another 2-3 feet expected during the week.

As I waited to pay my bill at the cafeteria line, I scanned around the dining area for an open seat. The hall was pretty crowded, although I did spot some space at a table near a big potted plant in one of the corners. As I took my food over toward the table, I noticed LaTasha Adams and Phyllis Drummond, two project managers in the Information Technology Infrastructure area, having lunch together at a table for four.

"Do you ladies mind if I sit next to you?" I asked.

"Not at all Tom. Please, have a seat." LaTasha said, moving her tray slightly to make more room.

I knew LaTasha and Phyllis casually, but did not know much about them or their work responsibilities. As I sat down, the two women eagerly returned to their conversation, which was fine by me as I had missed breakfast and was quite hungry for my burger and fries. I hadn't gotten one bite down, however, before LaTasha turned to me out of the blue with a question.

"Say, Tom, while you are sitting here, do you mind if I ask you a question?"

"Of course not," I mumbled, trying to chew my food quickly.

LaTasha said she had been a project manager for a year, and thought she did a good job of allocating work and managing her staff. However, she was less comfortable with her ability to actually help her team resolve the problems they encounter. The biggest obstacle was that she was not very strong in the technology her team was using.

"I know my team members expect me to be able to help them when problems arise, but often times I simply am unable to help," she said, putting down her fork. "I am concerned because I think the team thinks less of me because I do not have as strong a technical background as they do."

I was still chewing down the big bite of my burger when Phyllis jumped in. She was also a project manager, although she worked in the IT development group. She had a similar problem in the past and was able to provide some real world perspective on the role of a manager in resolving problems encountered by the team. I filled in some details where appropriate, but Phyllis, it turned out, gave her colleague most of the advice.

Story 46: Phyllis Fills in Nicely in the Mentor Role

Lesson #46 - Teach Your Staff How to Resolve Problems

I don't know of any manager who can do an effective job without being a good problem solver. Problems arise all the time – big problems and small ones. Sometimes these are within the control of the team to resolve, and other times the problems require outside help. Sometimes the way a problem is resolved has varying degrees of impact on people. Other times, the impact is the same regardless of the resolution – you just need to pick one and get moving again.

As a manager, there are two ways you can resolve problems affecting your team members. In one case, you know the answer to the problem or you have the ability to provide hands-on problem-solving expertise. In the other, you need to rely on general problem solving skills to help the team understand alternatives and make a final recommendation.

This is where Phyllis helped me out. She was able to articulate a good overall process for resolving problems. These techniques can be used regardless of whether the manager has strong expertise in the subject matter. The only requirement is to have a strong expertise in problem resolution techniques. Of course, formal problem-solving techniques are to be used for larger problems. Small problems may be resolved with a quick, arbitrary solution, or even a short-term band-aid solution. However, here is what Phyllis proposed to resolve those larger and trickier problems:

1. **Formalize the problem.**

   One reason that teams struggle with problem resolution is that they do not take the time to articulate the problem. A problem that cannot be documented will be hard to communicate to others. If you cannot communicate the problem effectively, others will have difficulty understanding the nature of the problem, which will handicap their ability to help. You should be able to define:
   - The nature of the problem.
   - The cause of the problem (if you are not sure of the cause, describe the symptoms. The symptoms should help you get to a cause later).
   - The impact. This helps you determine the relative priority of spending time on this problem and helps you gauge whether the cost of the proposed solution is justified.
   - The likely result if the problem is not resolved. Again, this provides a sense for the relative priority and how fast the situation should be resolved.

2. **Determine the people that need to be involved in the resolution.**

   This is very important to identify up-front. You can get these people involved in the problem resolution immediately, or you can give them an initial heads-up that you will need to get them involved with the final resolution at some point in the future.

3. **Assign one person to be responsible for the problem and the resolution.**

   It is important for someone to have ownership of the problem so that it does not get dropped. In many instances, since these are larger problems, the manager may take ownership. In other cases, the problem is brought to the manager's attention, but the problem resolution process is owned by someone else. It is also important to note that this

Story 46: Phyllis Fills in Nicely in the Mentor Role

assignment does not mean the problem owner has to do all the work. It just means they are responsible for getting the right people in place to determine the proper resolution.

4. **Research the problem to determine the cause.**

   This is where good problem-solving techniques come into play. Two good ways to resolve problems is through cause and effect analysis, and root cause analysis.

   Cause and Effect Analysis

   This problem solving technique is a way to analyze complex problems that appear to have many interrelated causes. One of the key aspects of the technique is the use of a cause-and-effect diagram. Because of the appearance of the diagram, this technique is also called a Fishbone Diagram. Benefits of this technique include:

   - It allows various categories of causes to be explored.
   - It encourages creativity through a brainstorming process.
   - It provides a visual image of the problem and potential categories of causes.

   You can use the following process to create a cause and effect Fishbone diagram.

   1. Describe the problem on the far right side of the diagram. This may be the actual problem or it may be a symptom - at this point you are not exactly sure.
   2. Draw a long horizontal arrow pointing to the box. This arrow will serve as the backbone from which further major and minor causes will be categorized and related.

   3. Identify potential causes and group them into major categories. Examples of major categories include people, processes, material, equipment, environment, etc. The major categories are identified using brainstorming techniques, so at this point you are not worried if there is disagreement about whether a category holds the potential cause or not. Just put them all up. Make sure to leave enough space between the major categories on the diagram so that you can add minor detailed causes later. Each of these major categories will be explored in more detail.

Story 46: Phyllis Fills in Nicely in the Mentor Role

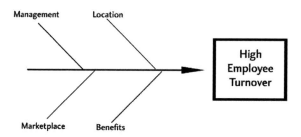

4. Continue to brainstorm the causes by looking at more detailed explanations for each of the major cause categories identified above. Write the more detailed causes on slanted lines that hook up to the appropriate major category lines.

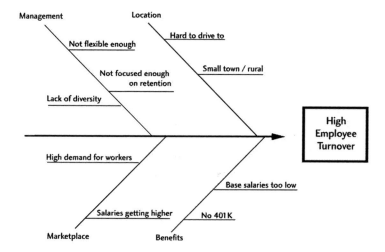

5. When you are done brainstorming major categories and more detailed potential causes, begin analyzing the information you have compiled. Evaluate each major cause and the potential detailed causes associated with it. Remember that the original list was compiled by brainstorming where all ideas are included. Now, you must determine which items seem like they are more likely to be the cause (or one of the causes). Circle the items that are most promising and should be investigated further.

6. If there is not an obvious consensus on the top areas to investigate, use some sort of voting system to formally narrow down the top choices with the most chance of success. For each item circled, discuss how the item impacts the problem.

Story 46: Phyllis Fills in Nicely in the Mentor Role

7. Create an action plan for resolving the circled causes. Remember that there may be a number of potential causes that interact together to create the problem. The action plan must account for these interdependencies. If the detailed causes are still complex, or if not enough information is known, they may be assigned to one or more people for further analysis outside of the meeting.

Root Cause Analysis

Sometimes when you try to resolve a problem, you find that it is really a related symptom, not the actual cause of the problem itself. Consider the following classical example:

A plant manager walks past the assembly line and notices a puddle of water on the floor. Knowing that the water is a safety hazard, he asks the supervisor to have someone get a mop and clean up the puddle. The plant manager is proud of himself for fixing a potential safety problem. The supervisor looks for a root cause by asking 'why?' He discovers that the water puddle is caused by a leak in an overhead pipe. He asks 'why' again, and discovers that the pipe is leaking because the water pressure is set too high. He asks 'why?' again and discovers that the water pressure valve is faulty. He asks 'why?' again, and does not get a further answer. So, the valve is replaced, which solves the symptom of water on the factory floor.

Root cause analysis is a way to identify the ultimate cause of a problem. In the example above, there were many opportunities for solving the wrong problem. First, the plant manager could have ordered more mops to be available on the factory floor. The supervisor likewise could have ordered that the overhead pipe be replaced. However, these solutions would have ultimately been wasteful and they would not have solved the problem since they only addressed symptoms - not the problem itself.

Root cause analysis is usually accomplished by asking a series of "why" questions. Just as the example above illustrates, you ask yourself "why" a problem exists. Then you come up with one of more causes. For each of these causes, ask "why" again. If you can answer that question again, then the first answer is probably a symptom brought on by the more fundamental cause. Continue to ask "why" for each answer until you can no longer generate a logical response. This lowest level is likely to be a root cause and is what generates the observed symptoms. You may discover more than one root cause through this analysis.

When you have identified the root cause(s), put an action plan in place to solve the problem. The symptoms should go away as well.

5. **Once the cause(s) are determined, look for solutions.** The key here is to look at a number of alternatives that might make sense to resolve the problem. For each solution proposed, determine the impact of the solution and the cost. The team should also come up with a recommendation.

6. **Take the alternatives and the recommendation to the decision-makers.** This is the reason you identified the people that need to be involved in the resolution. Now that you have alternatives and recommendations, you can take it to the decision-makers for a final resolution.

Phyllis and I were able to walk through this problem resolution process in a logical manner and LaTasha picked up on the general idea pretty quickly. The key points we stressed from a

Story 46: Phyllis Fills in Nicely in the Mentor Role

management perspective were that no one expects you to have all of the answers. However, your team members do expect that you know the proper questions to ask and that you know how to resolve problems. As a manager, this is where you can provide the most value.

Story 47:

Warren Actually Wants to Work on the Most Important Projects First

I was excited to be meeting with Warren Yount, an older gentleman in his late 50s who had been at Mega more than 30 years and risen from the mailroom to Division Vice President. I had gotten to know Warren well during my time on the merger committee, but I had not spoken to him for almost three months. Warren had dark grey hair and an athletic build. He looked at least a dozen years younger than he really was, and I found him to be very intelligent.

Warren had asked me to do some research on Portfolio Management for our meeting today, and I came prepared to discuss this topic thoroughly. I arrived a few minutes early to his office and his assistant asked me to have a seat as he was finishing up a meeting with his senior staff. I waited about 10 minutes before I saw the door to his office open and several people come streaming out. The last at the door was Warren, who waved and shook my hand as I walked in.

"Thanks so much for waiting a few minutes, Tom. I really hate to keep you waiting."

"Not a problem Warren. I was here a few minutes early, so I had a chance to reread some of my notes on Portfolio Management."

"Great! Why don't you have a seat and let me fill you in on what's going on over here."

Warren began talking about his department and the people he had on board. As he spoke, he walked around the room collecting files and moving things around, obviously straightening things up after his last meeting. The heart of his conversation had to do with making sure the people in his division were working on the most important activities.

"Money and resources are too precious to have people working on things that are not absolutely critical to the business," he said, finally sitting down.

Warren assumed that all managers were making staffing decisions in the best interest of the company. However, he was uneasy about the way each department within the division was determining the work that was most important. Part of the question had to do with making sure every department used a similar process to allocate work to their staff. But how could he be sure that the work was important from a Division or company perspective?

"Even if I could ensure that all of the right priorities were set at the beginning of the year, I know that things change. When new high-priority work arises, each manager needs to determine how to get the work done. Since we rarely hire new staff, this usually means that some other important work must get dropped or postponed."

Again, Warren wondered how all of these allocation decisions were made.

"I've been reading a lot about Portfolio Management, which is why you are here today, to give me more info."

Story 47: Warren Actually Wants to Work on the Most Important Projects First

Lesson #47 - Use Portfolio Management Techniques to Ensure People are Allocated to the Right Work

No company has the resources to meet all of the business requests placed upon it. This is true in the best of times and the worst. Even if you have all the money you need, you certainly do not have all the people capacity to complete everything you would like.

The typical response to managing scarce resources against unlimited demand is to come up with some type of prioritization process to ensure that the approved work will provide the most value. As you peel back the onion layers, however, you get the inevitable question of how you know that you are applying resources against the highest priority and highest value work.

This is a tough question to answer, and it certainly cannot be answered in isolation. What you really need to understand is your overall business strategy and where you are trying to move your company. Then you have some context in which to make decisions about what work is most important. In fact, you may turn down projects that have a huge return on investment because the project does not really help you execute your business strategy.

Many people are familiar with the term "portfolio management" in the financial sense. You want to manage your money in a way that maximizes your return and minimizes your risk. This includes understanding the different investment alternatives available and picking the ones that best meet your overall financial goals. One size does not fit all. The investment decisions you make are different if you are 30 years old than if you are 55. You don't look at each investment in isolation, but in the context of the entire portfolio.

For instance, you may have a bond fund that is not doing as well as your stock funds. However, you may decide to keep it because it provides overall balance to your entire portfolio and helps reduce your overall risk. Depending on market conditions, you may find that your stock funds are suddenly down, but your bond fund is now providing the counterbalancing strength.

In more recent times, this same "portfolio management" concept has become popular as a way to manage business investments. At a high-level, many of the same concepts are involved. You have a limited number of resources to apply to your investments. You want to manage these resources as a portfolio to maximize the overall value and to allow you to reach your goals.

Portfolio management is a way to plan, prioritize and manage the totality of work that is in the organization. Furthermore, it helps you come up with the baseline that you use to subsequently measure how well you are managing the portfolio to meet the company's needs.

Just as with the financial portfolio, the first place you need to start is by gaining an understanding of who you are and where you want to be in the future. You cannot start a portfolio management process by simply putting a prioritization process into place. You can't prioritize work unless you have a context to guide your decision making.

If you go way back to the beginning, the place to start is with a Current State Assessment. This assessment tells you about your organization today. After you know where you are today, you need to define how your organization wants to look in the future – usually in a three-to-five year horizon. This is the Future State Analysis. Next, compare the current state of your organization against the future state to create a Gap Analysis that shows what has to change to

Story 47: Warren Actually Wants to Work on the Most Important Projects First

get you from where you are today to where you want to be in the future. The Gap Analysis, in turn, leads to your strategy.

Your strategy is a high-level set of directions that articulates how the organization will achieve its mission and move toward its future vision. The strategy is important because it provides this context under which you can make prioritization decisions. For example, let's say you receive a proposal to save a substantial amount of money by rewriting a business solution using newer technology. Do you do the work? In the past, you might have looked at the ROI and if it looked good, the project might be approved.

When you manage your project as a portfolio, however, you don't look at projects one at a time, but as pieces of a larger puzzle. You would check your strategy to see whether this type of project will help you get to your future state. If it does not, it should be rejected – even if it has a compelling ROI. If it falls under your strategy (say, to reduce costs and be more efficient), you would still need to balance the project against all of the other projects in the portfolio. If your portfolio is filled for the year, you would need to determine what work will not get done so that this new project can be completed.

Fortunately, Warren's organization does a good job of updating a year's set of objectives based on a three-to-five year set of business goals and strategies. So, his division will be able to determine whether a project aligns to the strategy or not. It may not be an easy process because of different managers' interpretations. However, they should at least have the basis for an intelligent discussion.

Generally, there are two points when organizations make prioritization decisions. The first is at defined points when you do formal business planning. The second is when new work surfaces during the year and needs to be evaluated at that time. Most companies have a defined business planning cycle. Typically this occurs on an annual basis. Depending on the size of your organization, this might start four to six months before the end of your fiscal year.

Regardless of how the initial planning process proceeds, at some point you have identified the amount of work that is requested for the coming year. This work is always more than the company is willing to pay for, and it is also more work than what you have resources to accomplish. This is where the portfolio prioritization process comes in. It works something like this:

1. **Mandatory.** This is work that you have to do.
2. **Business critical.** This is where you start to look at work that is not mandatory, but must be done to support the business. However, one of the key aspects of this work is that you have some discretion over how much you spend.
3. **High priority.** Now you start to look at work that you think must get done. You might break this work into two more areas based on the impact to the business – strategic and tactical. Strategic work is usually larger and more expensive, but helps you transform the business. Tactical work usually costs less and has a more short-term payoff. However, the value is incremental, not transformational.
4. **Everything else.** Everything else goes here. It is possible to break this work down into

Story 47: Warren Actually Wants to Work on the Most Important Projects First

medium priority or low priority, but usually neither category of work will get funded. Low priority work should certainly not get funded. Approving low priority work is throwing money away.

Once the work is prioritized at a high-level, an overall funding request is made from each organization to the company. The company then comes back and tells each organization what their budget will be for the coming year. Sometimes an organization with compelling needs gets all the funding they ask for. Usually, however, each organization gets less than they requested. Normally, you then apply this budget funding to the approved list of work, starting with mandatory work and moving down through the priorities until the funding runs out. The remaining work will not be funded unless the business situation changes favorably to allow more funding, or the work priority of a project changes during the year.

When you are managing work as a portfolio, you must create a plan that schedules out the work for the entire year. You don't want to be in position where a major project ends and you are not sure what to do with the available resources. Likewise, you do not want to schedule a major initiative only to find out that you do not have the resources available to support the effort.

Just as a project manager schedules out the detailed activities on a workplan, the senior managers need to create a master schedule of work for the portfolio. The portfolio schedule must be updated to reflect the current projected end dates of projects in progress, estimated project start dates, support schedules, new hire availability, etc. If possible, you should schedule a smooth staffing line throughout the year, but the timing of work from a business perspective may not allow it. In those cases, you may have to bring in contract staff to handle peak workloads.

The job of managing a large portfolio of work would be difficult enough if everything could be executed as planned. However, you know that you rarely have that luxury. Instead, you barely have time to get a stake in the ground when business changes put your carefully constructed plans in flux. You know the causes. Profits and revenue are down. Budget cuts are required. New management comes in with different priorities. Your company acquires another company. Government regulations change. Someone comes up with a new, great idea.

If you manage work as a portfolio, you should be able to respond intelligently. You should already have an up-to-date portfolio plan that accounts for all the work going on today, with a mapping of how and when the remaining work will be scheduled. When work priorities change, you should go back to your previous prioritization process to determine how to proceed.

Sometimes changes in business priority mean that previously-approved work is stopped or canceled. In this scenario, your portfolio team now should have additional capability to do other work. If previously-approved work is canceled, you might think that the division with the cancelled work should be able to approve the replacement work. In many organizations, that is how it works today. However, in true portfolio management, there are no "automatic

Story 47: Warren Actually Wants to Work on the Most Important Projects First

replacements." Instead, all of the stakeholders are informed of the current status, and all of them should have a chance to offer up their highest-priority work as a replacement.

Changes also evolve as a result of normal fluctuations in approved work. For instance, if approved projects start to go over their budget or deadline estimates, you could be in trouble. This situation will be offset somewhat by any projects that come in early and under budget. However, it seems like there are never enough early ones to make up for the late ones. As you are updating and rescheduling the portfolio each month, you may find you cannot get all of the approved work done. Your first priority will be to put corrective action in place to try to get on target for the portfolio. However, if you cannot, you will need to get the clients involved to determine if you can get incremental funding to cover all the work, or whether some projects need to be dropped. Remember that just because a project starts later in the year does not mean that it is a lower priority, so the process of determining what work will be postponed and then re-balancing the work for the remainder of the year becomes even more complex.

Warren and I had a good discussion about portfolio management and how it might be used by his management team to better allocate resources across the division. I always caution managers that no process is a silver bullet. It takes hard work and focus to implement portfolio management. However, the benefits may be great as well.

Story 48:

Chris Risks Much with His Ideas for Compensation Changes

Another major snowstorm pounded Dickens the second week of December, closing down schools and several area businesses. It took me an extra 30 minutes to shovel out our driveway, and by the time I arrived at my office I found Chris Carpenter waiting for me. Chris was in his mid 30s and was the father of four children. He was from a family of seven himself, and had always wanted a big family of his own. I found out all of this last May at our annual Cinco De Mayo party at the office. Chris and I sat next to each other at the party and talked casually for about 15 minutes.

Chris was one of five IT Development Managers. He had talked to our HR Director about whether it would make sense to set up an incentive-based compensation program for his staff. I was the logical choice to talk further with Chris because of my background in IT, as well as my role as management coach.

When I met with Chris, he explained the purpose of the discussion.

"I am trying to respond to the concerns of my client managers who are frustrated by the inability of the IT staff to complete projects on time and within budget."

Chris' thoughts were simple: if project managers and team members have a personal financial incentive, they might be more focused on delivering within the agreed-upon expectation. After all, these incentive-based compensation programs seem to be the norm in other areas such as Sales and Marketing. If they make their numbers, they are compensated fully. If they do not make their numbers, they make less. This is the amount that is "at-risk" and is paid based on performance. Chris wanted to try a program like this in his group as a pilot to see if it would drive better performance. If he was successful, perhaps the model could be expanded throughout all of IT.

Chris stated that he would actually place part of his team member's salaries, say 20 percent, on the line. If they achieve their project objectives, they will earn back the 20 percent, plus an additional reward. If they don't hit their objectives they may make less money. For the project managers, his goal is to provide a powerful incentive to complete their projects on time and within budget. If they do they will make more money. If they don't, they will make less.

I could tell that Chris was really fired up and so I wanted to look at the concept closely. For this discussion, I just wanted to talk through some of the pros and cons, and then we would see what made sense for next steps.

Lesson #48 - Be Very Savvy When Implementing At-Risk Compensation Plans

At-risk pay presents some interesting scenarios - some very good and some very bad. On the surface, these compensation programs seem like a very good way to gain employee buy-in to the common goals and objectives of the company. If the person's objectives are met, then the

Story 48: Chris Risks Much with His Ideas for Compensation Changes

individual's pay objectives will be met as well. In Chris's department, this would translate into helping the organization do a better job of meeting project commitments for deadline and budget.

Chris and I started our meeting by discussing some of the basic philosophies about at-risk compensation plans. There are many people who have risk-based compensation. Salespeople deal with this all the time. They might receive a base salary, but part of the base might be tied to achieving a minimum level of sales. If the sales revenue does not come in, their base salary may go down. On the other hand, if the exceed their target; they usually can make a lot of extra money. Senior management also has at-risk pay in many companies, especially if the company is sales-focused.

On the other hand, at-risk compensation does not work for everyone in the organization. People need to feel that they have control over making the at-risk pay. If they are too low on the organization chart, they may feel they have a limited ability to control their own fate. Of course, all team members contribute to the overall success, or the lack of success, on a project. But 20 percent at-risk might be steep for them. If people see their base salary cut and don't feel they can control getting the money back, there will be problems. If we moved forward with this proposal, perhaps 5 percent would be a better at-risk number for them.

The next thing Chris and I discussed was a sample at-risk pay scenario. This was important to make sure both of us were on the same page in terms of our understanding of his proposal. One thing that Chris did not mention, for instance, was that at-risk pay normally needs to be balanced with the incentive to make more money if all objectives are met or succeeded. If we only talk about withholding money and then giving people an ability to make that same money back, there will not be the buy-in that we need from the staff.

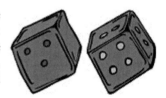

In fact, they will see the program as one where they are taking all the risk and the company is not taking any. Therefore, we must be prepared to provide an honest chance for each person to make more money than they would have, in exchange for also recognizing that the individual could make less.

We walked through a scenario of moving from a traditional compensation plan to one where some portion of the pay is at-risk. In our example, we assumed that 20 percent of the total salary is at-risk, but there is also a 20 percent additional pay incentive available for high achievers. Just so we can use round numbers, we will take the case of a specific individual that currently makes $100,000 per year. Chris would sit down with her and explain the new compensation program – specifically that she would now be making a base salary of $80,000, with an additional $40,000 paid if she achieves a certain set of objectives.

These objectives could be strictly project-based or they could be a combination of personal objectives and project objectives. So, it is possible that the person might lose up to $20,000 from her salary, but also possible that she could end up making an additional $20,000. Of course, she could also end up anywhere within that range. This provides a very powerful positive incentive to achieve the stated project objectives.

Story 48: Chris Risks Much with His Ideas for Compensation Changes

I then played devil's advocate and we talked through a number of risks to the organization if Chris' proposal moved forward. First, Chris needs to understand that people in IT are not used to these types of compensation plans. One practical problem is that people have cash-flow needs and monthly obligations that take much (or all) of the take-home pay. Not everyone can absorb a lower monthly salary, in the hopes of coming out whole (or ahead) in the end. If people cannot afford to live at the reduced pay level, there will be problems.

Generally speaking, then, there is a risk that people will rebel against the new compensation plan and they will simply leave the company. As we discussed previously, the reasons might be because of cash-flow needs or because they do not feel they have the control that they need. I'm sure that Chris will agree that many of the problems with project delivery are organizational and cultural. Therefore, even project managers may feel that they do not have the level of control needed to ensure that a project completes within deadline and budget expectations. I don't know whether at-risk compensation plans can work even at the project manager level, unless the IT organization was really willing to give them the responsibility and authority to get their job done.

If people feel that the new plan will not work for them, they may leave and not stay around to see if they can prosper more under the new plan. If their skill sets are in demand in the market, they may or may not have a tolerance for putting base pay at risk. If it looks like they are not going to make the money they need, they will just go somewhere else.

As I mentioned earlier, the purpose of this discussion was not to make any decisions, but to discuss the overall proposal and look at the pros and cons. At-risk pay programs can be innovative and bold. Of course, there are many risks as well that must be overcome. Chris would need to decide if the potential benefit to his organization was worth the potential risk, or if he would be better off applying some more traditional remedies.

If Chris decides to proceed with the recommendation, I am sure he will need to overcome a skeptical IT and HR management team. However, Chris is the champion of this idea. If he thinks it can work and is willing to make the business case, perhaps he can get approval for a limited trial program. If the trial program is a success, who knows where it could lead. As our meeting ended, I don't know whether Chris was willing to invest the time and effort to push this initiative forward. However, I congratulated him for thinking outside the box and wished him good luck. You never know. The idea looks to be a long shot. On the other hand, stranger things have happened at Mega.

Story 49:

"Give it Up" to a Self-Managed Team

It was the last week of the year, and things at Mega were quiet and for the first time all year – dull. Many people had taken extra time off because of the inclement weather, and many more decided to get an early jump on Christmas by taking a few extra days of vacation. As a reward to its employees for a record year, Mega had given everyone the days off between Christmas and New Year. Many people took advantages of this by scheduling extra vacation time prior to Christmas.

As I reviewed my calendar for the day, I noticed only one appointment. It was with Jed Holley, a manager in the Manufacturing Division. Jed was responsible for a group of supervisors and their staffs who work on the shop floor in the widget manufacturing process.

Jed arrived at my office wearing black pants and a blue shirt with a blue Santa Claus tie.

"How many kids do you have Jed?" I asked as he walked into my office.

"Two Tom. How did you know I had kids?"

"I've got a few ties like that one at home in my drawer, too. Gifts from my son over the years."

We both chuckled at the reality of the "dreaded" Christmas tie. Jed eventually took a seat and we got down to business. Jed went to a class a few weeks ago that described the benefits of creating self-managed teams. He would like to try out the concepts in his department and see if there may be some benefits to the organization.

He had received permission from Human Resources to start one self-managed team as a pilot. If the team worked out well, he could try to expand the concept further. Expanding the concept would require him to work with Human Resources on changes to job descriptions, reporting relationships, etc. Human Resources was skeptical that the concept would work, but they were giving Jed the okay to try the concept out and see how it went.

Lesson #49 - Use Self-Managed Teams

Teamwork can provide many benefits in the business world. Through teamwork, employees become more motivated and enthusiastic, develop new ideas to improve company performance, and assume greater responsibility in putting these plans into action. Teamwork results in decreased absenteeism, work-related injuries, conflicts, and quality defects while employee productivity and customer satisfaction increase.

A Self-Managed Team, or SMT, is a specific type of team that maintains a high degree of cohesion and collaboration, and manages itself, with the goal of becoming a very high-performing team (sometimes in a manufacturing setting these are also called "production teams"). With SMTs, specific performance goals are established, tracked and evaluated on an ongoing basis. Trust grows among the team members as work progresses and they become motivated to accept more difficult challenges. The focus in these types of groups is on performance, as well as on

Story 49: "Give it Up" to a Self-Managed Team

teamwork. Their success requires strong personal and company commitment, available time, skill development, and support from team members and management.

To make the most of the benefits that SMTs can offer, companies have to consider factors such as team size, resource allocation, performance challenges, and decision-making authority. The team members must be trained and typically the team must have all of the skill sets needed to complete some specific work product. In other words, the team is not made up of a group of specialists who do one thing, but rather enough people that they can complete an entire process or sub-process.

Of course, they cannot be trained in every possible contingency. One of the objectives of a self-management team is to be flexible enough to resolve unforeseen problems when they occur. No amount of training and planning can bring perfect results. Unforeseen problems will certainly arise, and teams must be prepared to invest adequate resources and energy even after the implementation stages.

When Jed and I talked, I stressed to him the need to provide training to his team to specifically prepare the members to work in an environment such as this. A very common mistake is to throw people into a self-managed environment without adequate preparation. This results in chaos, frustration and paralysis. Self-managed teams can be powerful motivators for team members to do their best. However, it may not be intuitively obvious how individuals are meant to behave in this environment. Many team members have spent their careers basically taking orders from a supervisor, or doing the same job over and over again. If they have exercised any spontaneity or creativity, it has been within the narrow confines of their individual job responsibilities. Now they are being asked to view their job as a part of a process and to look for ways that the entire process can be performed more effectively and efficiently.

The best time to offer training is when the need for learning arises. For SMTs, that time would be when the team is first formed and when the team encounters situations it cannot handle. The initial training should give the team a good start, but the company should be prepared to offer ongoing training as required.

When companies implement SMTs, they shift their focus from the concept of "supervisors" to "coaches," or team leaders. While a supervisor's role is to make decisions and instruct team members in how to tackle any situation, the role of a coach is to guide team members and help them improve their decision-making skills through experience. Thus, the skills expected of coaches are quite different from those of supervisors. Their responsibilities shift from getting work done to developing the capabilities of team members. This is done by encouraging discussions, asking questions and providing explanations to raise the team's level of thinking.

To be successful, an SMT should work as a single unit, not as a group of individuals. Seeking out individual team members to deal with breakdowns or unexpected situations may bring quick solutions, but it hampers teamwork in the long run.

It is important to remember that when dealing with SMTs, all issues and requests should be brought to the team and not directly to the coach or to individual team members. Such

Story 49: "Give it Up" to a Self-Managed Team

interactions hinder the SMT's sense of collective responsibility. Employees outside the SMT should respect its identity to help facilitate its growth.

One of the biggest mistakes committed during the implementation of SMTs is selecting a formal "team leader." The "leader" is then usually assigned important tasks such as running team meetings, scheduling work, and attending meetings with other groups. At first glance, this approach seems to be in the best interest of the SMTs. It assigns extra responsibility to one team member and hopefully ensures that the tasks will be completed with the best possible results. Unfortunately, this could lead to some harmful consequences.

The other team members might tend to shirk responsibility and ownership. This hampers the team's development. One option is to rotate leadership and assign each team member one or two leadership tasks for a period of time. Rotating leadership has several advantages. It fosters learning, increases empathy, and gives each member an opportunity to learn a range of tasks. Also, rotation enhances overall commitment because over time, each member has a chance to perform each task and take on each responsibility.

It is usually the case that implementation, not design, is the toughest part of introducing a self-managed team. In many areas, including Jed's shop floor group, the people are used to working as cogs in a big machine. They are not really used to seeing themselves as team members. One common problem that is encountered when people start to work as a more coherent team is that personality conflicts arise.

When people start to express their opinions and ideas in a team environment, they don't always know how to provide feedback and receive feedback in the most mature way. People who do not provide constructive feedback in a positive manner can cause personnel problems. In the same respect, team members may not be used to receiving feedback, and they can look at criticism of their ideas as being a personal criticism of themselves. This is an example of an area where the team should first be trained because a lot of unnecessary friction can arise from people giving and taking feedback.

My overall advice to Jed was along the following set of points:

- The introduction of a self-managed team has the ability to make a large positive difference in his department. However, this is definitely a big change in how people do their jobs today. Therefore, Jed needs to implement this as a culture change initiative. The plan must be holistic and address both processes and people. The initiative must also have staying power. It may be six months to a year before this first team is starting to truly function as a Self Managed Team.

- The team should have a coach or team leader and not a specific manager. The coach must be someone trained in coaching teams. The coach cannot be a production supervisor or else the team will still informally look to that person for direction and guidance.

- The SMT must have some specific direction and objectives to point them in the right direction and keep them focused. The point of the team is to complete an entire process or subprocess more efficiently and effectively than they can today as a series of individual contributors.

Story 49: "Give it Up" to a Self-Managed Team

- The team should have responsibility over a process or subprocess. If necessary, some additional people may need to be a part of the team – either full-time or part-time. In Jed's case, he is considering adding a quality engineer and a financial analyst to the team on a part-time basis to make sure that the SMT has a complete set of skills to understand the entire process they are responsible for.

- Lastly and perhaps most importantly, Jed needs to give the team the responsibility and the authority to make changes. Larger decisions still might need to be approved, but the team should have some reasonable level of authority. One common problem with self-managed teams is that managers want to give them a high level of responsibility and give them lofty expectations, but then give them very little authority. This then becomes a powerful de-motivator to the team and often results in the team only giving lip service to the new paradigm.

As the sponsoring manager, Jed needs to make sure he is supportive of the team, while at the same time curbing his normal tendency as a manager to want to manage and control the group. In some respects this will be as much a challenge to Jed as it is to the rest of the team to take up the management slack.

There is going to be initial resistance and conflict. This is normal with any culture change initiative. With the right level of coaching, training and support, the team will gradually get the problems under control. The team members can then focus on suggesting and implementing positive change to the processes they control. The team will hopefully perform at a higher level than the combination of their individual contributions before. In a best-case scenario, the team will become super efficient and independent and move into the realm of a high-performing team. This will not happen overnight, but it can be a great payoff for the initial cost and management focus Jed invests in the group.

Story 50:

Morale Problems Don't Take Holidays

My last meeting of the year was with Gerry Tyson, a somber man in his early 40s who had worked at Mega for about eight years after moving to Dickens from San Francisco. Although Mega Manufacturing was doing well in general, Gerry's manufacturing organization had some rough problems to deal with. There was recently a well-publicized incident of a product recall that focused on a manufacturing glitch that was not caught. His organization had also been outsourcing more and more work – not because of poor quality, but because of pure financial considerations.

When Gerry arrived at my office, he was looking pretty glum.

"Is everything OK Gerry?" I asked as I shook his hand.

"I can't say that it is, Tom. As I think you know, it has been a very difficult year for me and my manufacturing team. It seems like one bad thing after another has happened to us this year. I would not be surprised if my whole team is let go as a result of this merger with Acme."

I knew that would not be the case, although I did not know if certain members of his team, or perhaps even Gerry himself, might be let go.

"I know you've had some rough patches, and I am sure it has made for some difficult decisions. Is that why you came to see me today?"

"Indeed. The string of bad news and tough times has not surprisingly led to some significant morale problems."

Gerry said that the pressure to reduce manufacturing costs was everywhere and he had to make some tough decisions including layoffs. All this (and more) had left staff morale at a low level. The staff was grumbling about being blamed for quality problems, while at the same time having to manufacture to a higher level of quality with less people. Gerry saw the problem, but wasn't sure what to do about it.

"I was thinking about sponsoring some fun event-related days for our folks next year, like 'jeans and sweatshirt' day, but I don't think anything simple like this is going to help at this point."

Knowing his staff, I had to agree.

Lesson #50 - Respond Carefully to Significant Morale Problems

If you are running a project or if you have a small team, you have more flexibility in terms of resolving morale problems. If you find there are problems at the team level that are within your control, you can address them directly. If there are problems that are outside your control, you can recognize that as well and start to address some of the symptoms as best you can.

Story 50: Morale Problems Don't Take Holidays

When I met with Gerry, he seemed to have already performed these first few steps. That is, he has validated that there is a morale problem and he is pretty sure it is impacting the productivity and quality of the manufacturing process. He has also uncovered a set of probable causes, as follows:

- The biggest concern seems to be job security. Although the manufacturing division still employs thousands, they have seen their numbers shrink over the past few years. It seems that all of the remaining staff knows one or more people that have been laid off over the past few years. The remaining staff wonders if it is just a matter of time before they are in the same position as well. In hindsight, Gerry realizes that the prior layoffs could have been handled better, and should have been handled better.

- There is no doubt that the recent quality-related recall had a short-term impact on morale as well. No one likes to be told that their work is no good, and this recall received plenty of press coverage. Even though only a portion of the staff was involved, the general manufacturing process received a black eye and the entire division was tainted.

- There is a sense of management callousness toward the workers. In other words, the employees feel that the managers simply don't care about them and their concerns.

When you are managing a larger organization, the root causes, the symptoms and the resolutions to a morale problem are tougher to deal with. This does not mean that the causes are harder to determine. In fact, they may be easier to ascertain. In Gerry's case, for instance, he is able to track back the major causes to job insecurity and the quality problem. However, once the root causes are determined, the solutions are more complex to implement. You will find that the root causes that are out of the control of each individual team now become more within the control of the extended organization.

After hearing Gerry give his perception of the employee concerns, I thought for a minute on how best to help him address them. He is right that a "Jeans and Sweatshirt Day" is probably not going to overcome these fundamental problems. Of course, these types of job-security problems are not unique to Mega Manufacturing and they are not unique to the Manufacturing Division. Many of these same concerns exist throughout corporate America. Even the Information Technology organization is feeling the pressure of cost cutting and outsourcing.

On the other hand, even if we agree that the concerns are large, it doesn't mean we throw our hands up and give up on the problem. That would be abdicating our management responsibilities and allowing the matter to just get worse. To Gerry's credit, he is not taking that approach. He would like to try to turn the situation around and has begun to think of some ideas to help.

So, the question is whether you can resolve the morale problem by focusing on the symptoms or whether you can address the root causes. It can be more challenging to address the root causes, but let's start there.

In Gerry's case, the primary causes appear to be the long-term uncertainty around job security and the short-term quality incident. I have arranged them this way because the quality problem

Story 50: Morale Problems Don't Take Holidays

is not a common one for the organization and if there are no additional quality problems over some period of time, the morale problem associated with this cause will fade away.

Gerry and his management team must understand the reasons for the quality lapse and address them. This might include additional training, additional quality control procedures, etc. From a morale standpoint, Gerry might want to have a pep-talk for the staff and underscore his faith in the people and the work processes. He can also assure the staff that the management team understands that everyone shares in the accolades and the shortcomings of the manufacturing process and that everyone takes their role seriously. He can also encourage process improvement ideas from the staff. However, because this is a one-time event (so far), the morale problems will go away naturally if the problem does not reoccur.

The longer-term problem of job security is one that Gerry may also choose to address head on. If the layoffs were a short-term response to a short-term problem, Gerry could also take a more one-time approach to building back morale. He could reassure everyone that their jobs are safe and morale will slowly build back up again. Improved morale could be accelerated by the "Jeans and Sweatshirt Days" and other fun events.

However, in this case, Gerry understands that the organization may face more layoffs and outsourcing pressures in the future. Therefore, it would be bad for the organization to give people false hope and then dash that hope at a later time. This approach might take years to recover from.

That is why addressing the root cause in this case is more difficult. If Gerry and his management team do not think they can address the root causes of the job loss scenario, they would be wrong to try to address the morale problem with a rah-rah approach. On the other hand, if they think they can deal with the root cause, they have a powerful case to be made to work with the staff toward a set of common objectives and goals. Gerry and his team can determine what it will take to keep the job situation stable.

For instance, if they can show a declining cost to manufacture a widget, they might be able to keep their jobs stable. In this case, the place to start building morale is through communication and striving toward a common goal. People love to strive toward a goal as a part of a team. It gives everyone something to rally around.

So, Gerry needs to feel pretty comfortable that if he can get manufacturing efficiencies to a certain level, there would be no incentive to outsource the work. He can get the entire manufacturing organization to focus on this problem. It will not be easy but there are a number of things that can help.

- **Talk about the business value of the work.** Make sure people see the value of their work and know they are providing benefits to the business. Better yet, have your customer explain how they use your product and the value it provides. If people think they are doing something important, they will feel better about their work.
- **Get everyone involved.** People can set up small teams to discuss ways to become more efficient. Group events around efficiency can be organized, etc. If you want to improve everyone's morale, try to get everyone involved. Instead of having people complain

Story 50: Morale Problems Don't Take Holidays

privately, get the team together to build solutions and share ideas. If people really feel a part of a team, they are bound to pull together and not let the team down.

- **Publicize the results.** The division needs to sharpen its metrics and make sure that they are measuring the right things. All of the collected metrics should be displayed prominently so that the staff sees how they are doing on an ongoing basis. This is a powerful motivator and will get everyone pulling in a common direction.

- **Recognize people and ideas.** Recognition can go a long way toward improving morale. Make sure that you recognize people for a job well done. Praise people in front of the team. Recognize good performance to your managers. Ask your customer to praise the team for a job well done.

- **Have fun.** Okay, so do not give up on the fun stuff. Go ahead and have the "Jeans and Sweatshirt Day" – not in isolation but as part of a coordinated and well-rounded strategy. There is a lot that can be done to have fun in an organization. This can include pizza lunches (the team can chip in if your company won't pay). You can take turns bringing in donuts for breakfast. Give people certificates for offbeat accomplishments like being the tallest on the team. Get your most outgoing people to plan some quirky events for the team. Fun is contagious. If staff members see others enjoying themselves, they will feel better too.

I think that is the fundamental decision Gerry and his team need to make. If they think they can do it, he and his management team can pull the entire organization together to work toward the common goals around being more cost efficient. If they are successful, everyone in the division will benefit. If they do not reach their goals, there may be further consequences, but at least people will know where they stand.

On the other hand, if he and his management team don't think they can reach the efficiency level needed to stave off more layoffs and outsourcing, they should not go down this path, since they will just be introducing false hope. Instead, they should take other actions, perhaps around retooling portions of their staff, providing better severance packages and dealing as best they can with a declining workforce.

YEAR-END RECAP

I guess it's a sign of growing older that it seems that entire years get gobbled up in one swallow. I can't believe another year has come and gone. However, I can look back at the prior year and honestly say that it was a most interesting and challenging year. I was able to meet many new people and become exposed to many new parts of the organization. Best of all, I felt like I was able to help people perform better on their jobs.

Managers have to deal with many diverse problems. One of the frustrating parts about managing people is seeing problems and not knowing how to address them. It is especially difficult with people problems because of the personal interaction required. To a certain extent the problems are as diverse as the people involved. The larger your company, the more types of problems you will face.

My job as a <u>management coach</u> is to better arm managers with skills and tools to help them resolve problems. That is why I don't tell them that I will solve their problems for them. Instead I show them a technique or skill that they can use to work through the problem on their own. That way, they will own the experience and they will be the ones that are maturing as managers.

I hope that these stories of my year as a management coach were helpful to you as well. Although the situations reflected in these stories may not be exactly the ones that you face, it is my hope that they are similar enough that you can see how the lessons that were applied in these stories could also be applied to your situation. Remember that for every personnel problem there is at least one solution (maybe more). Your challenge is to work through the situation and to arrive at the best solution that works for you, your company and the people involved.

I wish you good luck in the future. Solve those problems!